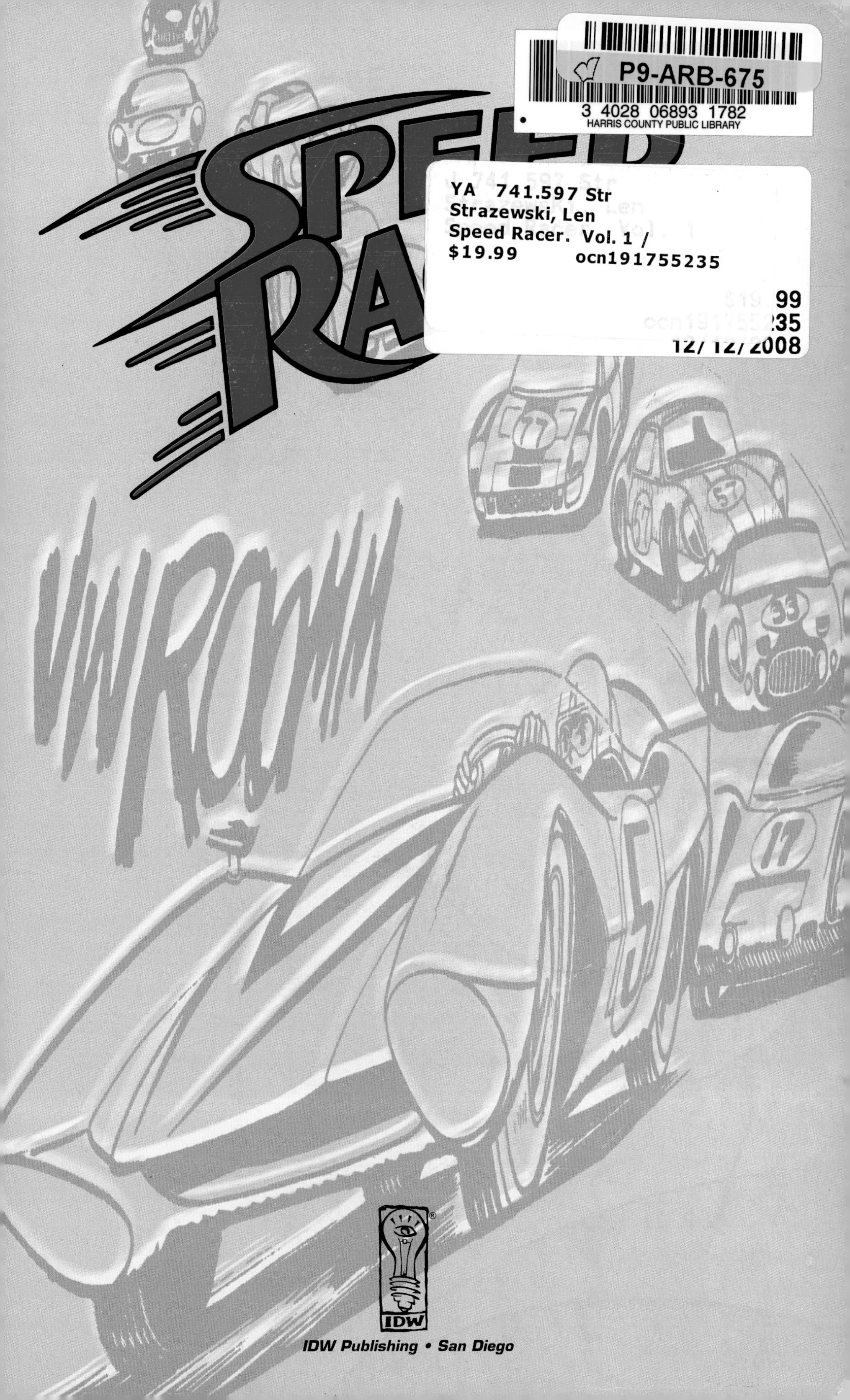

IDW Publishing • San Diego

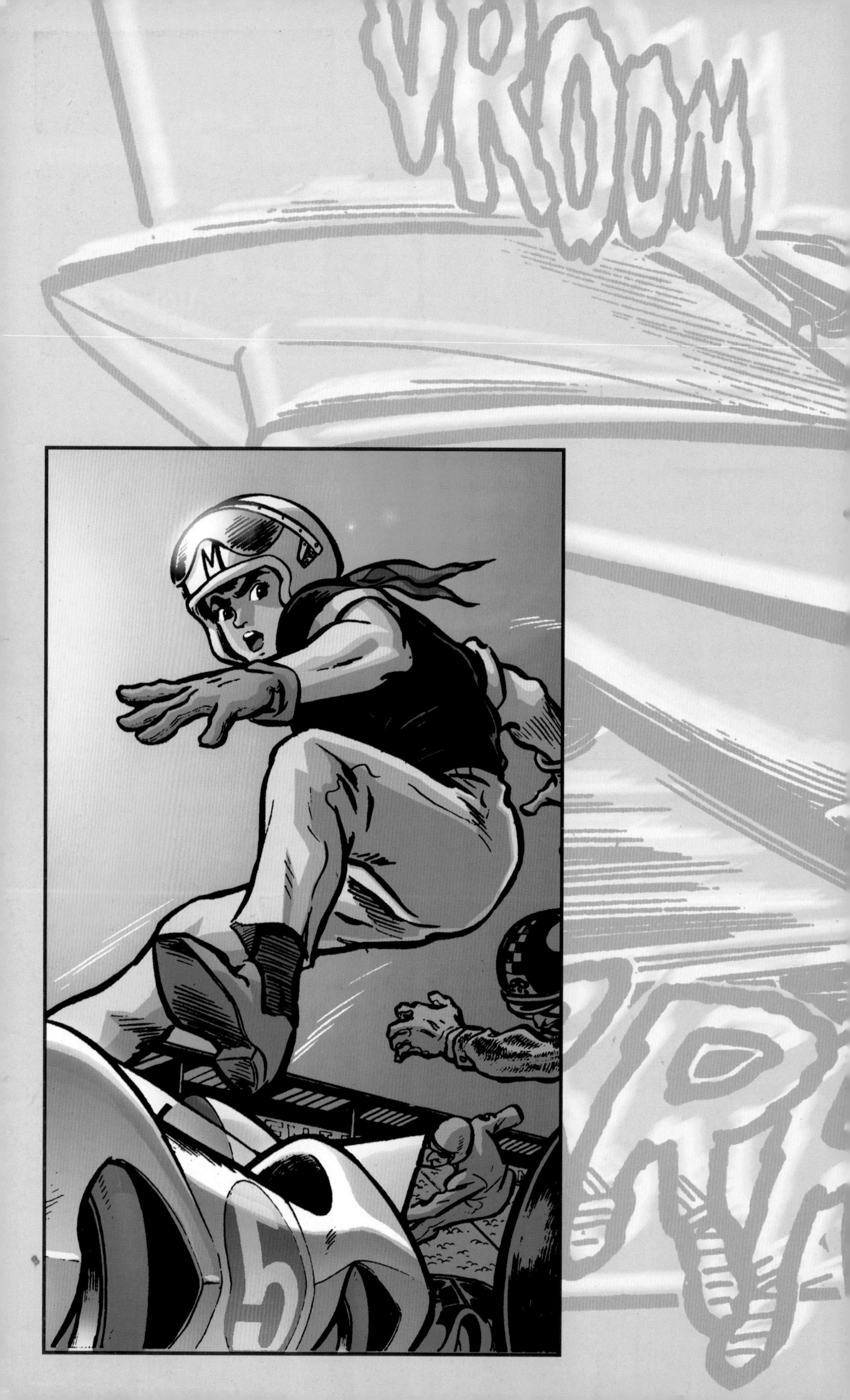
VROOM

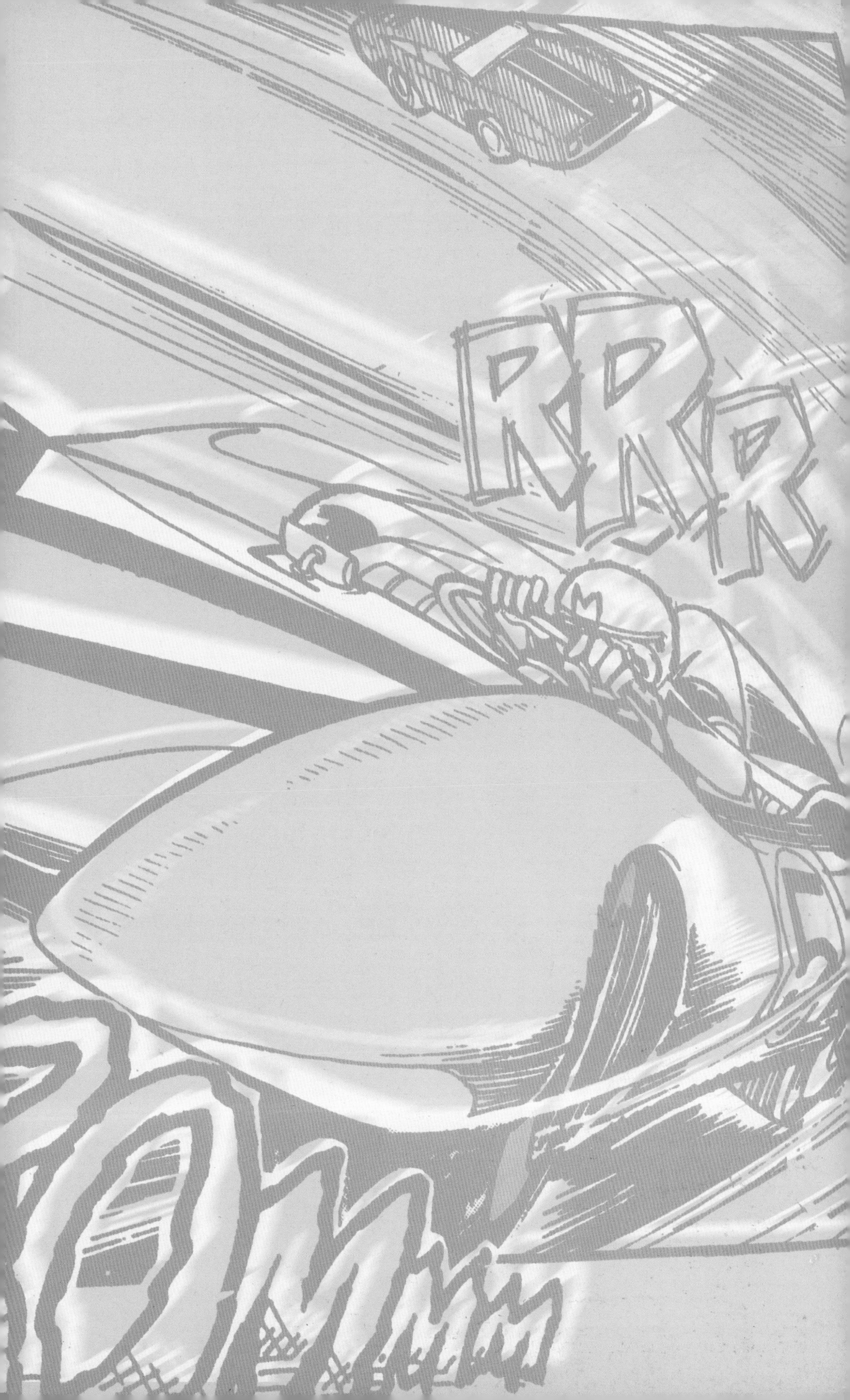
RRR

IDW Publishing is:
Ted Adams, *President*
Robbie Robbins, *EVP/Sr. Graphic Artist*
Chris Ryall, *Publisher/Editor-in-Chief*
Clifford Meth, *EVP of Strategies/Editorial*
Alan Payne, *VP of Sales*
Neil Uyetake, *Art Director*
Tom Waltz, *Editor*
Andrew Steven Harris, *Editor*
Chris Mowry, *Graphic Artist*
Amauri Osorio, *Graphic Artist*
Dene Nee, *Graphic Artist/Editor*
Matthew Ruzicka, *CPA, Controller*
Alonzo Simon, *Shipping Manager*
Kris Oprisko, *Editor/Foreign Lic. Rep.*

www.idwpublishing.com
www.speedracer.com

ISBN: 978-1-60010-174-8
11 10 09 08   1 2 3 4 5

Speed Racer #1
page 6
Written by ***Len Strazewski***
Pencilled by ***Gary Washington***
Inked by ***Brian Thomas***
Lettered and Colored by ***Ken Holewczynski***
Edited by ***Brian Augustyn***

Speed Racer #2
page 32
Written by ***Len Strazewski***
Pencilled by ***Gary Washington***
Inked by ***Rodney Dunn***
Colored by ***Rodney Dunn & Ken Holewczynski***
Lettered by ***Deborah Marks***
Edited by ***Brian Augustyn***

Speed Racer #3
page 54
Written by ***Len Strazewski***
Pencilled by ***Jill Thompson***
Inked by ***Brian Thomas***
Lettered and Colored by ***Ken Holewczynski***
Edited by ***Brian Augustyn***

Speed Racer #4
page 76
Written by ***Len Strazewski***
Pencilled by ***Gary Washington***
Inked by ***Brian Thomas***
Lettered and Colored by ***Ken Holewczynski***
Edited by ***Brian Augustyn***

Speed Racer #5
page 98
Written by ***Brian Thomas***
Pencilled by ***Jill Thompson***
Inked by ***Brian Thomas***
Lettered and Colored by ***Ken Holewczynski***
Edited by ***Tony Caputo***

Speed Racer Vol. 1 TPB

Cover by ***Ken Steacy***

Edited by ***Dene Nee***

Design and Remaster by ***Tom B. Long***

Speed Racer #1

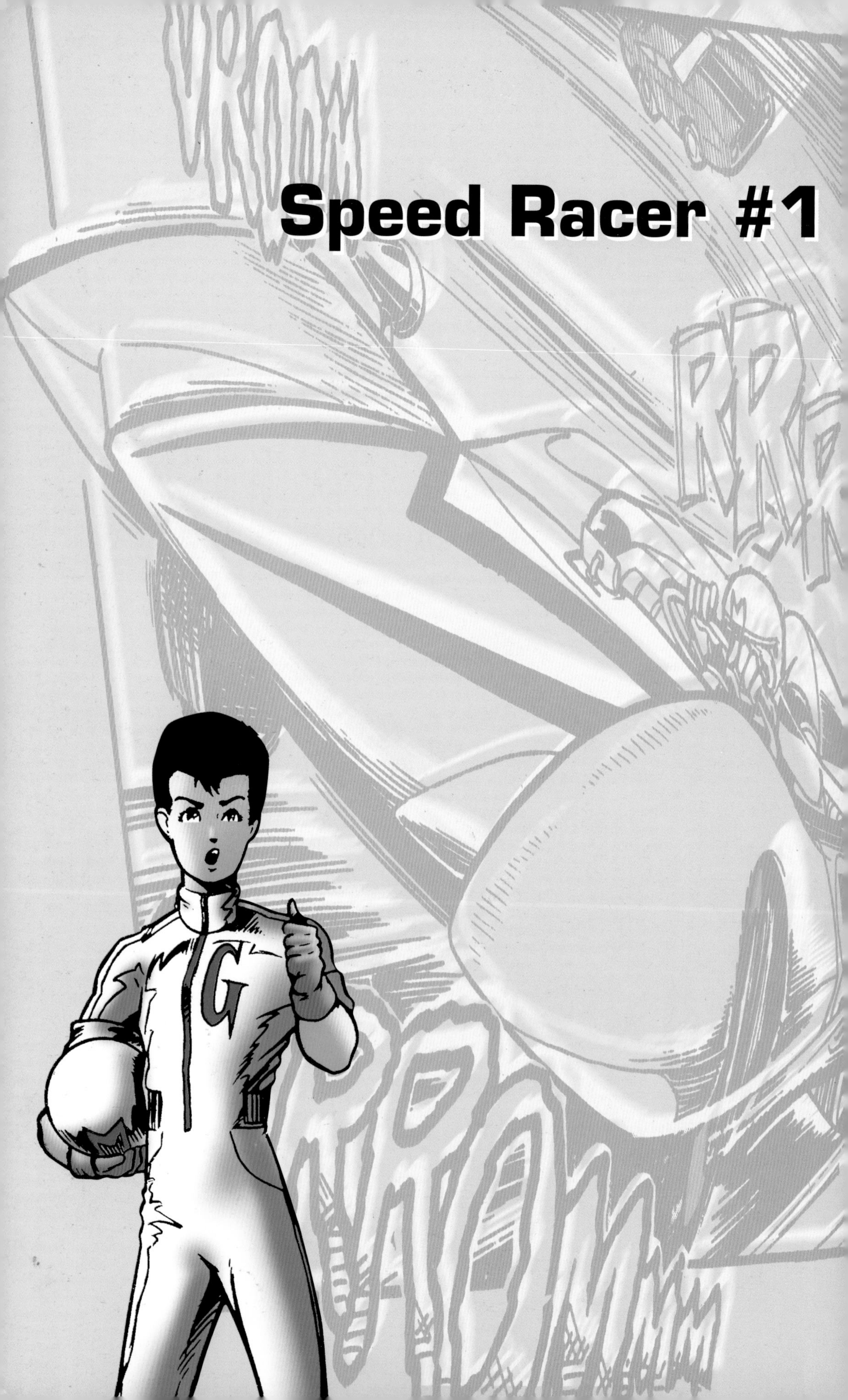

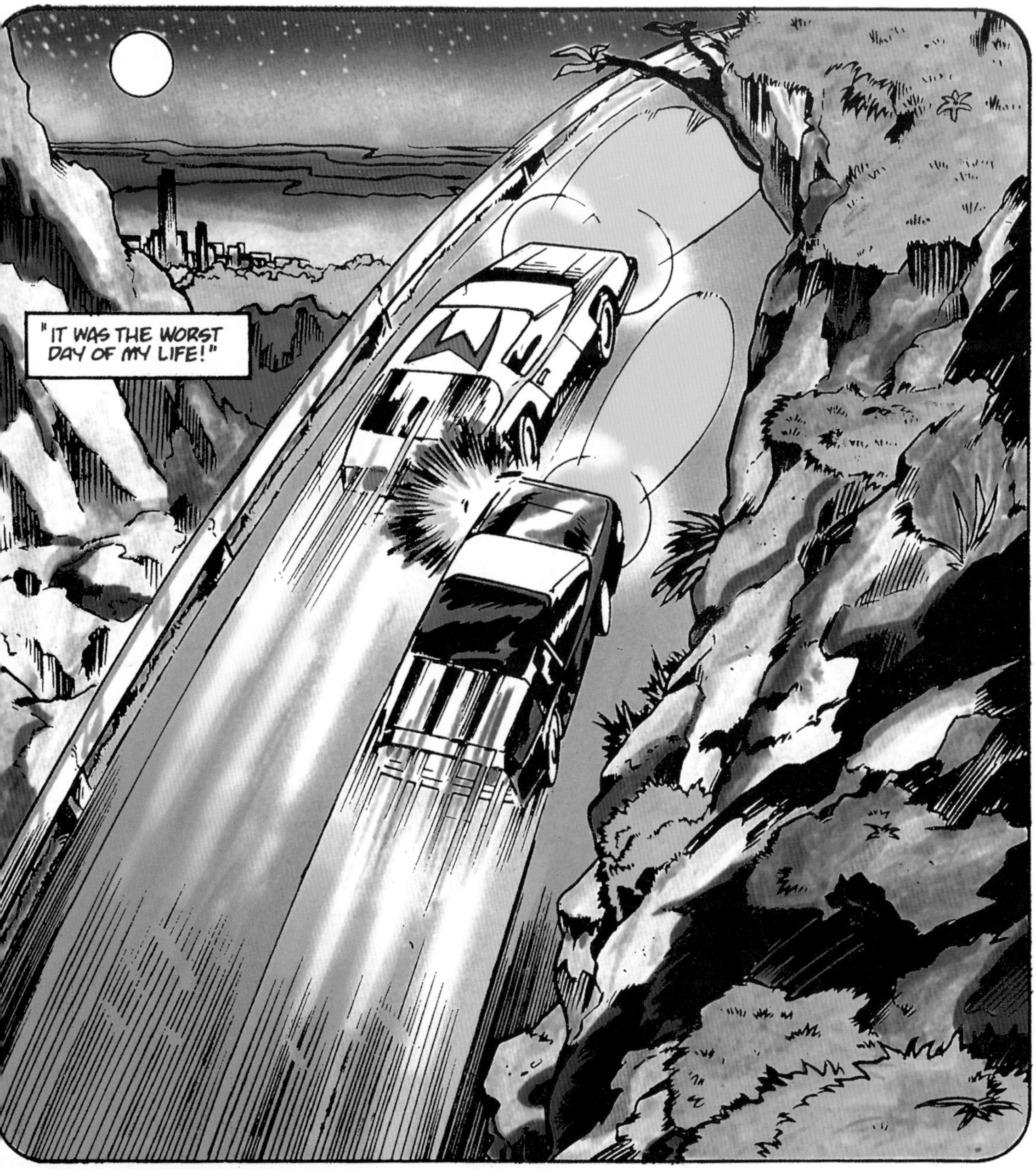
"IT WAS THE WORST DAY OF MY LIFE!"

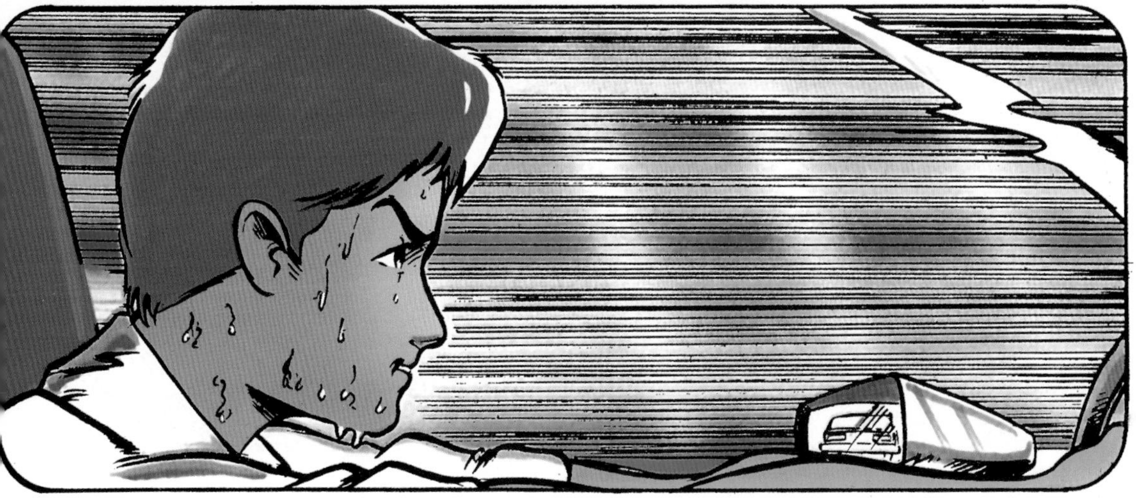

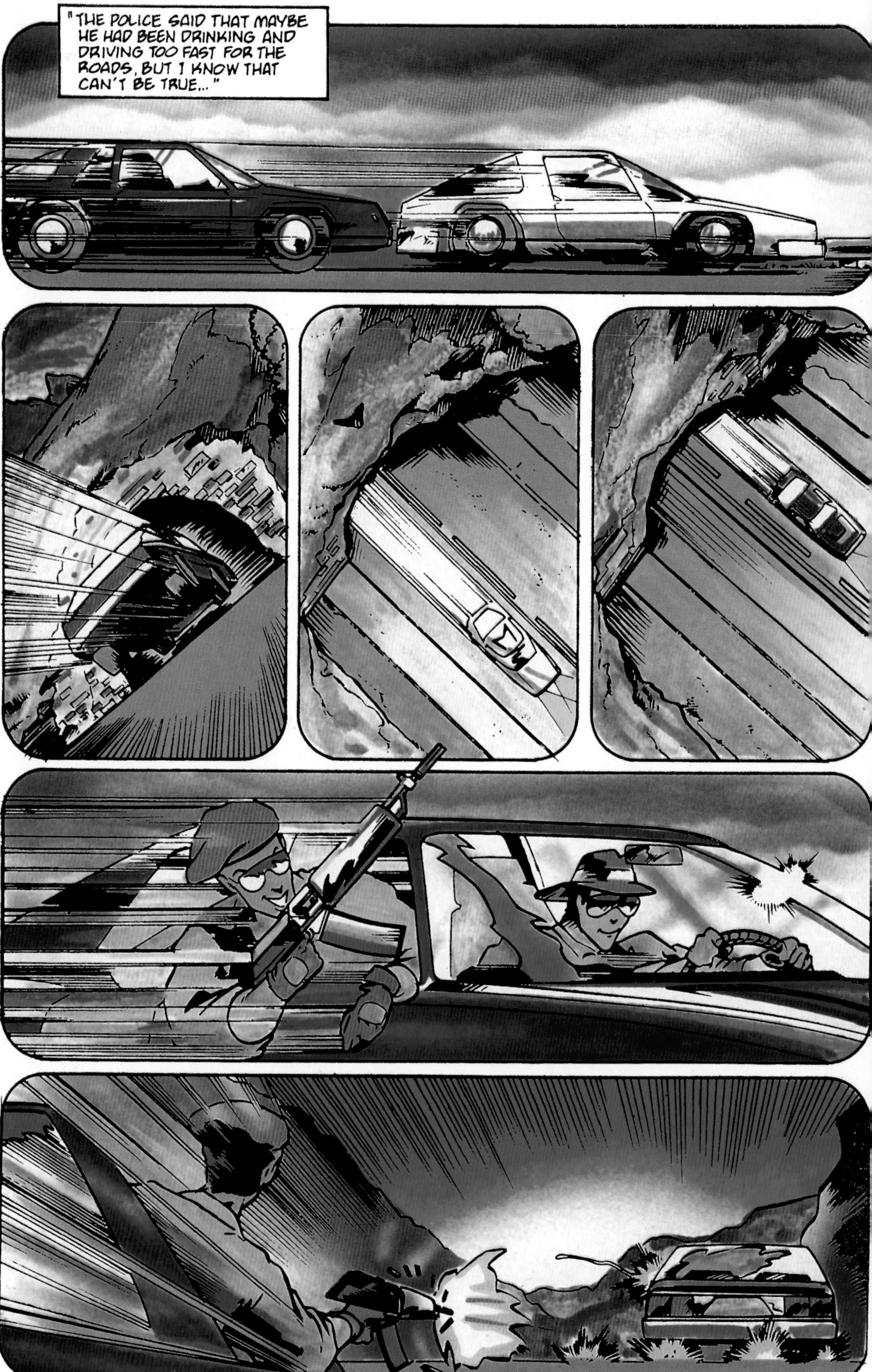
"THE POLICE SAID THAT MAYBE HE HAD BEEN DRINKING AND DRIVING TOO FAST FOR THE ROADS, BUT I KNOW THAT CAN'T BE TRUE..."

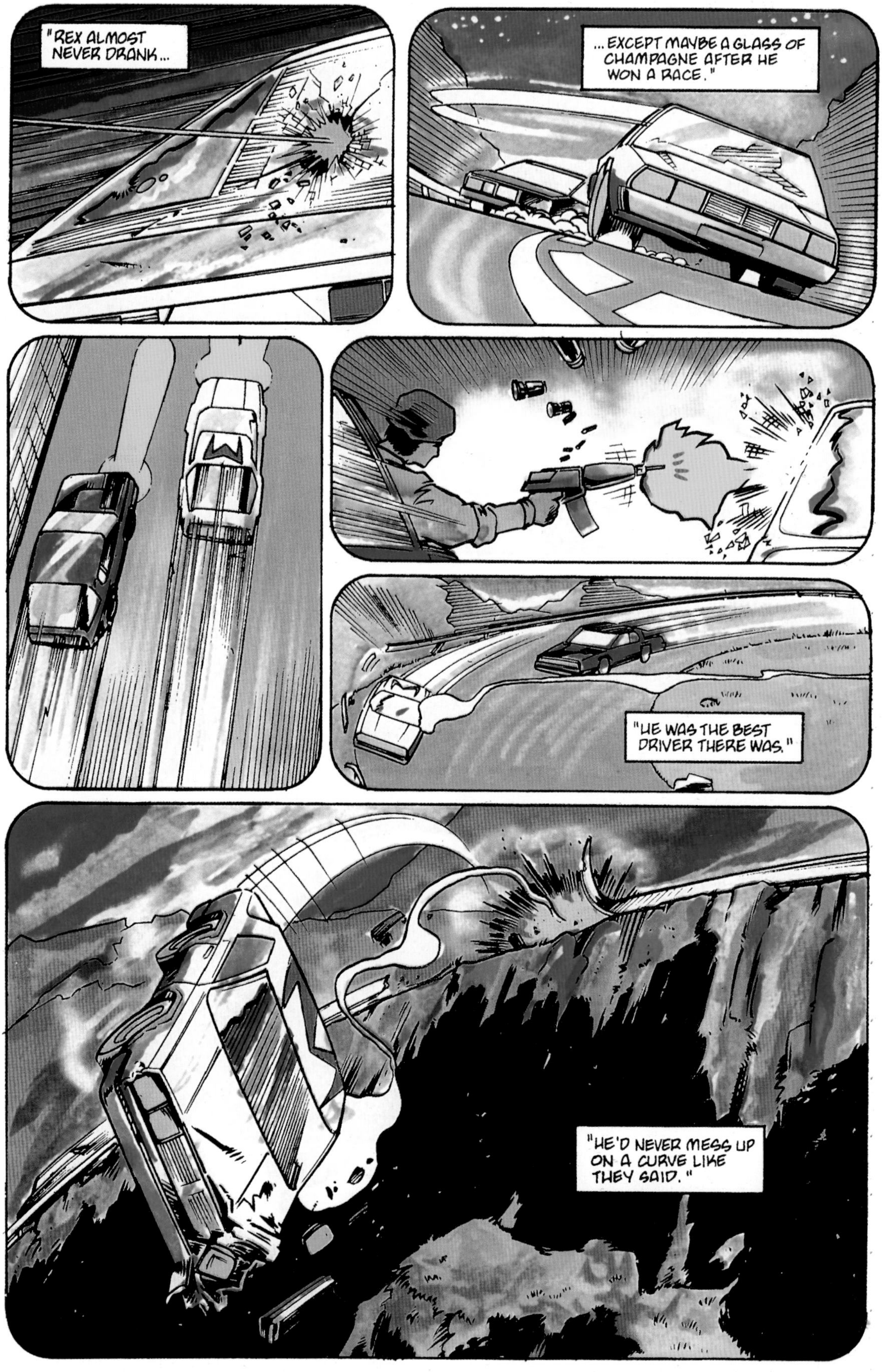
"REX ALMOST NEVER DRANK...
...EXCEPT MAYBE A GLASS OF CHAMPAGNE AFTER HE WON A RACE."
"HE WAS THE BEST DRIVER THERE WAS."
"HE'D NEVER MESS UP ON A CURVE LIKE THEY SAID."

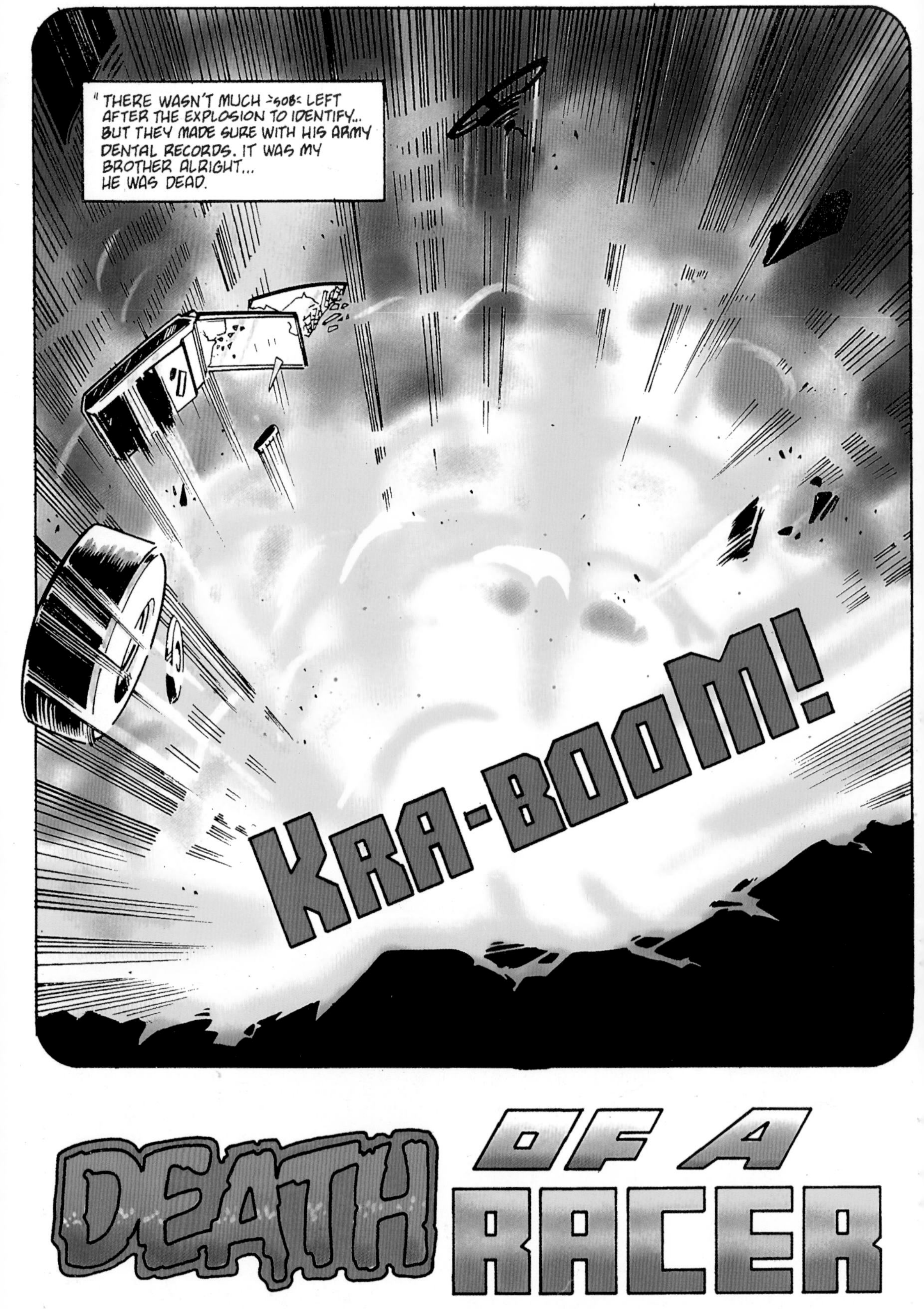
"THERE WASN'T MUCH >SOB< LEFT AFTER THE EXPLOSION TO IDENTIFY... BUT THEY MADE SURE WITH HIS ARMY DENTAL RECORDS. IT WAS MY BROTHER ALRIGHT... HE WAS DEAD.
KRA-BOOM!

DEATH OF A RACER

WRITER - LEN STRAZEWSKI • PENCILLER - GARY THOMAS WASHINGTON • INKER - BRIAN THOMAS
LETTERER/COLORIST - KEN HOLEWCZYNSKI • STORY EDITOR - BRIAN AUGUSTYN

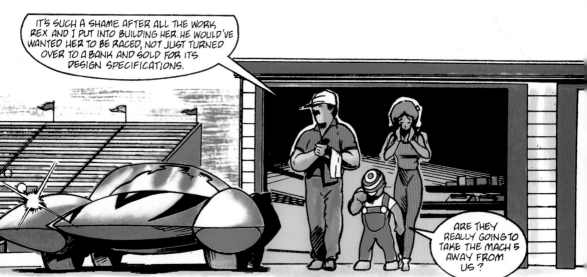

IT'S SUCH A SHAME AFTER ALL THE WORK REX AND I PUT INTO BUILDING HER. HE WOULD'VE WANTED HER TO BE RACED, NOT JUST TURNED OVER TO A BANK AND SOLD FOR ITS DESIGN SPECIFICATIONS.

ARE THEY REALLY GOING TO TAKE THE MACH 5 AWAY FROM US?

YES, SON. IT'S TRUE. REX AND I PUT EVERYTHING WE HAD INTO HER... AND IT'S THE GREATEST RACE CAR IN THE WORLD. WITH MY ENGINE AND REX'S COMPUTERS... THERE'S NO CAR THAT CAN BEAT HER.

BUT WE HAD TO PUT THE BANK'S MONEY INTO HER AS WELL AND WE HAVE TO WIN RACES TO PAY OFF THE LOANS.

...BUT I'M NOT THE DRIVER REX WAS... AND IT TAKES SPECIAL TRAINING TO USE THE COMPUTER ASSISTS CORRECTLY.

BUT CAN'T SOMEONE ELSE...

I'M AFRAID NOT, SON. ONLY REX UNDERSTOOD THAT ELECTRONIC STUFF.

THAT'S NOT TRUE!

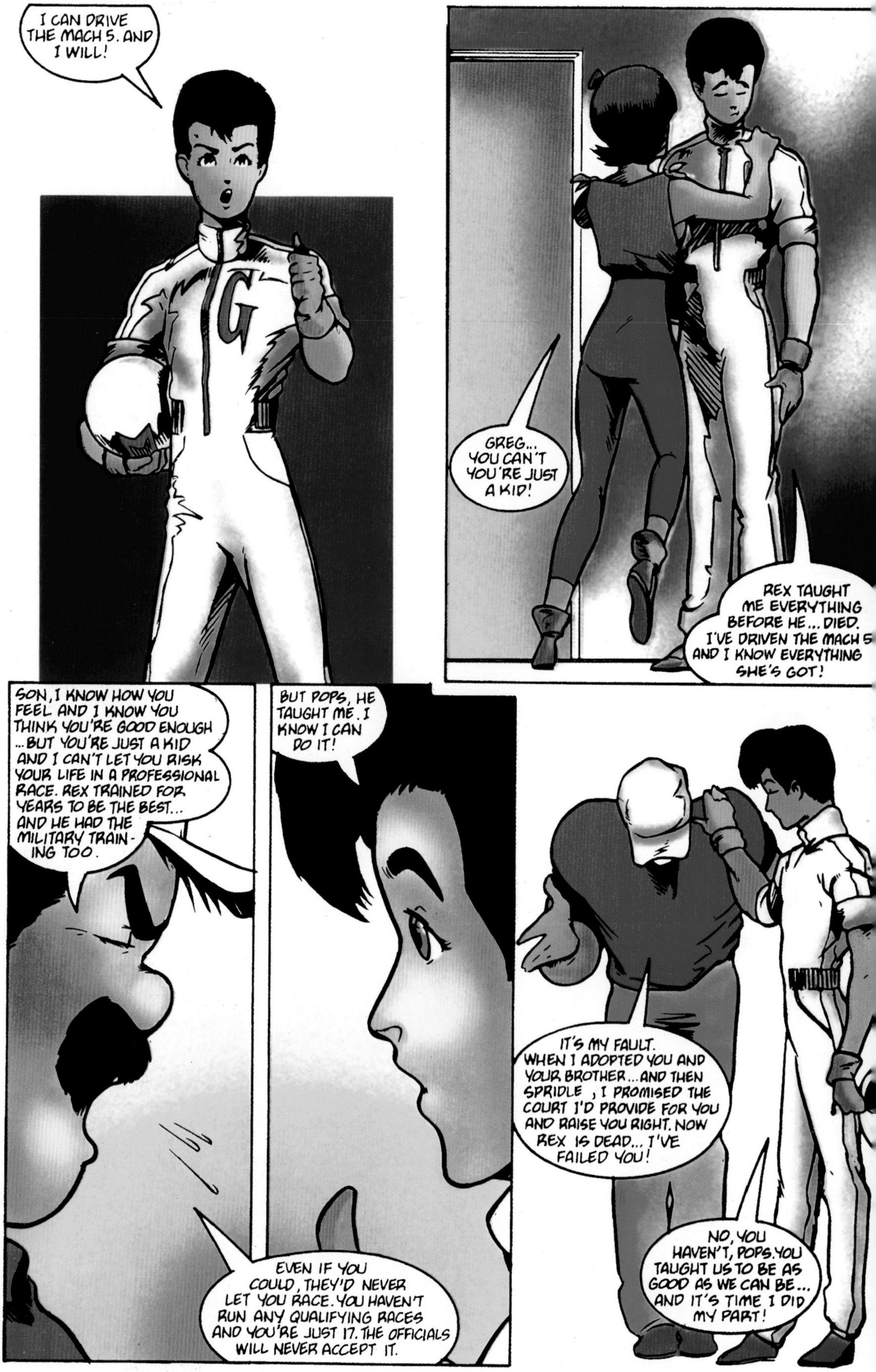
I CAN DRIVE THE MACH 5. AND I WILL!
GREG... YOU CAN'T YOU'RE JUST A KID!
REX TAUGHT ME EVERYTHING BEFORE HE... DIED. I'VE DRIVEN THE MACH 5 AND I KNOW EVERYTHING SHE'S GOT!
SON, I KNOW HOW YOU FEEL AND I KNOW YOU THINK YOU'RE GOOD ENOUGH ...BUT YOU'RE JUST A KID AND I CAN'T LET YOU RISK YOUR LIFE IN A PROFESSIONAL RACE. REX TRAINED FOR YEARS TO BE THE BEST... AND HE HAD THE MILITARY TRAINING TOO.
BUT POPS, HE TAUGHT ME. I KNOW I CAN DO IT!
EVEN IF YOU COULD, THEY'D NEVER LET YOU RACE. YOU HAVEN'T RUN ANY QUALIFYING RACES AND YOU'RE JUST 17. THE OFFICIALS WILL NEVER ACCEPT IT.
IT'S MY FAULT. WHEN I ADOPTED YOU AND YOUR BROTHER... AND THEN SPRIDLE, I PROMISED THE COURT I'D PROVIDE FOR YOU AND RAISE YOU RIGHT. NOW REX IS DEAD... I'VE FAILED YOU!
NO, YOU HAVEN'T, POPS. YOU TAUGHT US TO BE AS GOOD AS WE CAN BE... AND IT'S TIME I DID MY PART!

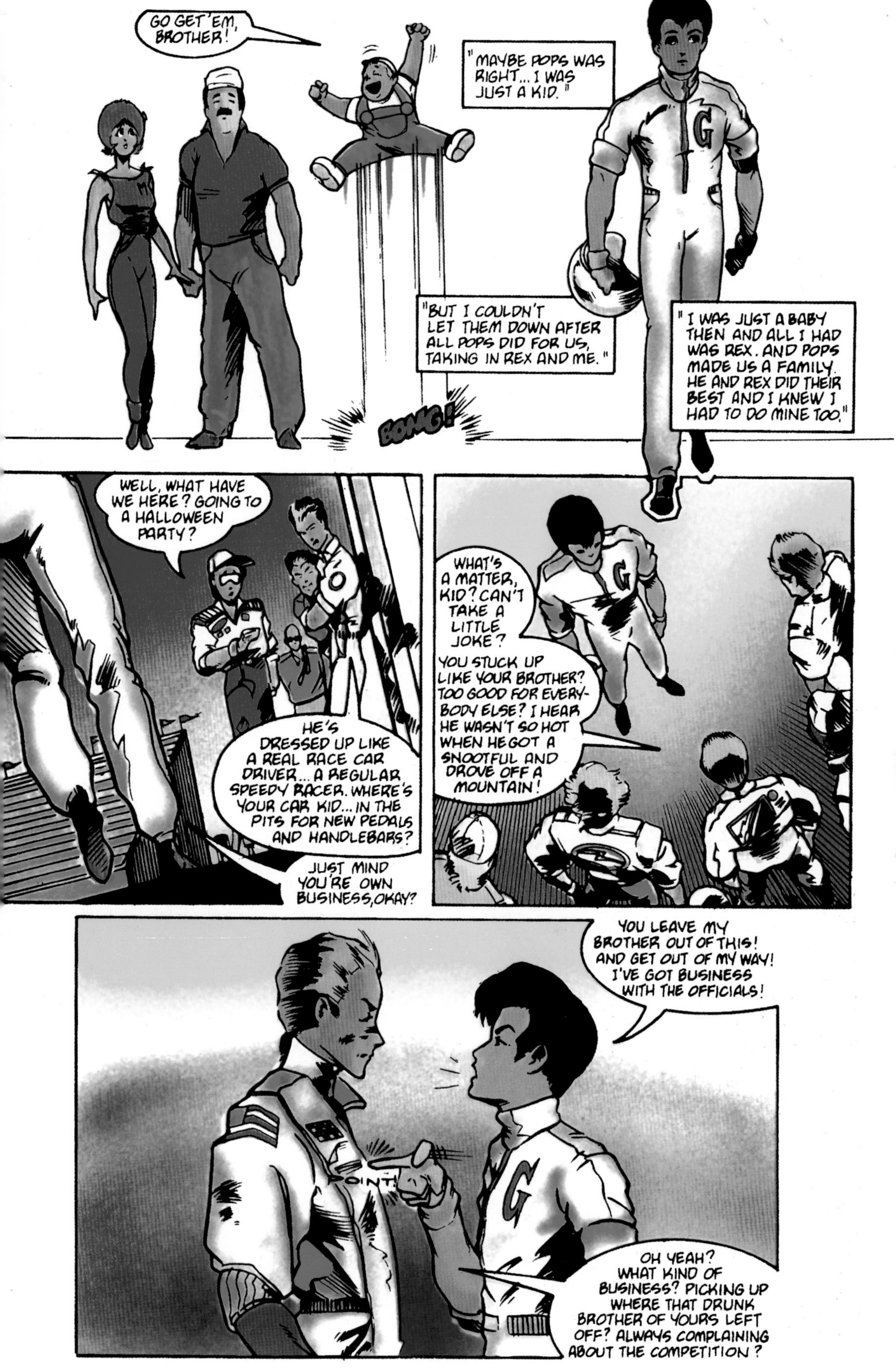
GO GET 'EM, BROTHER!
"MAYBE POPS WAS RIGHT... I WAS JUST A KID."
"BUT I COULDN'T LET THEM DOWN AFTER ALL POPS DID FOR US, TAKING IN REX AND ME."
" I WAS JUST A BABY THEN AND ALL I HAD WAS REX. AND POPS MADE US A FAMILY. HE AND REX DID THEIR BEST AND I KNEW I HAD TO DO MINE TOO."
BONG!
WELL, WHAT HAVE WE HERE? GOING TO A HALLOWEEN PARTY?
HE'S DRESSED UP LIKE A REAL RACE CAR DRIVER... A REGULAR SPEEDY RACER. WHERE'S YOUR CAR KID... IN THE PITS FOR NEW PEDALS AND HANDLEBARS?
JUST MIND YOU'RE OWN BUSINESS, OKAY?
WHAT'S A MATTER, KID? CAN'T TAKE A LITTLE JOKE?
YOU STUCK UP LIKE YOUR BROTHER? TOO GOOD FOR EVERY-BODY ELSE? I HEAR HE WASN'T SO HOT WHEN HE GOT A SNOOTFUL AND DROVE OFF A MOUNTAIN!
YOU LEAVE MY BROTHER OUT OF THIS! AND GET OUT OF MY WAY! I'VE GOT BUSINESS WITH THE OFFICIALS!
POINT!
OH YEAH? WHAT KIND OF BUSINESS? PICKING UP WHERE THAT DRUNK BROTHER OF YOURS LEFT OFF? ALWAYS COMPLAINING ABOUT THE COMPETITION?

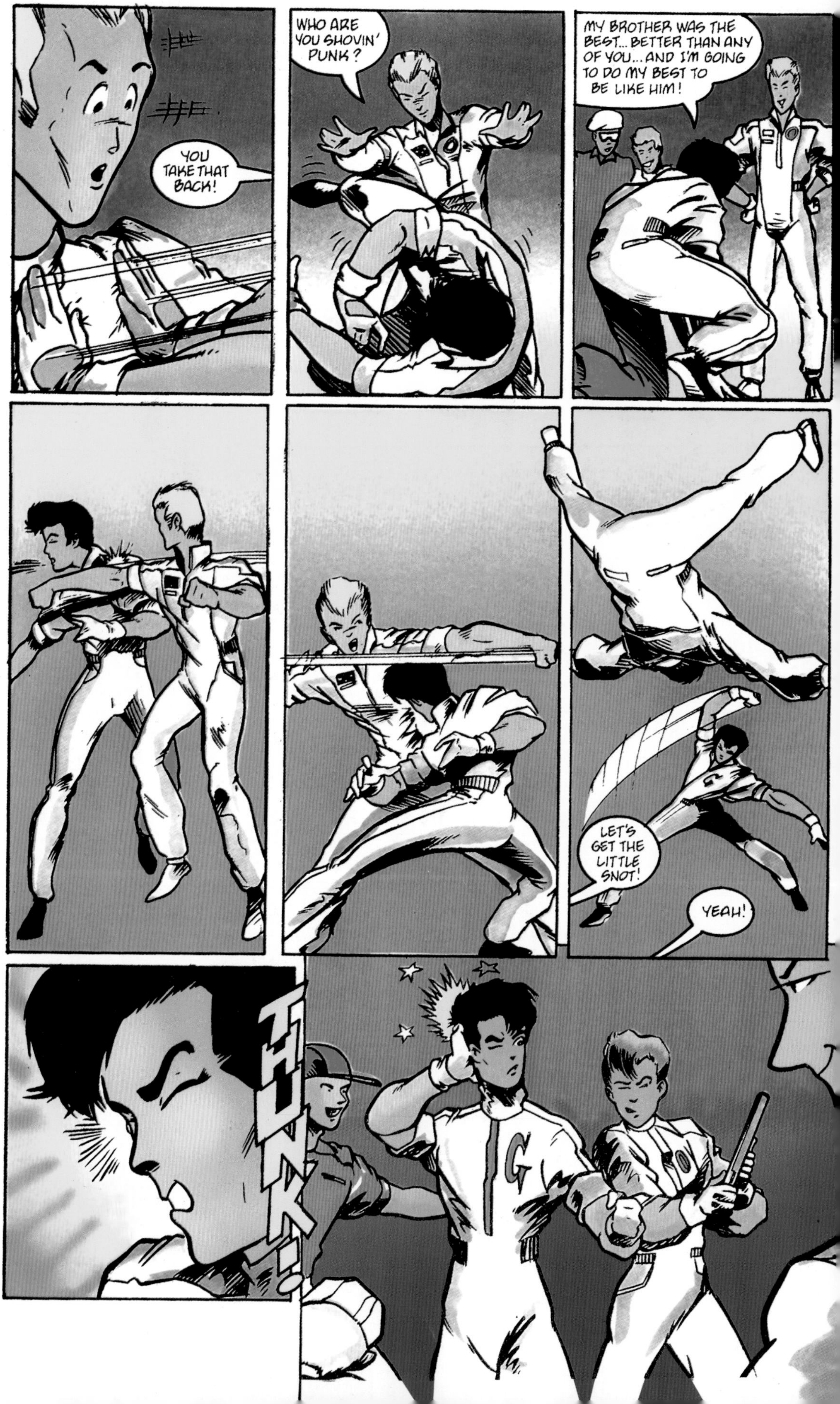
YOU TAKE THAT BACK!
WHO ARE YOU SHOVIN' PUNK?
MY BROTHER WAS THE BEST... BETTER THAN ANY OF YOU... AND I'M GOING TO DO MY BEST TO BE LIKE HIM!
LET'S GET THE LITTLE SNOT!
YEAH!
THUNK!

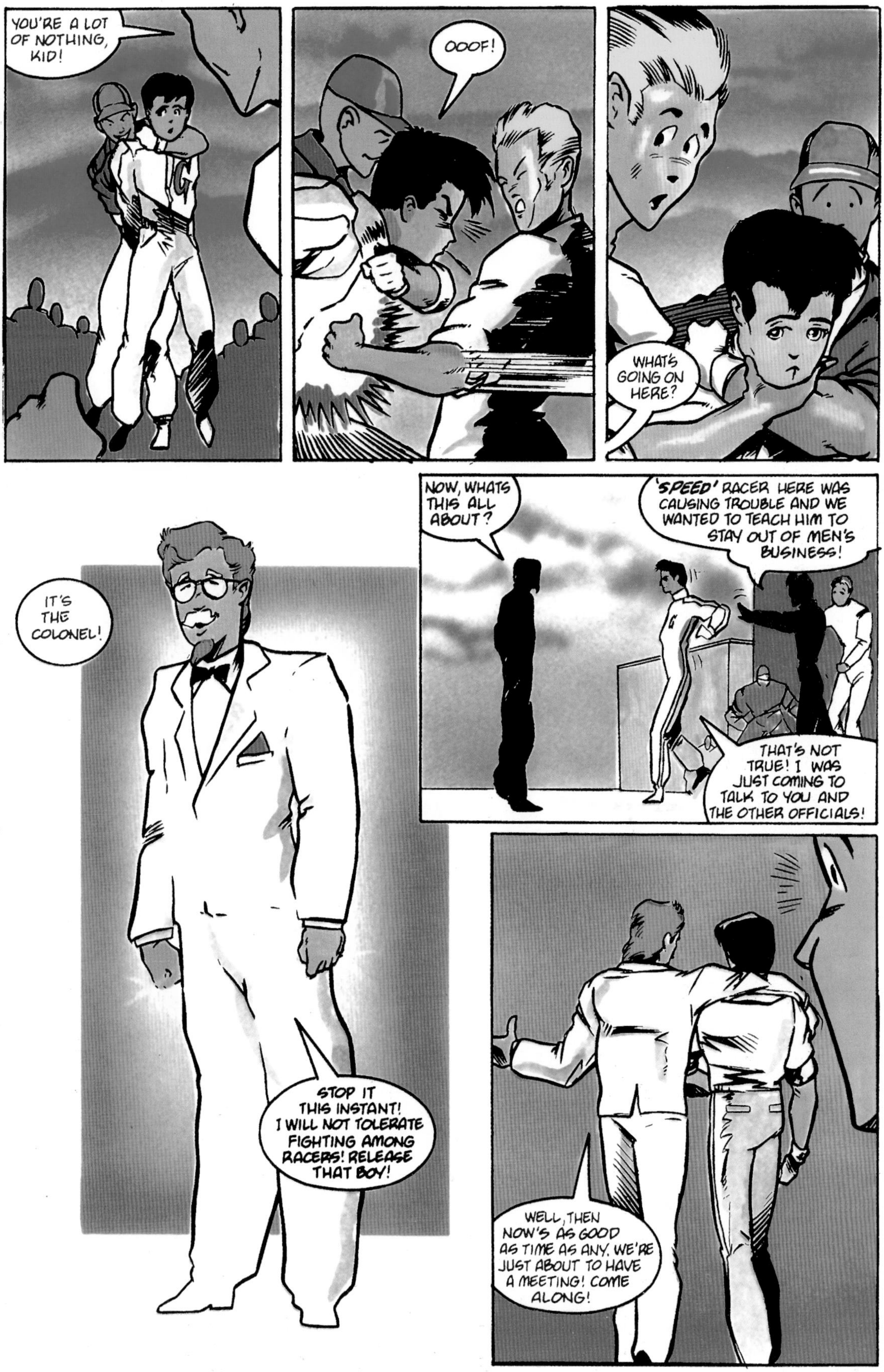
YOU'RE A LOT OF NOTHING, KID!
OOOF!
WHAT'S GOING ON HERE?
IT'S THE COLONEL!
STOP IT THIS INSTANT! I WILL NOT TOLERATE FIGHTING AMONG RACERS! RELEASE THAT BOY!
NOW, WHATS THIS ALL ABOUT?
'SPEED' RACER HERE WAS CAUSING TROUBLE AND WE WANTED TO TEACH HIM TO STAY OUT OF MEN'S BUSINESS!
THAT'S NOT TRUE! I WAS JUST COMING TO TALK TO YOU AND THE OTHER OFFICIALS!
WELL, THEN NOW'S AS GOOD AS TIME AS ANY. WE'RE JUST ABOUT TO HAVE A MEETING! COME ALONG!

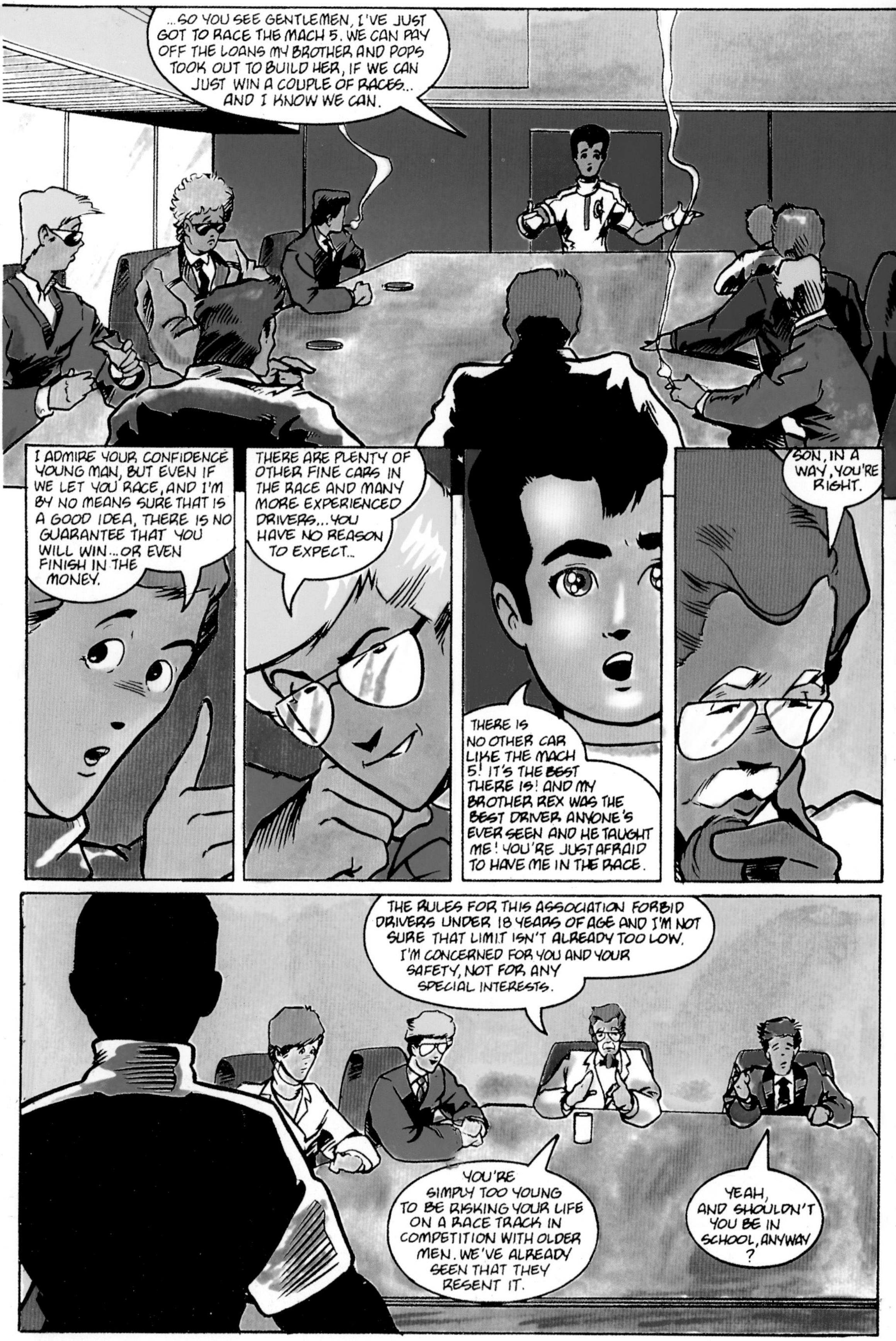
...SO YOU SEE GENTLEMEN, I'VE JUST GOT TO RACE THE MACH 5. WE CAN PAY OFF THE LOANS MY BROTHER AND POPS TOOK OUT TO BUILD HER, IF WE CAN JUST WIN A COUPLE OF RACES... AND I KNOW WE CAN.
I ADMIRE YOUR CONFIDENCE YOUNG MAN, BUT EVEN IF WE LET YOU RACE, AND I'M BY NO MEANS SURE THAT IS A GOOD IDEA, THERE IS NO GUARANTEE THAT YOU WILL WIN...OR EVEN FINISH IN THE MONEY.
THERE ARE PLENTY OF OTHER FINE CARS IN THE RACE AND MANY MORE EXPERIENCED DRIVERS... YOU HAVE NO REASON TO EXPECT...
THERE IS NO OTHER CAR LIKE THE MACH 5! IT'S THE BEST THERE IS! AND MY BROTHER REX WAS THE BEST DRIVER ANYONE'S EVER SEEN AND HE TAUGHT ME! YOU'RE JUST AFRAID TO HAVE ME IN THE RACE.
SON, IN A WAY, YOU'RE RIGHT.
THE RULES FOR THIS ASSOCIATION FORBID DRIVERS UNDER 18 YEARS OF AGE AND I'M NOT SURE THAT LIMIT ISN'T ALREADY TOO LOW. I'M CONCERNED FOR YOU AND YOUR SAFETY, NOT FOR ANY SPECIAL INTERESTS.
YOU'RE SIMPLY TOO YOUNG TO BE RISKING YOUR LIFE ON A RACE TRACK IN COMPETITION WITH OLDER MEN. WE'VE ALREADY SEEN THAT THEY RESENT IT.
YEAH, AND SHOULDN'T YOU BE IN SCHOOL, ANYWAY ?

I ALREADY HAVE MY HIGH SCHOOL DIPLOMA. I GRADUATED THIS PAST SPRING! BUT THAT'S NOT THE REAL ISSUE HERE, IS IT?

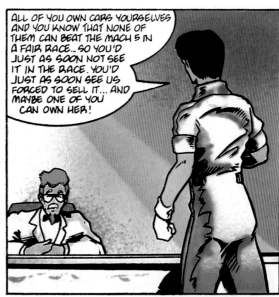

ALL OF YOU OWN CARS YOURSELVES AND YOU KNOW THAT NONE OF THEM CAN BEAT THE MACH 5 IN A FAIR RACE... SO YOU'D JUST AS SOON NOT SEE IT IN THE RACE. YOU'D JUST AS SOON SEE US FORCED TO SELL IT... AND MAYBE ONE OF YOU CAN OWN HER!

NOW HOLD ON, SON...

I'M NOT YOUR SON! I'M A RACER AND I'M AS GOOD OR BETTER THAN ANYONE... AND I CAN PROVE IT!

I'M SURE YOU CAN YOUNG MAN. AND I'M SURE YOU WILL...SOMEDAY. BUT FOR NOW, WE THINK IT BEST THAT YOU TRAIN FOR ANOTHER YEAR OR SO -- PERHAPS GET A JOB AS A PIT HAND WITH ONE OF THE MORE EXPERIENCED DRIVERS. YOUR FATHER IS A GOOD MECHANIC, I'M SURE HE CAN FIND WORK. WHY, I'LL EVEN TALK TO MY OWN CREW ABOUT A JOB FOR HIM. MAYBE WE CAN WORK OUT SOME- THING FOR THE PURCHASE OF YOUR CAR.

I'M SORRY BUT OUR DESCISION IS FINAL.

I APPRECIATE THAT SIR! BUT THE MACH 5 WAS BUILT AS A FAMILY AND WE'LL RACE IT THAT WAY! AND I'M READY TO RACE HER!

NOTHING IS FINAL UNTIL THE RACE IS OVER!

SLAM

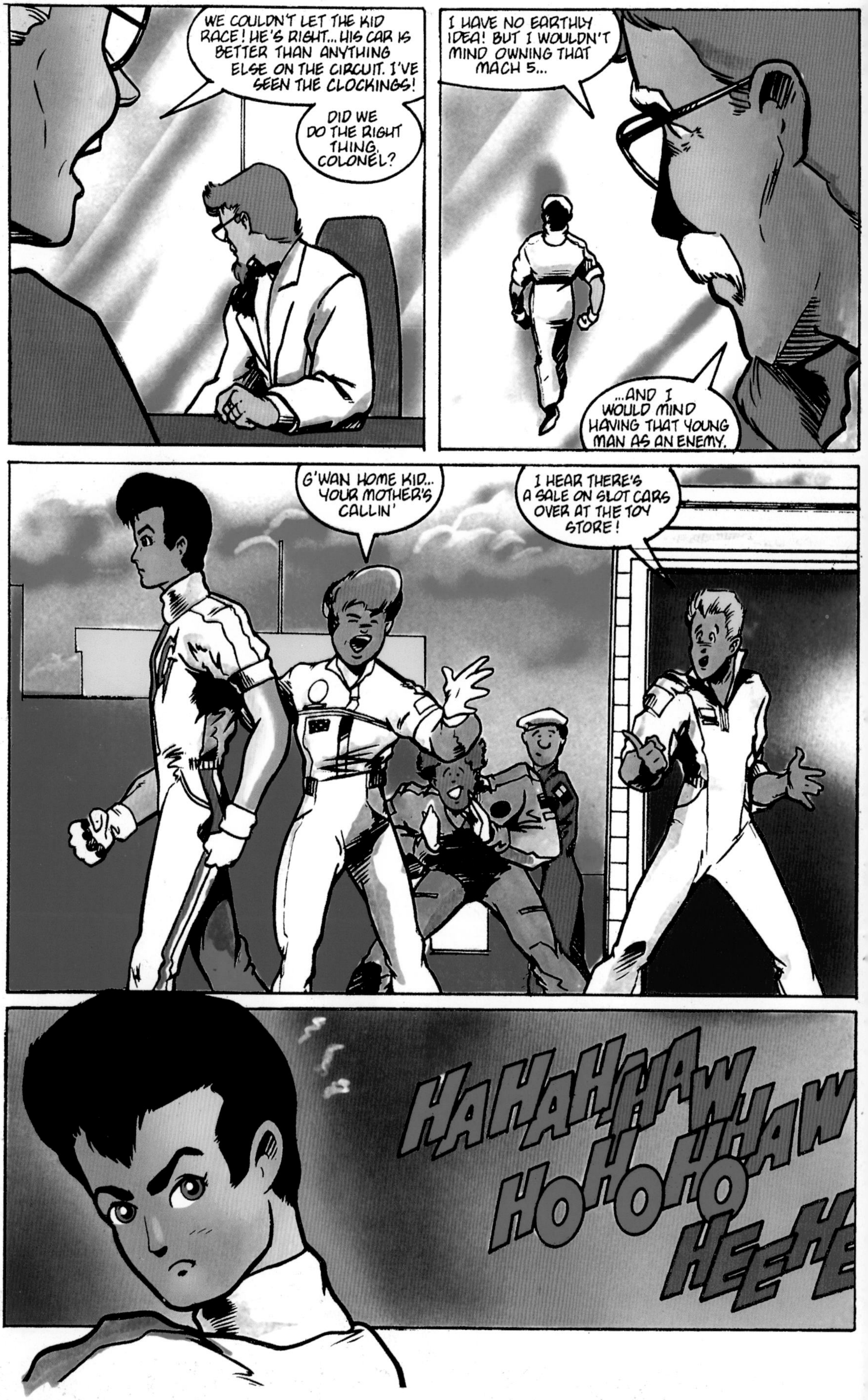

WE COULDN'T LET THE KID RACE! HE'S RIGHT... HIS CAR IS BETTER THAN ANYTHING ELSE ON THE CIRCUIT. I'VE SEEN THE CLOCKINGS!
DID WE DO THE RIGHT THING, COLONEL?
I HAVE NO EARTHLY IDEA! BUT I WOULDN'T MIND OWNING THAT MACH 5...
...AND I WOULD MIND HAVING THAT YOUNG MAN AS AN ENEMY.
G'WAN HOME KID... YOUR MOTHER'S CALLIN'
I HEAR THERE'S A SALE ON SLOT CARS OVER AT THE TOY STORE!
HAHAHHAW
HOHOHHAW
HOHO
HEEHE

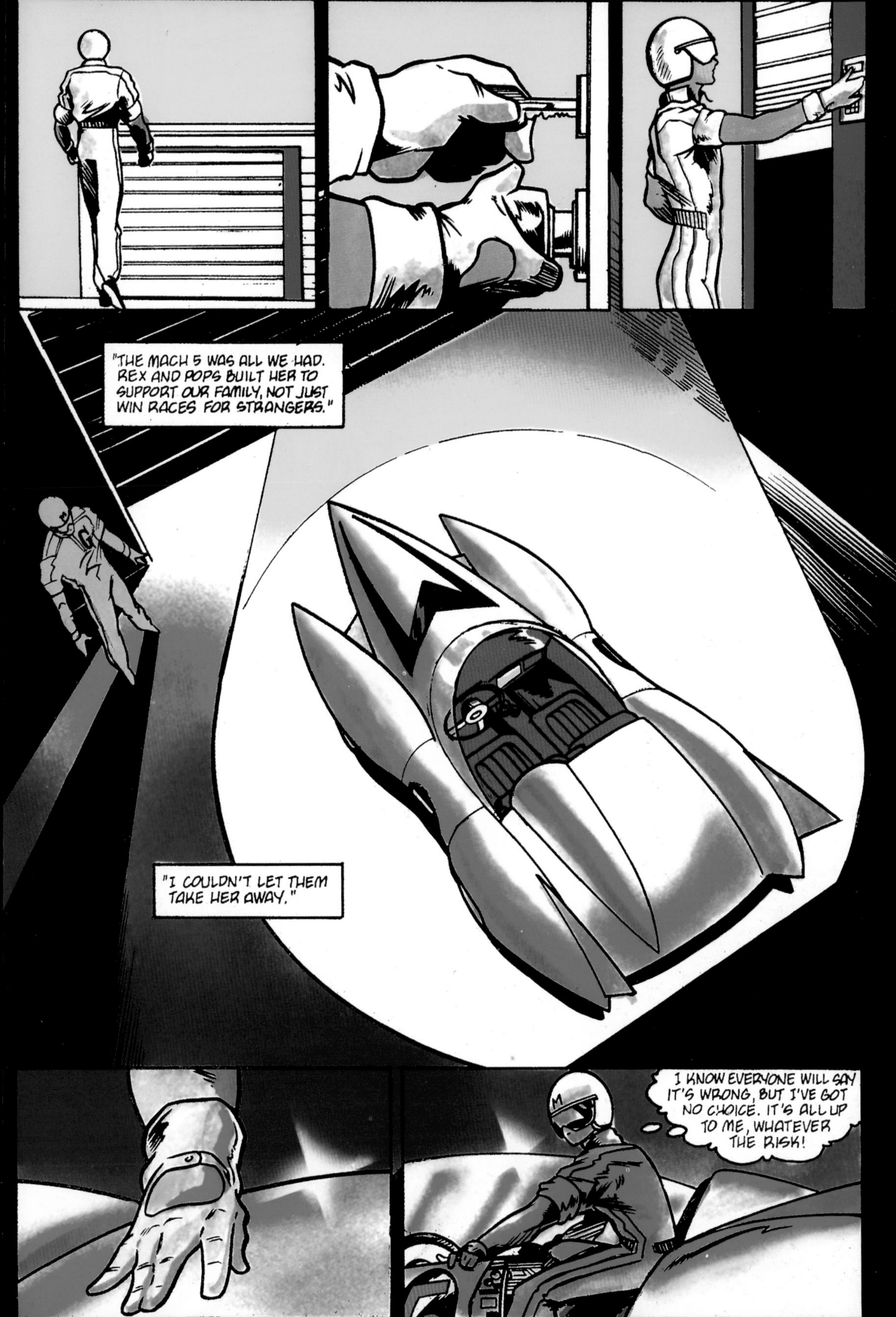
"THE MACH 5 WAS ALL WE HAD. REX AND POPS BUILT HER TO SUPPORT OUR FAMILY, NOT JUST WIN RACES FOR STRANGERS."
"I COULDN'T LET THEM TAKE HER AWAY."
I KNOW EVERYONE WILL SAY IT'S WRONG, BUT I'VE GOT NO CHOICE. IT'S ALL UP TO ME, WHATEVER THE RISK!

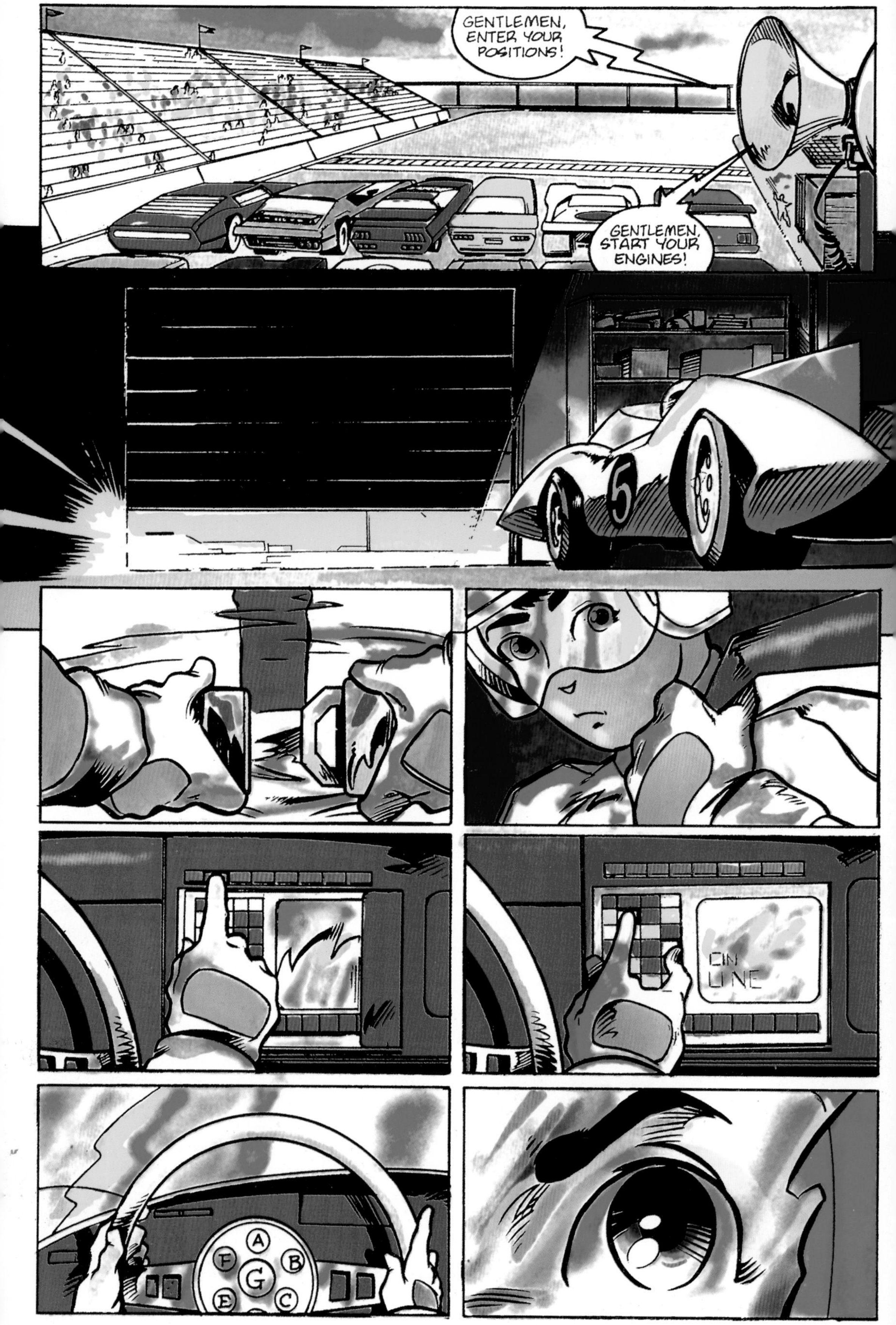
GENTLEMEN, ENTER YOUR POSITIONS!
GENTLEMEN, START YOUR ENGINES!
ON LINE
A
B
C
E
F
G

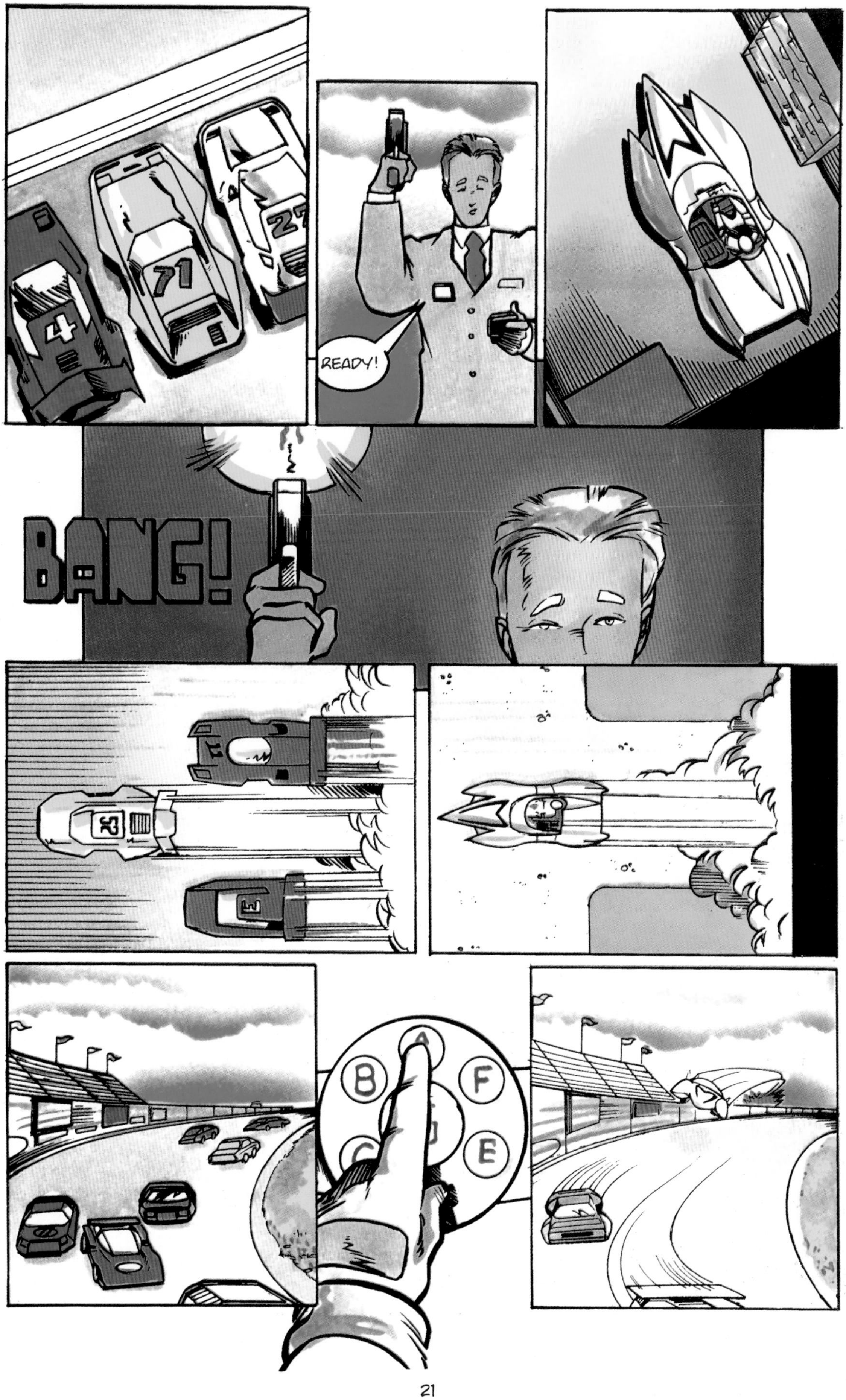
READY!
BANG!
A
B
F
E

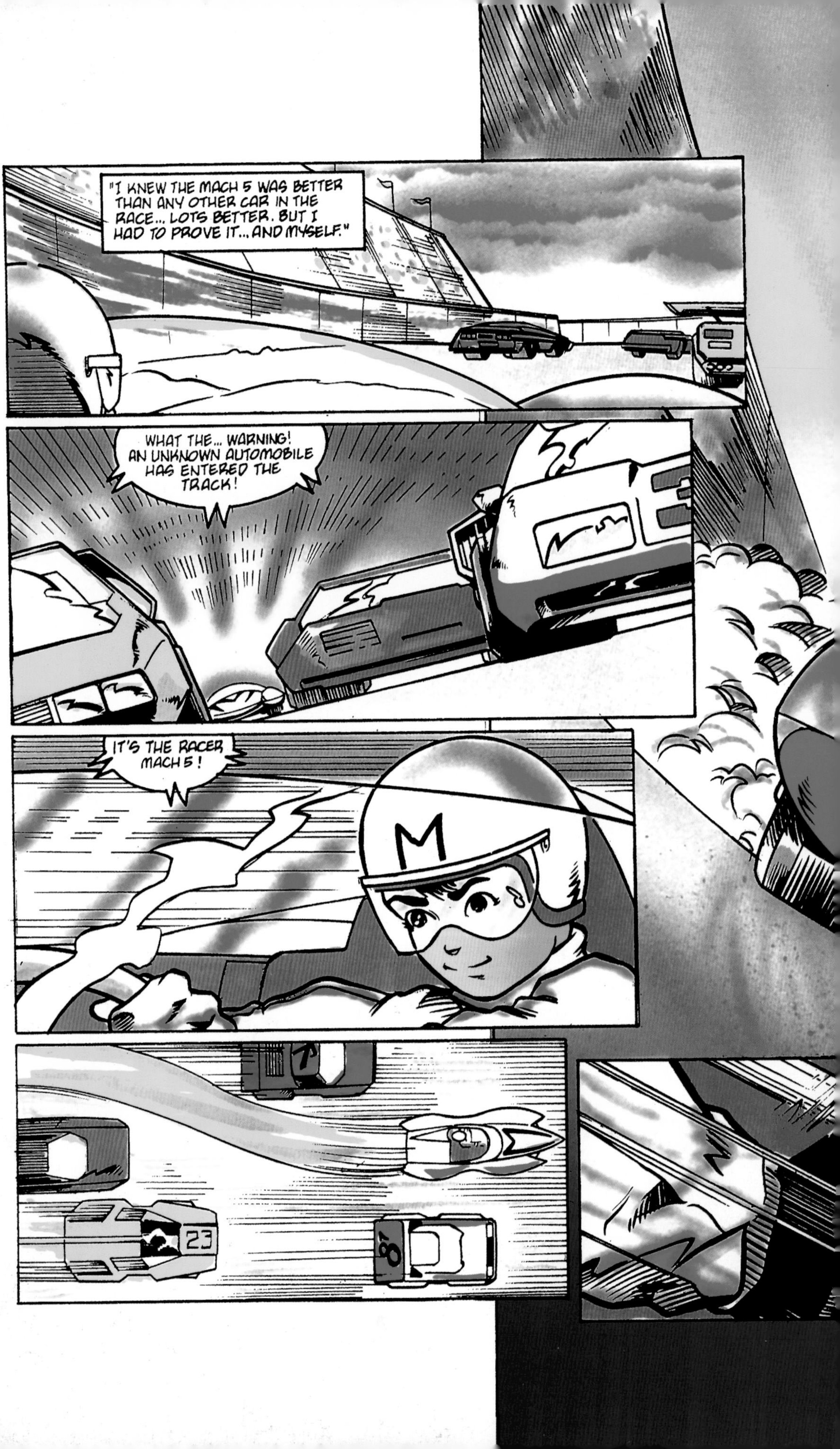
"I KNEW THE MACH 5 WAS BETTER THAN ANY OTHER CAR IN THE RACE... LOTS BETTER. BUT I HAD TO PROVE IT... AND MYSELF."
WHAT THE... WARNING! AN UNKNOWN AUTOMOBILE HAS ENTERED THE TRACK!
IT'S THE RACER MACH 5!
23
87

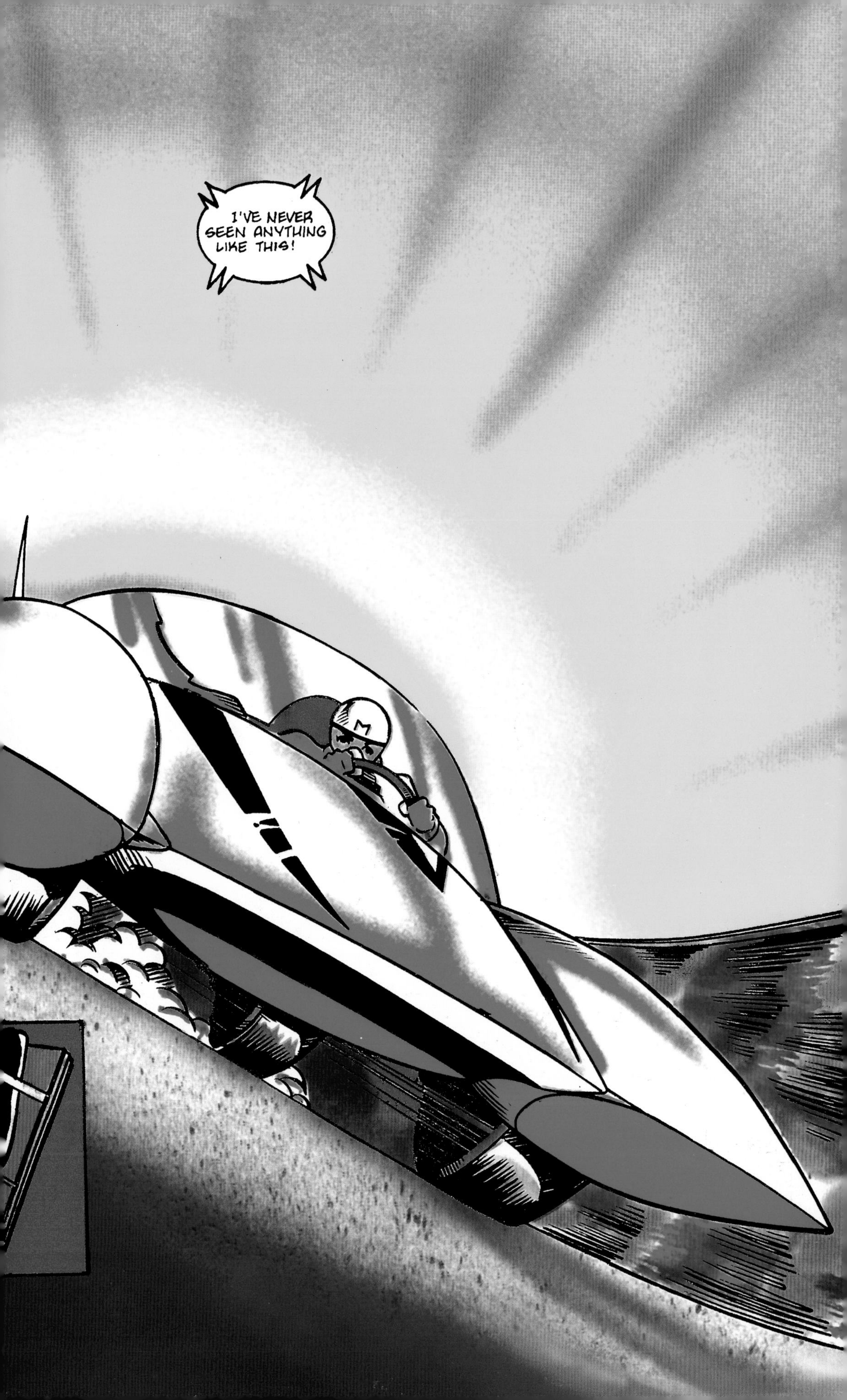
I'VE NEVER SEEN ANYTHING LIKE THIS!

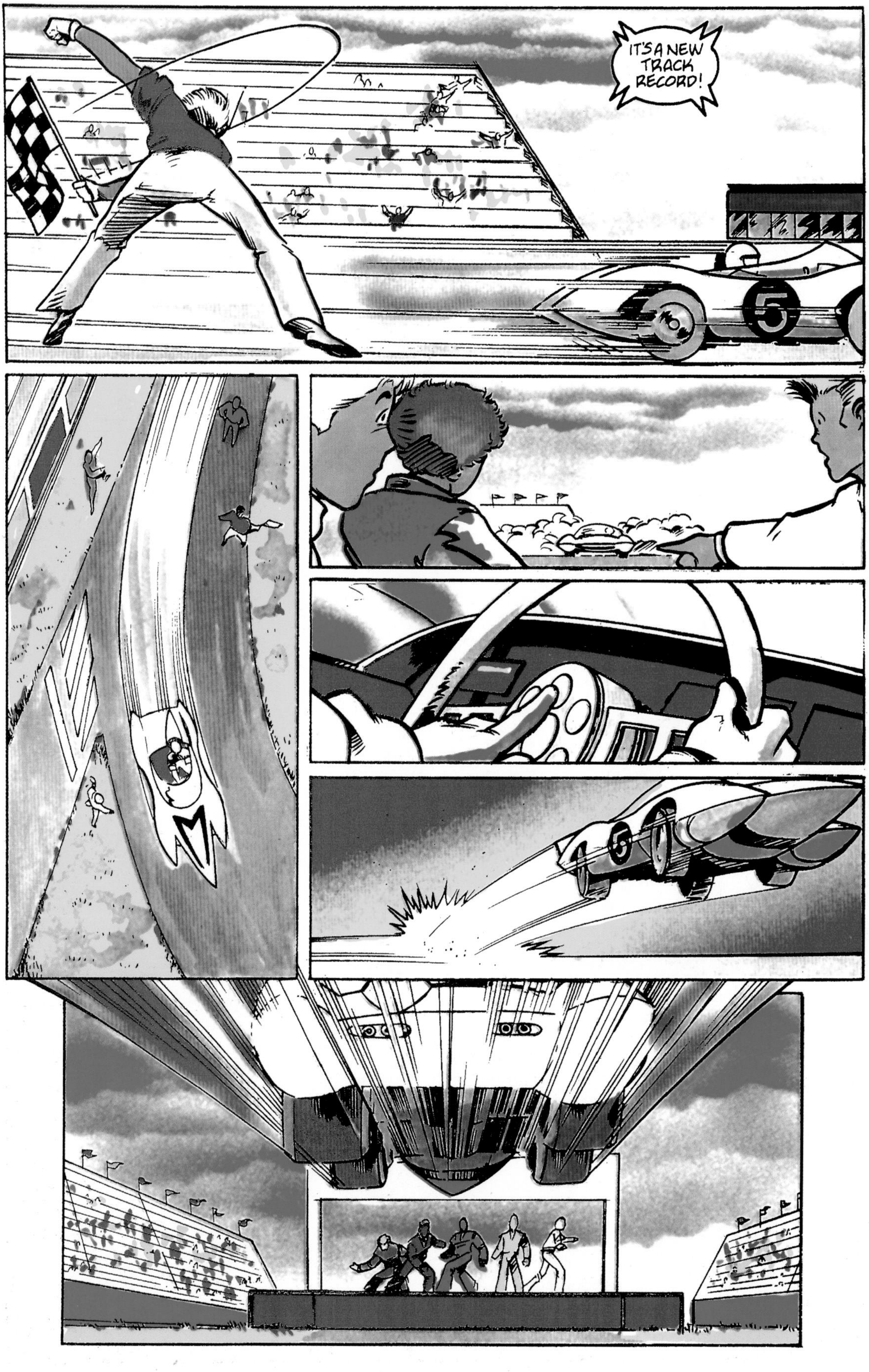
IT'S A NEW TRACK RECORD!

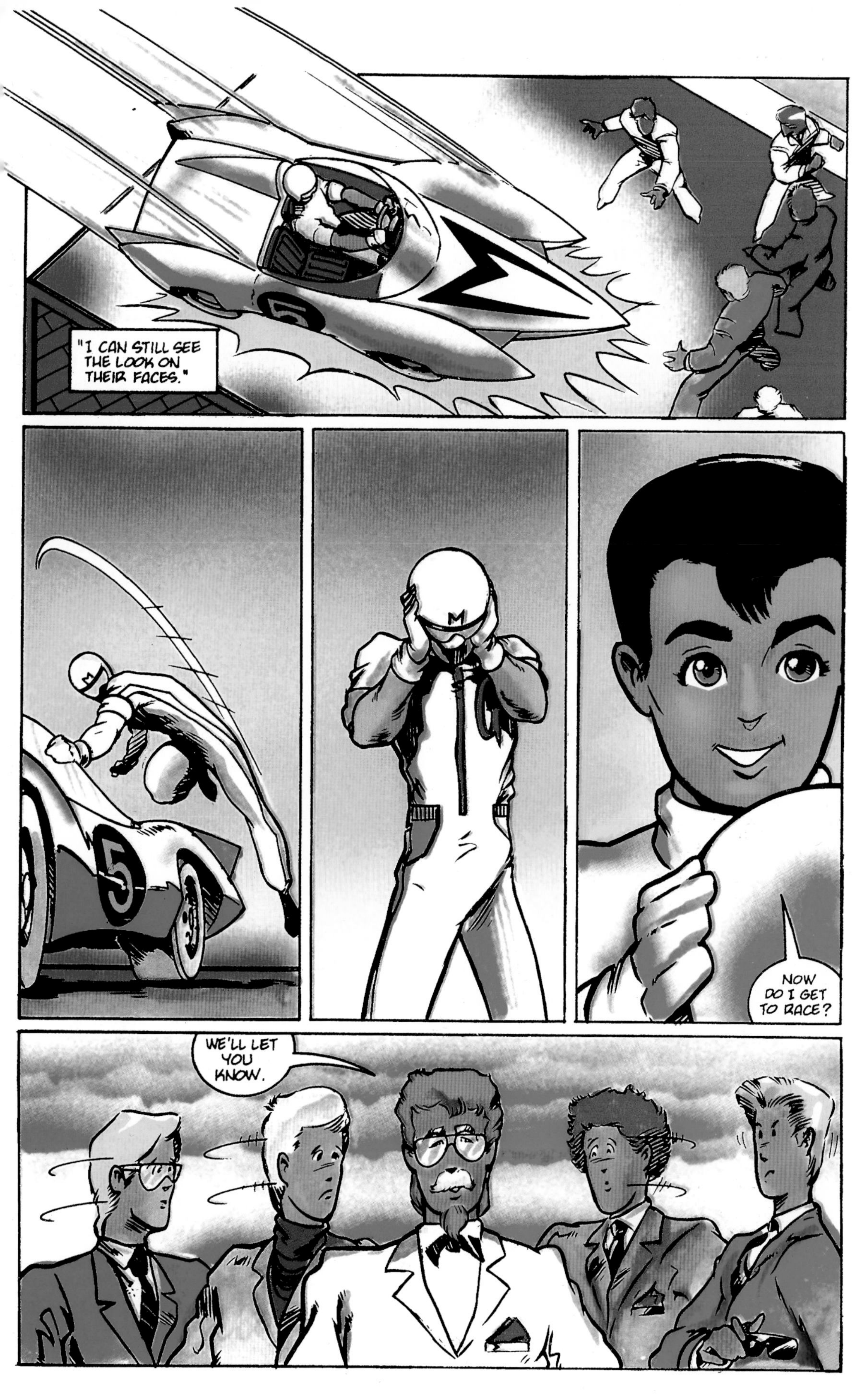
"I CAN STILL SEE THE LOOK ON THEIR FACES."
NOW DO I GET TO RACE?
WE'LL LET YOU KNOW.

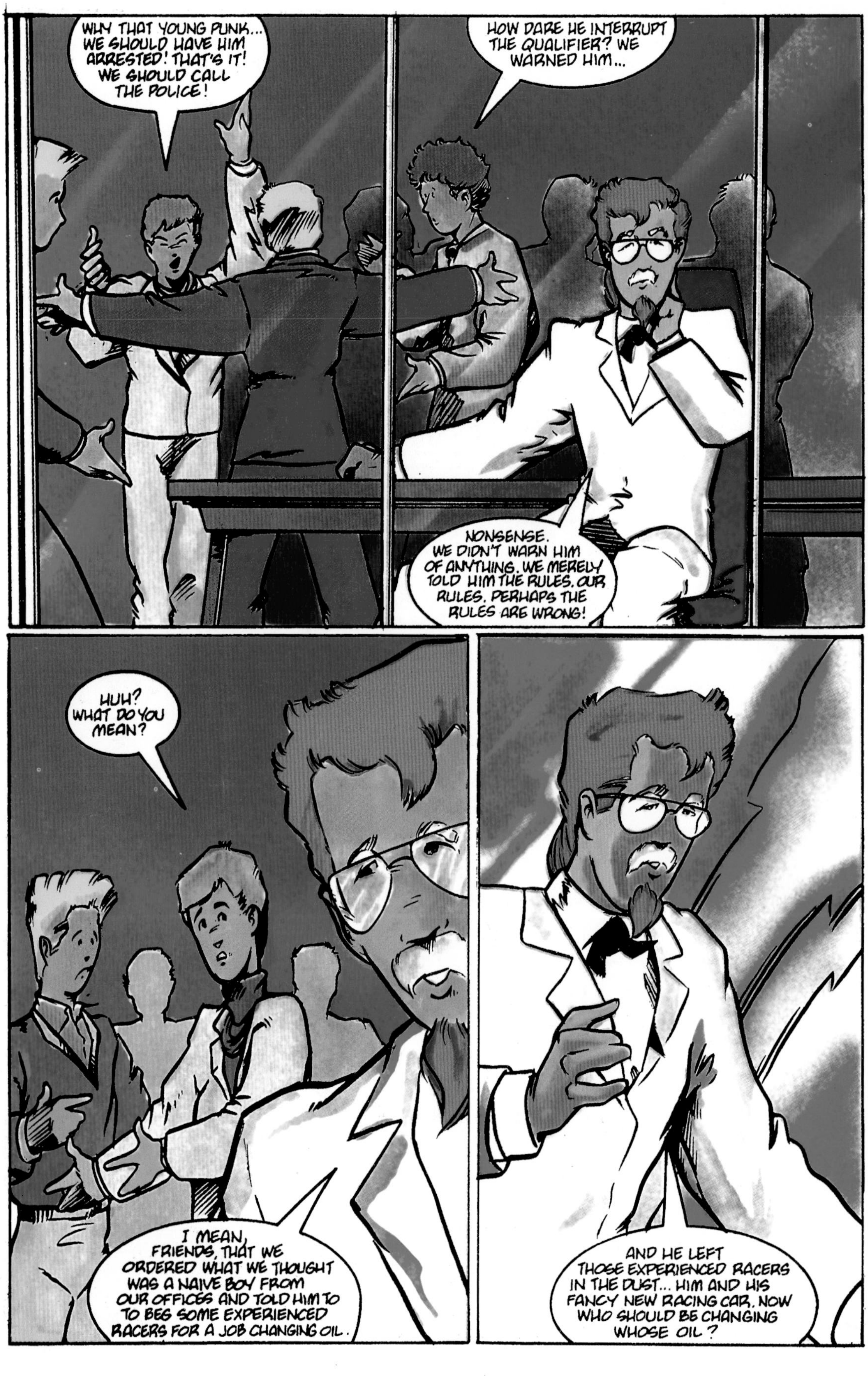
WHY THAT YOUNG PUNK... WE SHOULD HAVE HIM ARRESTED! THAT'S IT! WE SHOULD CALL THE POLICE!
HOW DARE HE INTERRUPT THE QUALIFIER? WE WARNED HIM...
NONSENSE. WE DIDN'T WARN HIM OF ANYTHING. WE MERELY TOLD HIM THE RULES. OUR RULES. PERHAPS THE RULES ARE WRONG!
HUH? WHAT DO YOU MEAN?
I MEAN, FRIENDS, THAT WE ORDERED WHAT WE THOUGHT WAS A NAIVE BOY FROM OUR OFFICES AND TOLD HIM TO TO BEG SOME EXPERIENCED RACERS FOR A JOB CHANGING OIL.
AND HE LEFT THOSE EXPERIENCED RACERS IN THE DUST... HIM AND HIS FANCY NEW RACING CAR. NOW WHO SHOULD BE CHANGING WHOSE OIL?

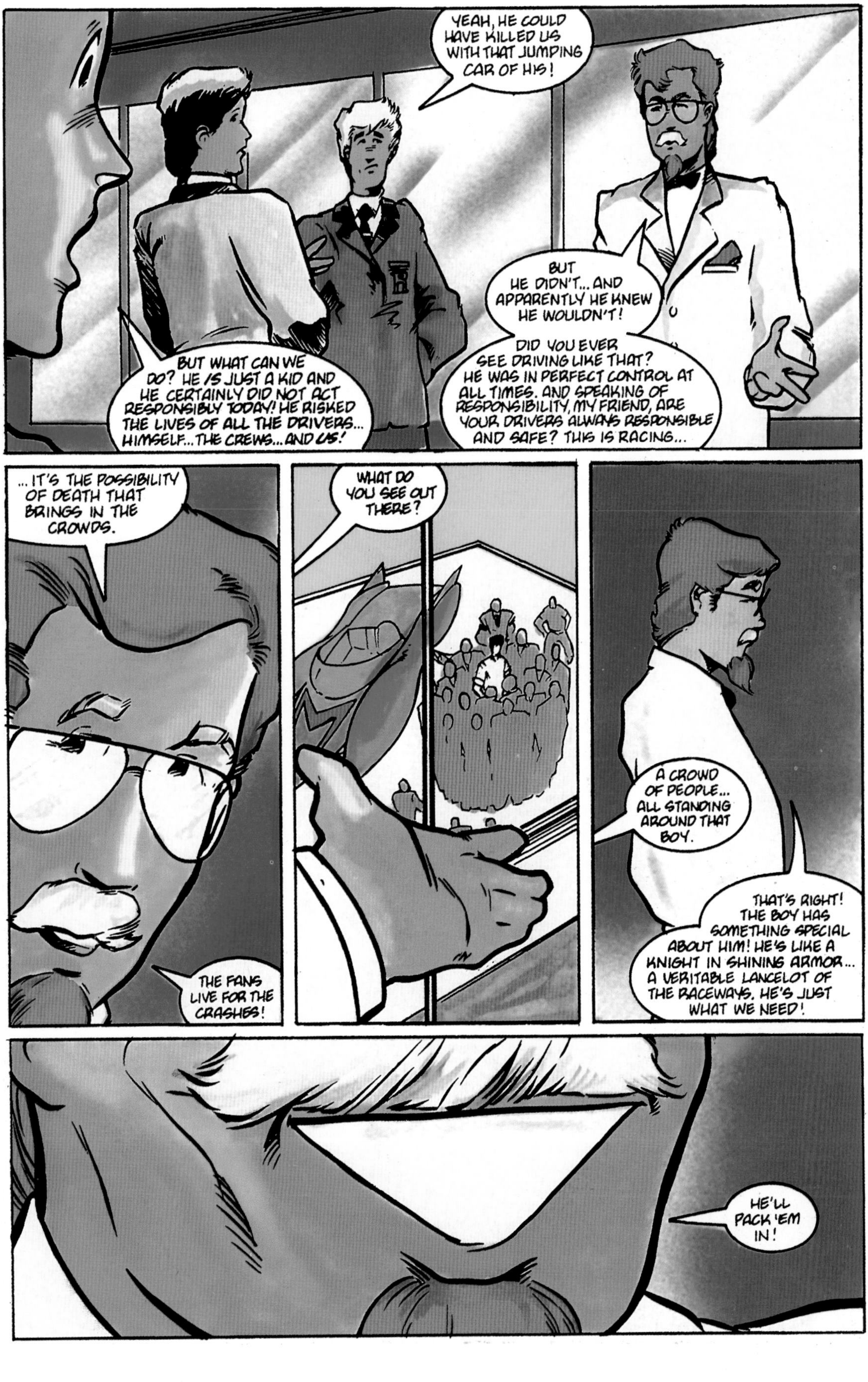
YEAH, HE COULD HAVE KILLED US WITH THAT JUMPING CAR OF HIS!
BUT WHAT CAN WE DO? HE IS JUST A KID AND HE CERTAINLY DID NOT ACT RESPONSIBLY TODAY! HE RISKED THE LIVES OF ALL THE DRIVERS... HIMSELF... THE CREWS... AND US!
BUT HE DIDN'T... AND APPARENTLY HE KNEW HE WOULDN'T!
DID YOU EVER SEE DRIVING LIKE THAT? HE WAS IN PERFECT CONTROL AT ALL TIMES. AND SPEAKING OF RESPONSIBILITY, MY FRIEND, ARE YOUR DRIVERS ALWAYS RESPONSIBLE AND SAFE? THIS IS RACING...
...IT'S THE POSSIBILITY OF DEATH THAT BRINGS IN THE CROWDS.
THE FANS LIVE FOR THE CRASHES!
WHAT DO YOU SEE OUT THERE?
A CROWD OF PEOPLE... ALL STANDING AROUND THAT BOY.
THAT'S RIGHT! THE BOY HAS SOMETHING SPECIAL ABOUT HIM! HE'S LIKE A KNIGHT IN SHINING ARMOR... A VERITABLE LANCELOT OF THE RACEWAYS. HE'S JUST WHAT WE NEED!
HE'LL PACK 'EM IN!

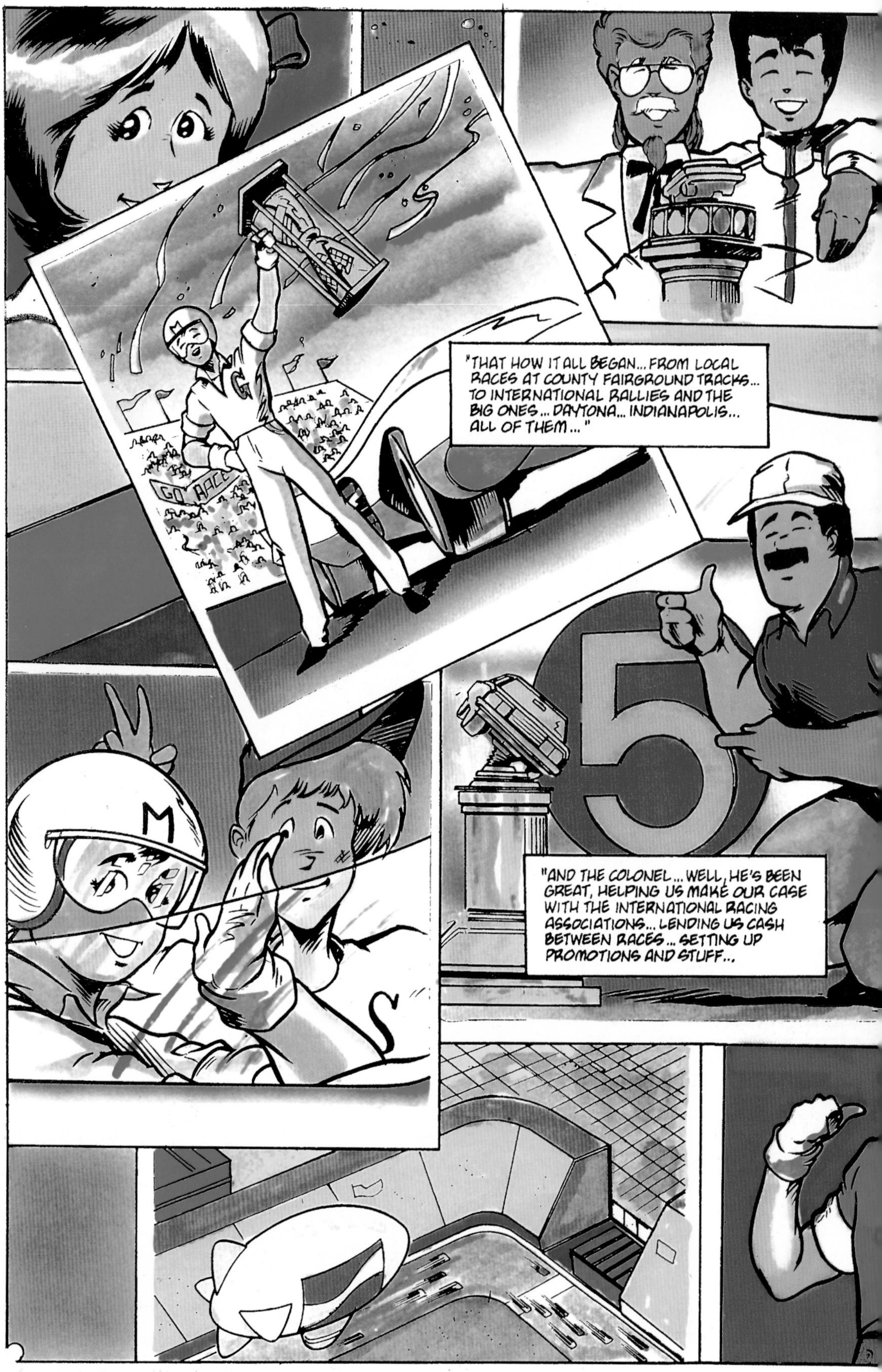
GO RACE
"THAT HOW IT ALL BEGAN... FROM LOCAL RACES AT COUNTY FAIRGROUND TRACKS... TO INTERNATIONAL RALLIES AND THE BIG ONES... DAYTONA... INDIANAPOLIS... ALL OF THEM..."
"AND THE COLONEL... WELL, HE'S BEEN GREAT, HELPING US MAKE OUR CASE WITH THE INTERNATIONAL RACING ASSOCIATIONS... LENDING US CASH BETWEEN RACES... SETTING UP PROMOTIONS AND STUFF...

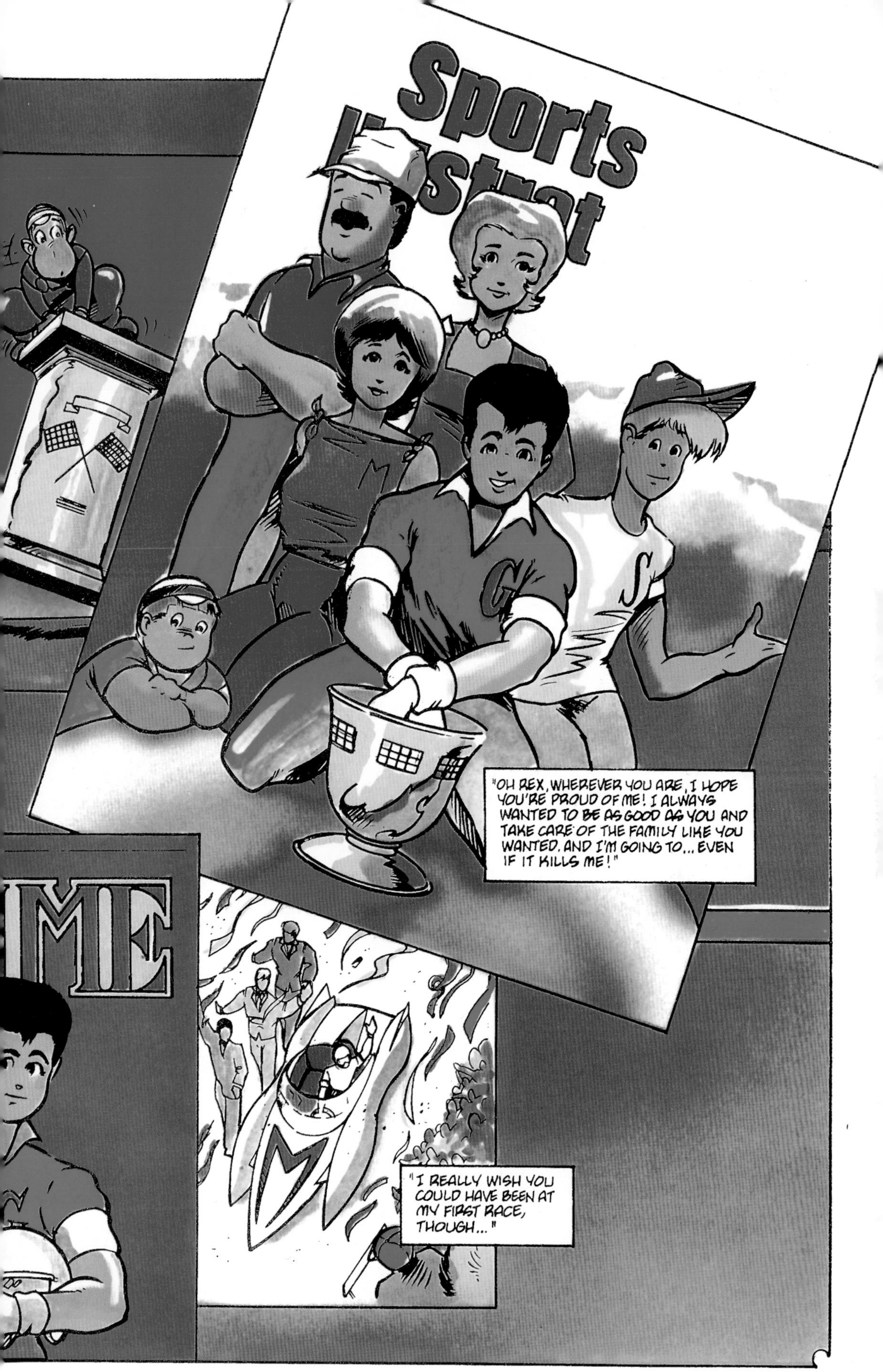
Sports Illustrat
"OH REX, WHEREVER YOU ARE, I HOPE YOU'RE PROUD OF ME! I ALWAYS WANTED TO BE AS GOOD AS YOU AND TAKE CARE OF THE FAMILY LIKE YOU WANTED. AND I'M GOING TO... EVEN IF IT KILLS ME!"
IME
"I REALLY WISH YOU COULD HAVE BEEN AT MY FIRST RACE, THOUGH..."

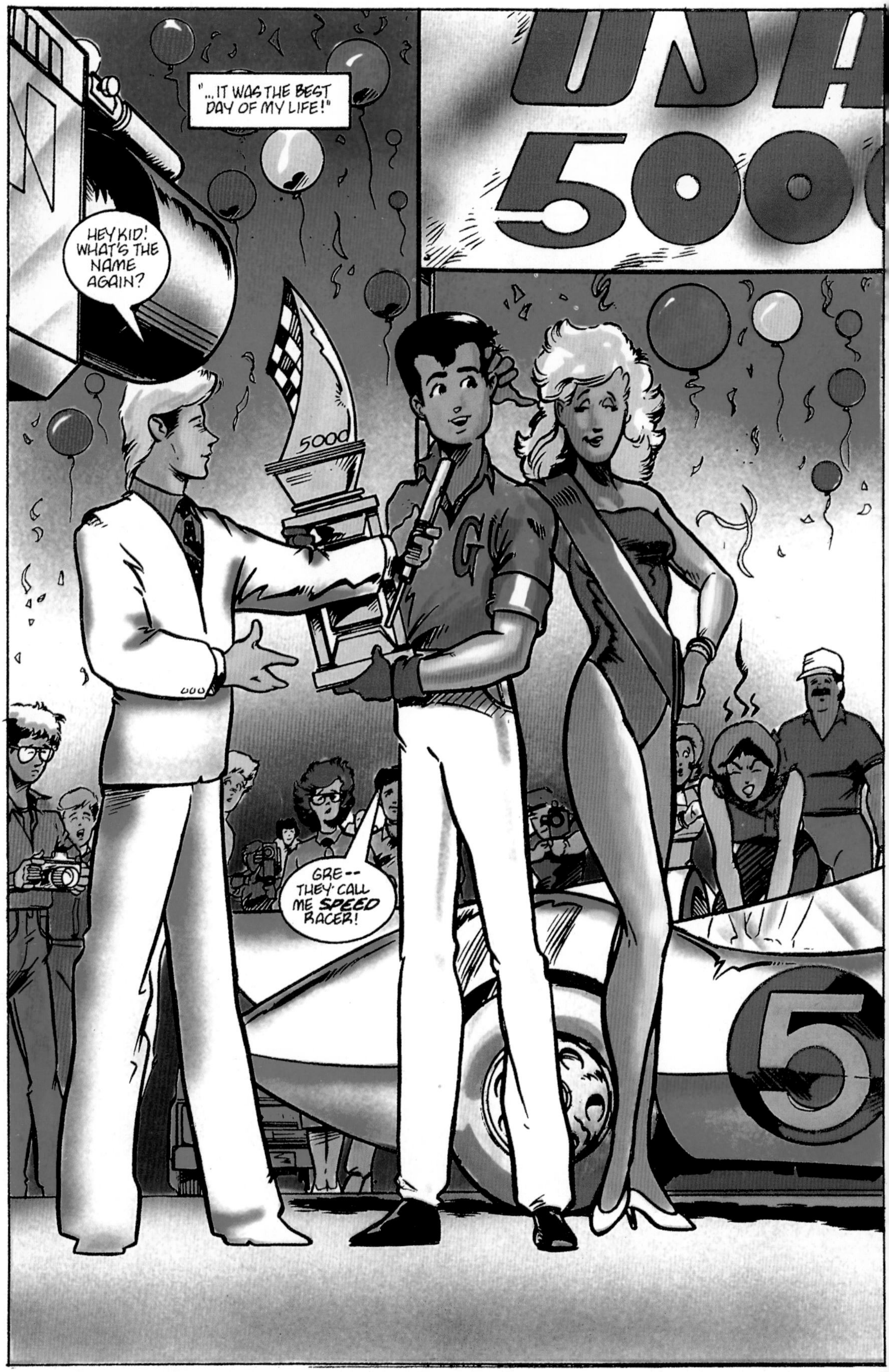
"...IT WAS THE BEST DAY OF MY LIFE!"
HEY KID! WHAT'S THE NAME AGAIN?
GRE-- THEY CALL ME SPEED RACER!

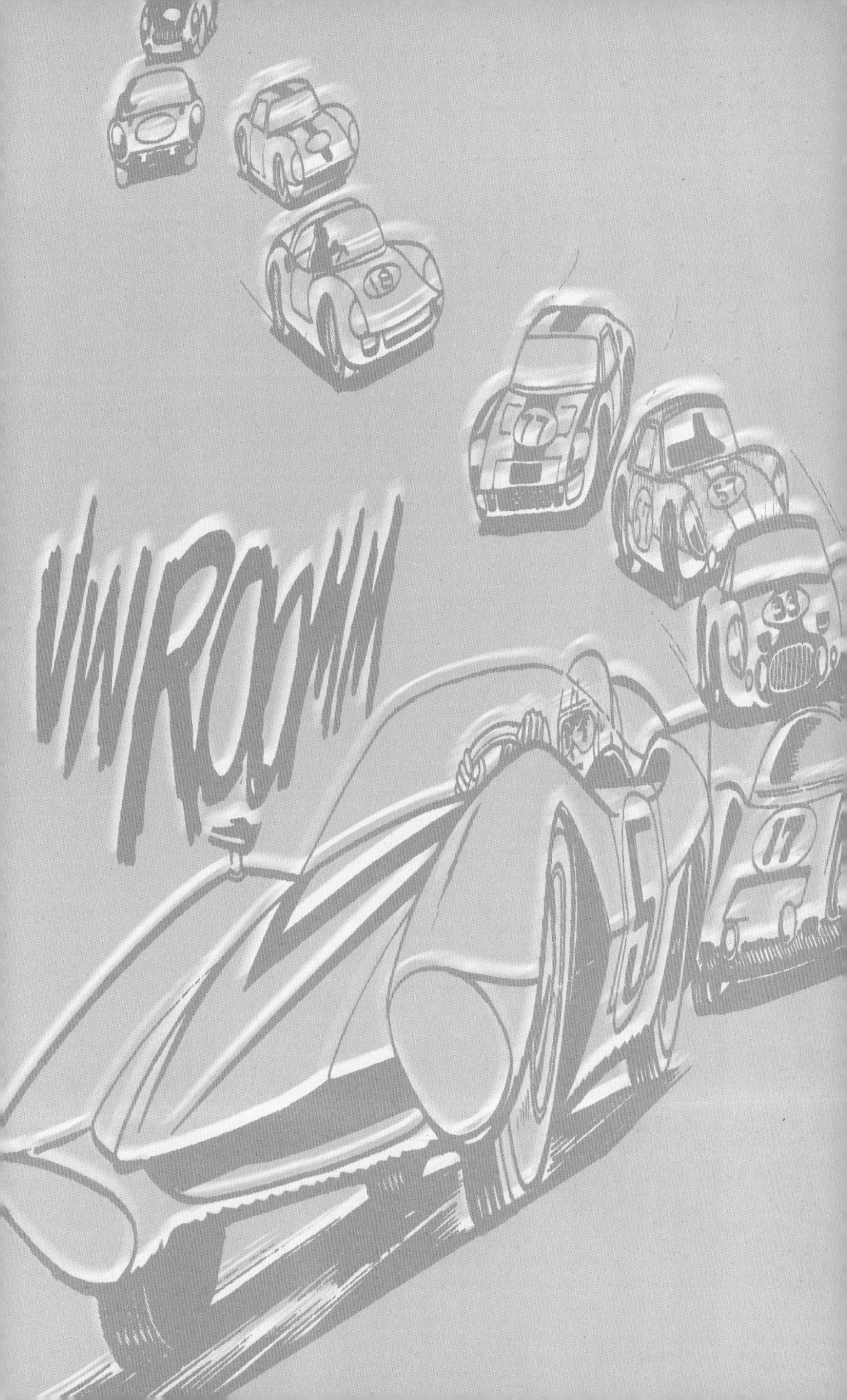
VWROOM

Speed Racer #2

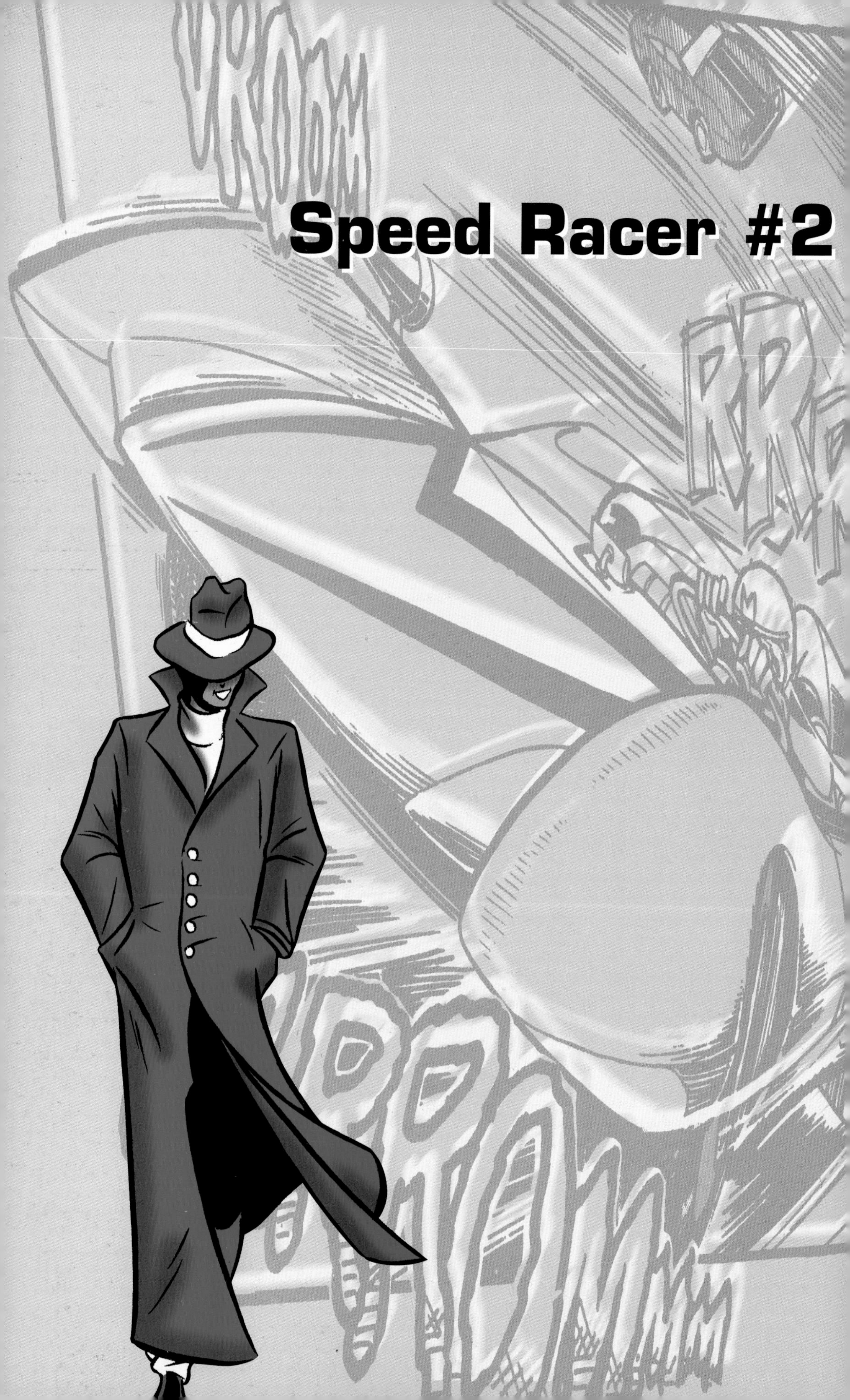

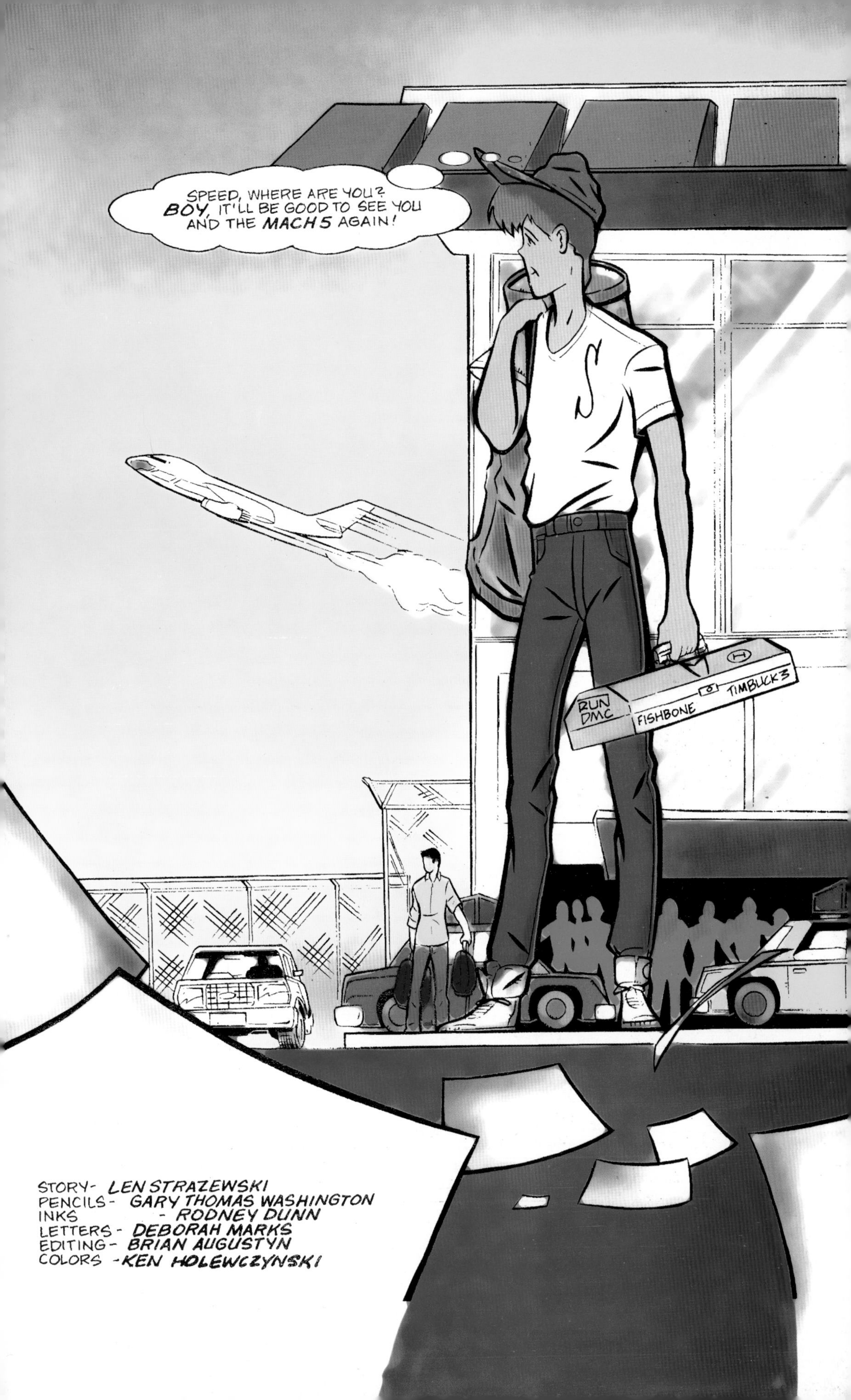
SPEED, WHERE ARE YOU? BOY, IT'LL BE GOOD TO SEE YOU AND THE MACH 5 AGAIN!
RUN DMC
FISHBONE
TIMBUCK 3
STORY- LEN STRAZEWSKI
PENCILS- GARY THOMAS WASHINGTON
INKS - RODNEY DUNN
LETTERS- DEBORAH MARKS
EDITING- BRIAN AUGUSTYN
COLORS -KEN HOLEWCZYNSKI

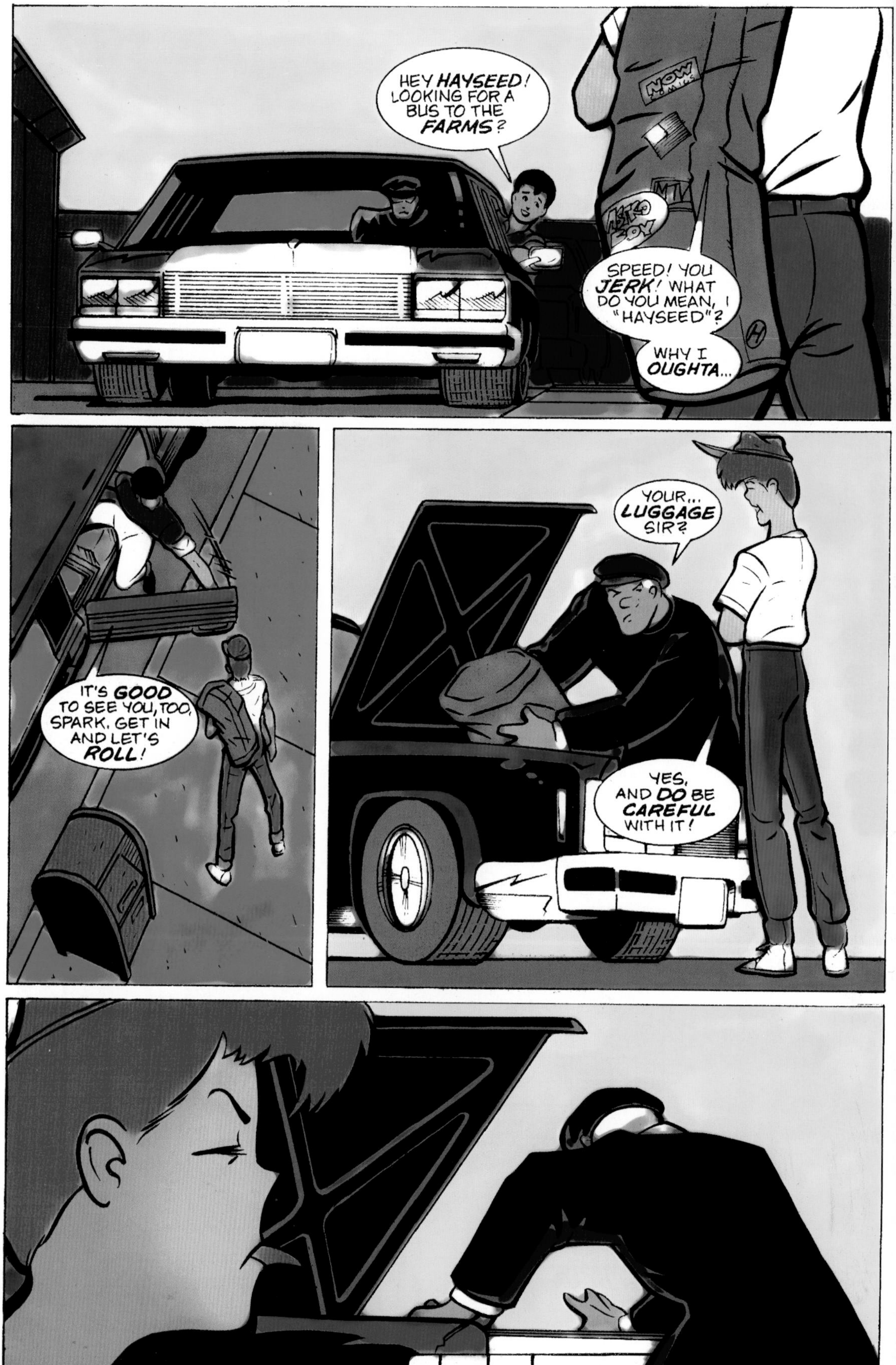
HEY HAYSEED! LOOKING FOR A BUS TO THE FARMS?
SPEED! YOU JERK! WHAT DO YOU MEAN, I "HAYSEED"?
WHY I OUGHTA...
IT'S GOOD TO SEE YOU, TOO, SPARK. GET IN AND LET'S ROLL!
YOUR... LUGGAGE SIR?
YES, AND DO BE CAREFUL WITH IT!

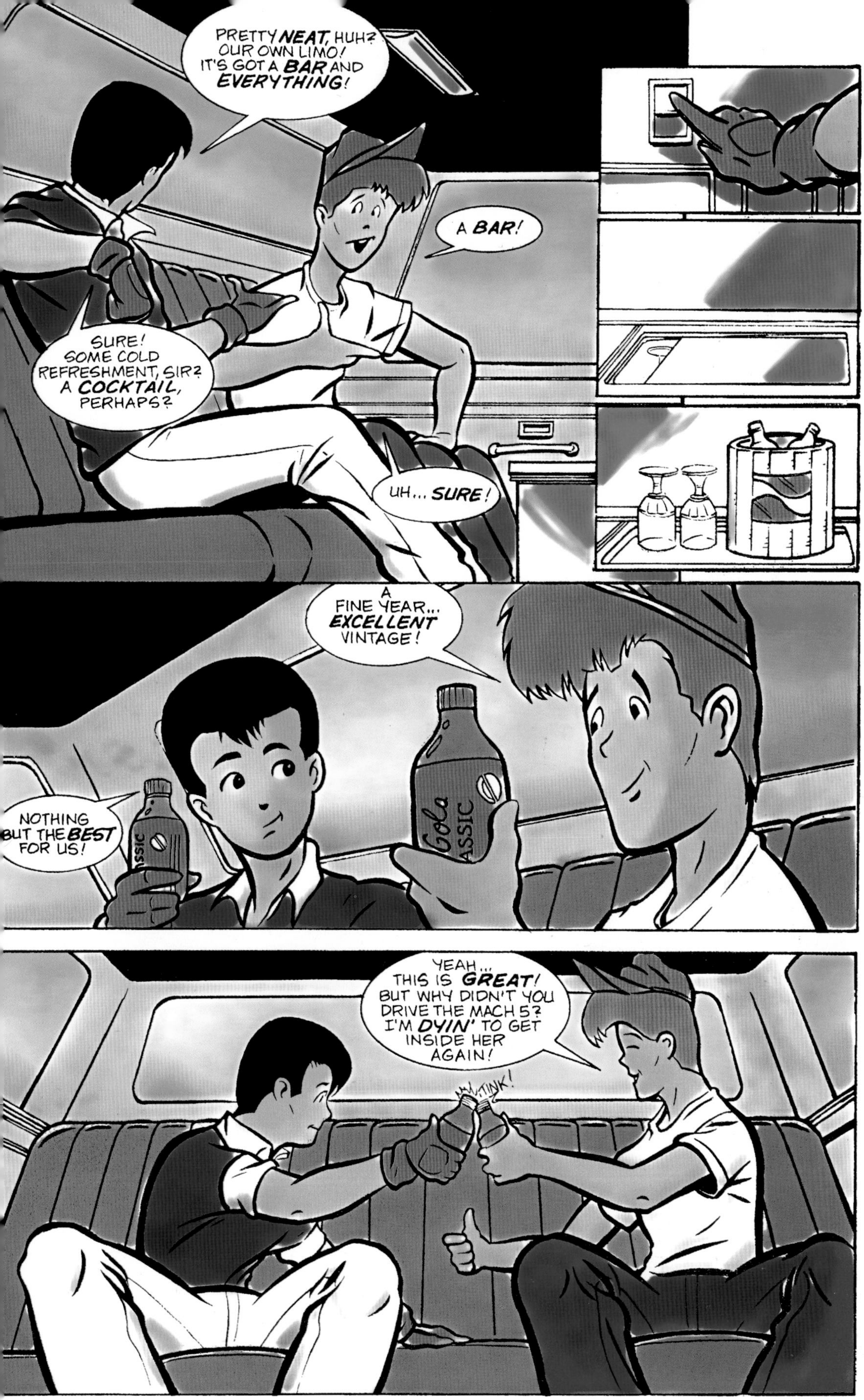
PRETTY NEAT, HUH? OUR OWN LIMO! IT'S GOT A BAR AND EVERYTHING!
A BAR!
SURE! SOME COLD REFRESHMENT, SIR? A COCKTAIL, PERHAPS?
UH... SURE!
A FINE YEAR... EXCELLENT VINTAGE!
NOTHING BUT THE BEST FOR US!
YEAH... THIS IS GREAT! BUT WHY DIDN'T YOU DRIVE THE MACH 5? I'M DYIN' TO GET INSIDE HER AGAIN!
TINK!

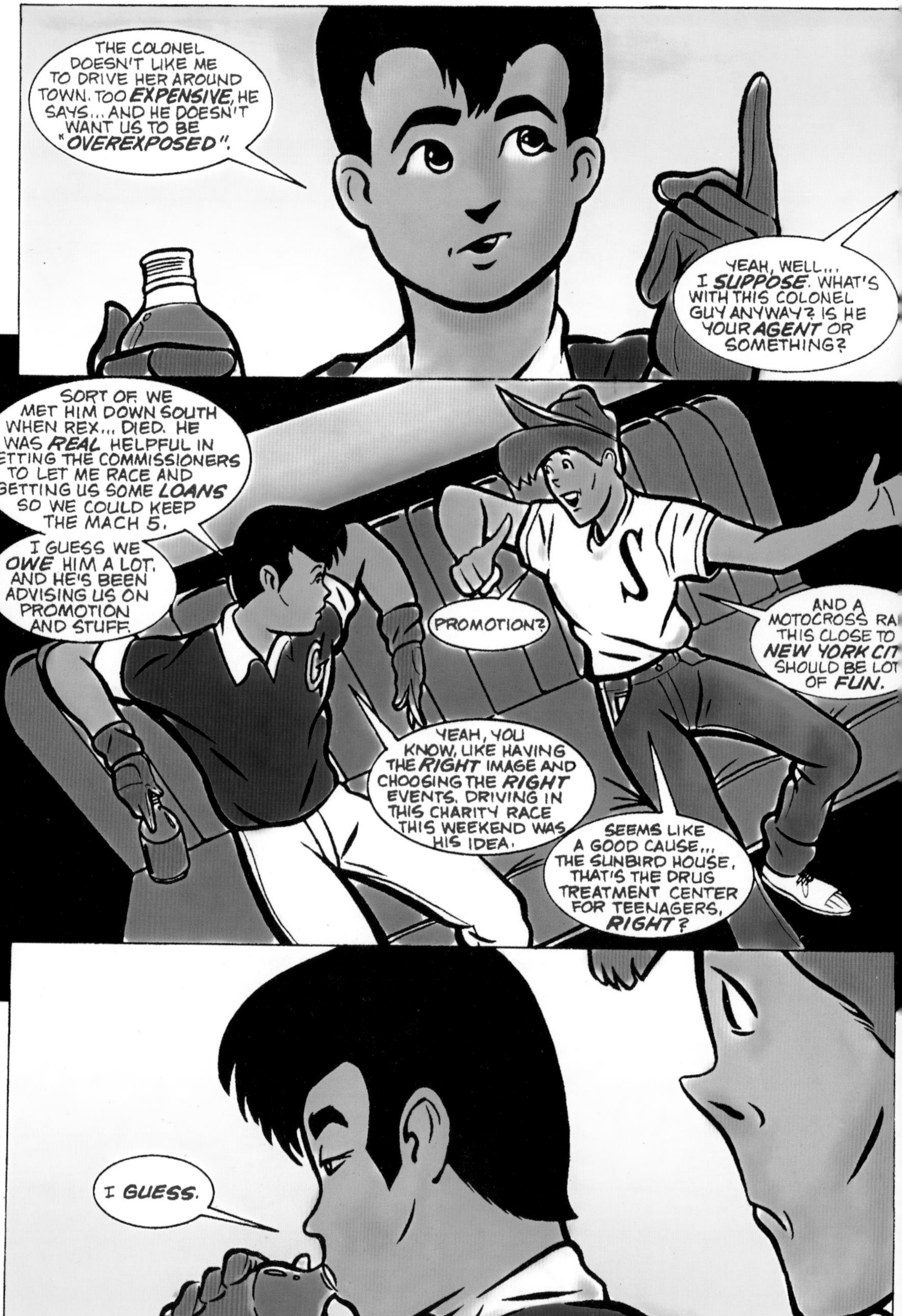
THE COLONEL DOESN'T LIKE ME TO DRIVE HER AROUND TOWN. TOO EXPENSIVE, HE SAYS... AND HE DOESN'T WANT US TO BE "OVEREXPOSED".
YEAH, WELL... I SUPPOSE. WHAT'S WITH THIS COLONEL GUY ANYWAY? IS HE YOUR AGENT OR SOMETHING?
SORT OF. WE MET HIM DOWN SOUTH WHEN REX... DIED. HE WAS REAL HELPFUL IN GETTING THE COMMISSIONERS TO LET ME RACE AND GETTING US SOME LOANS SO WE COULD KEEP THE MACH 5.
I GUESS WE OWE HIM A LOT. AND HE'S BEEN ADVISING US ON PROMOTION AND STUFF.
PROMOTION?
YEAH, YOU KNOW, LIKE HAVING THE RIGHT IMAGE AND CHOOSING THE RIGHT EVENTS. DRIVING IN THIS CHARITY RACE THIS WEEKEND WAS HIS IDEA.
AND A MOTOCROSS RA THIS CLOSE TO NEW YORK CIT SHOULD BE LOT OF FUN.
SEEMS LIKE A GOOD CAUSE... THE SUNBIRD HOUSE, THAT'S THE DRUG TREATMENT CENTER FOR TEENAGERS, RIGHT?
I GUESS.

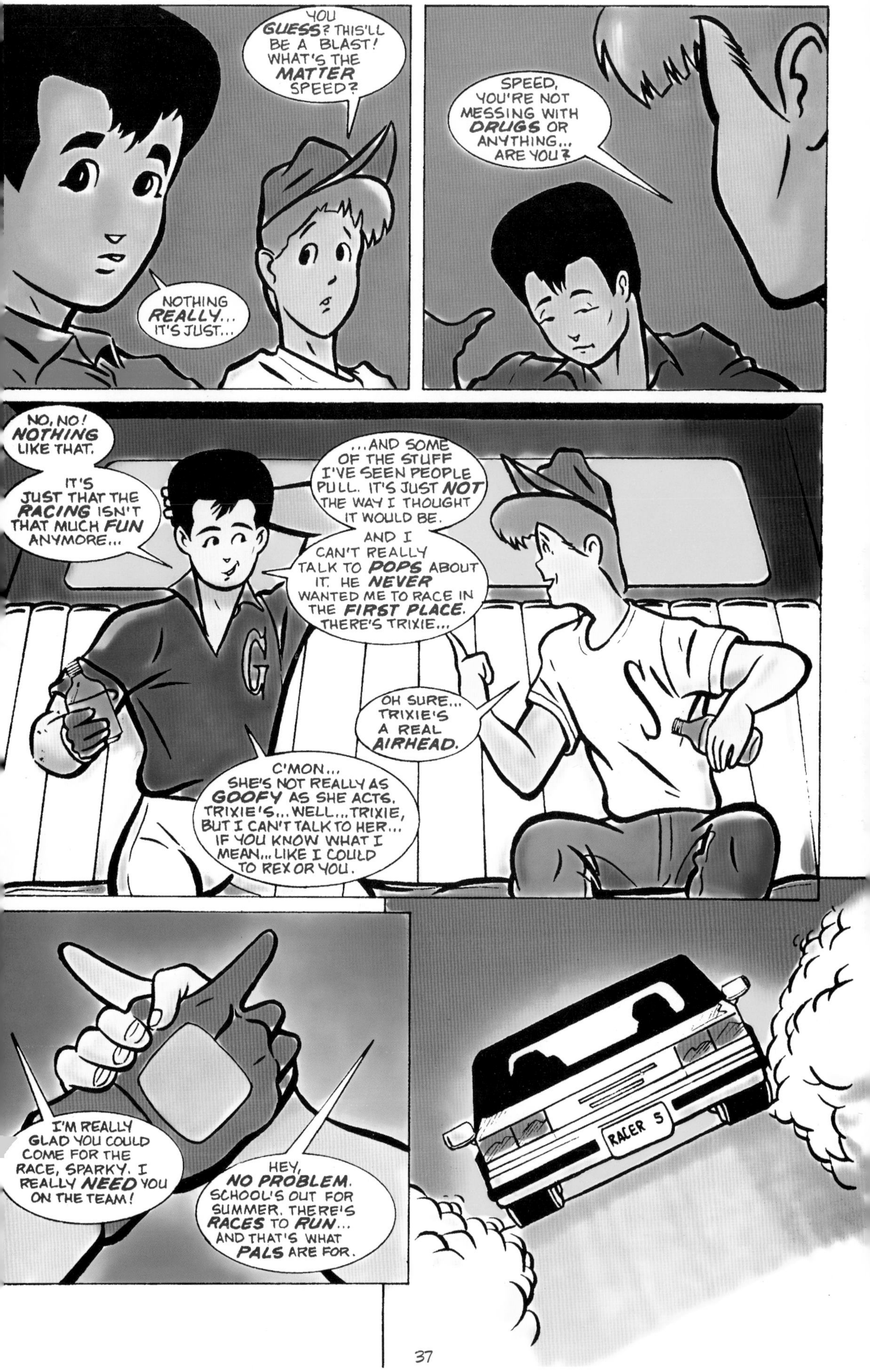
YOU GUESS? THIS'LL BE A BLAST! WHAT'S THE MATTER SPEED?
NOTHING REALLY... IT'S JUST...
SPEED, YOU'RE NOT MESSING WITH DRUGS OR ANYTHING... ARE YOU?
NO, NO! NOTHING LIKE THAT.
IT'S JUST THAT THE RACING ISN'T THAT MUCH FUN ANYMORE...
...AND SOME OF THE STUFF I'VE SEEN PEOPLE PULL. IT'S JUST NOT THE WAY I THOUGHT IT WOULD BE.
AND I CAN'T REALLY TALK TO POPS ABOUT IT. HE NEVER WANTED ME TO RACE IN THE FIRST PLACE. THERE'S TRIXIE...
OH SURE... TRIXIE'S A REAL AIRHEAD.
C'MON... SHE'S NOT REALLY AS GOOFY AS SHE ACTS. TRIXIE'S... WELL... TRIXIE, BUT I CAN'T TALK TO HER... IF YOU KNOW WHAT I MEAN... LIKE I COULD TO REX OR YOU.
I'M REALLY GLAD YOU COULD COME FOR THE RACE, SPARKY. I REALLY NEED YOU ON THE TEAM!
HEY, NO PROBLEM. SCHOOL'S OUT FOR SUMMER. THERE'S RACES TO RUN... AND THAT'S WHAT PALS ARE FOR.
RACER 5

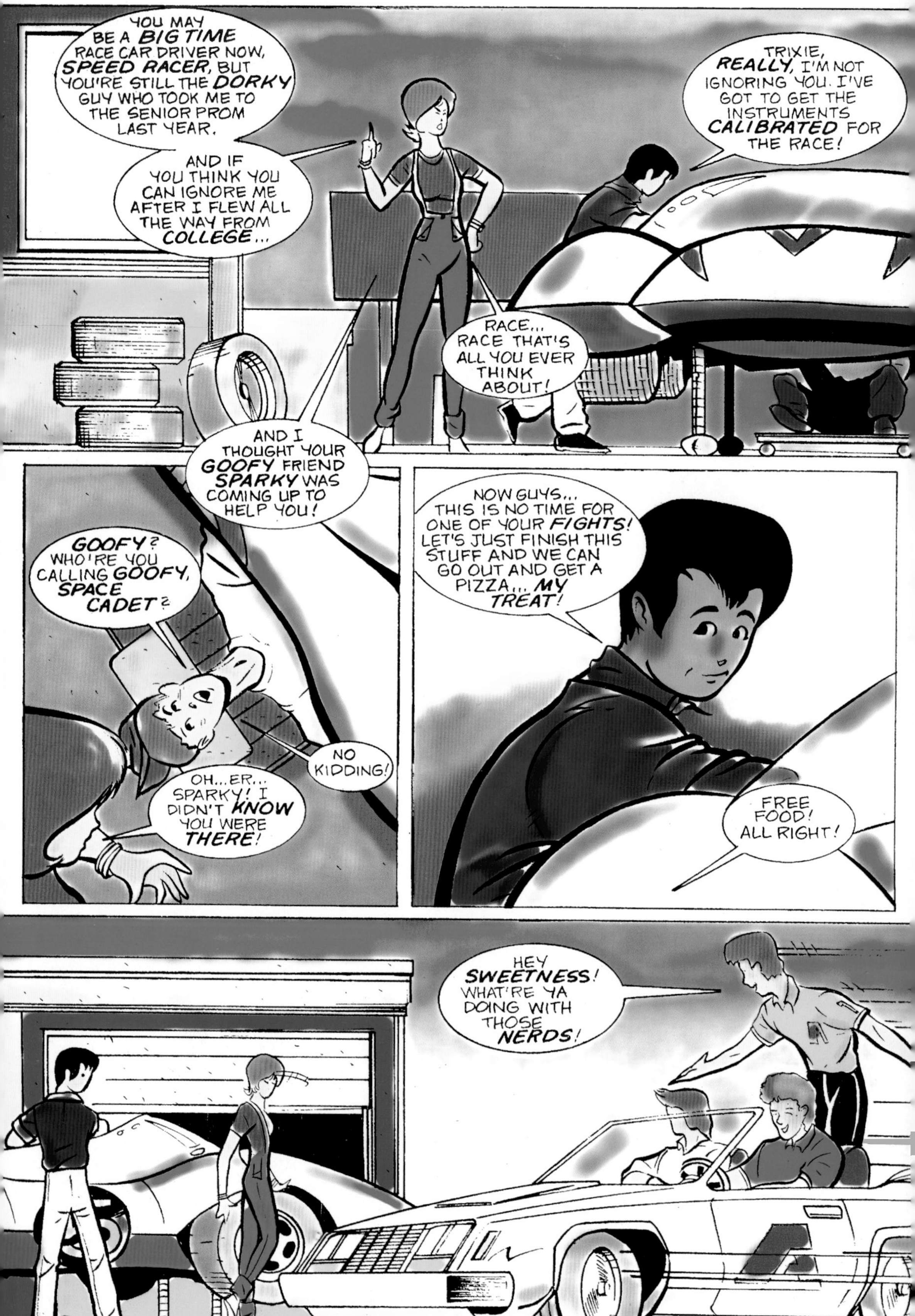
YOU MAY BE A BIG TIME RACE CAR DRIVER NOW, SPEED RACER, BUT YOU'RE STILL THE DORKY GUY WHO TOOK ME TO THE SENIOR PROM LAST YEAR.
AND IF YOU THINK YOU CAN IGNORE ME AFTER I FLEW ALL THE WAY FROM COLLEGE...
TRIXIE, REALLY, I'M NOT IGNORING YOU. I'VE GOT TO GET THE INSTRUMENTS CALIBRATED FOR THE RACE!
RACE... RACE THAT'S ALL YOU EVER THINK ABOUT!
AND I THOUGHT YOUR GOOFY FRIEND SPARKY WAS COMING UP TO HELP YOU!
GOOFY? WHO'RE YOU CALLING GOOFY, SPACE CADET?
NO KIDDING!
OH...ER... SPARKY! I DIDN'T KNOW YOU WERE THERE!
NOW GUYS... THIS IS NO TIME FOR ONE OF YOUR FIGHTS! LET'S JUST FINISH THIS STUFF AND WE CAN GO OUT AND GET A PIZZA... MY TREAT!
FREE FOOD! ALL RIGHT!
HEY SWEETNESS! WHAT'RE YA DOING WITH THOSE NERDS!

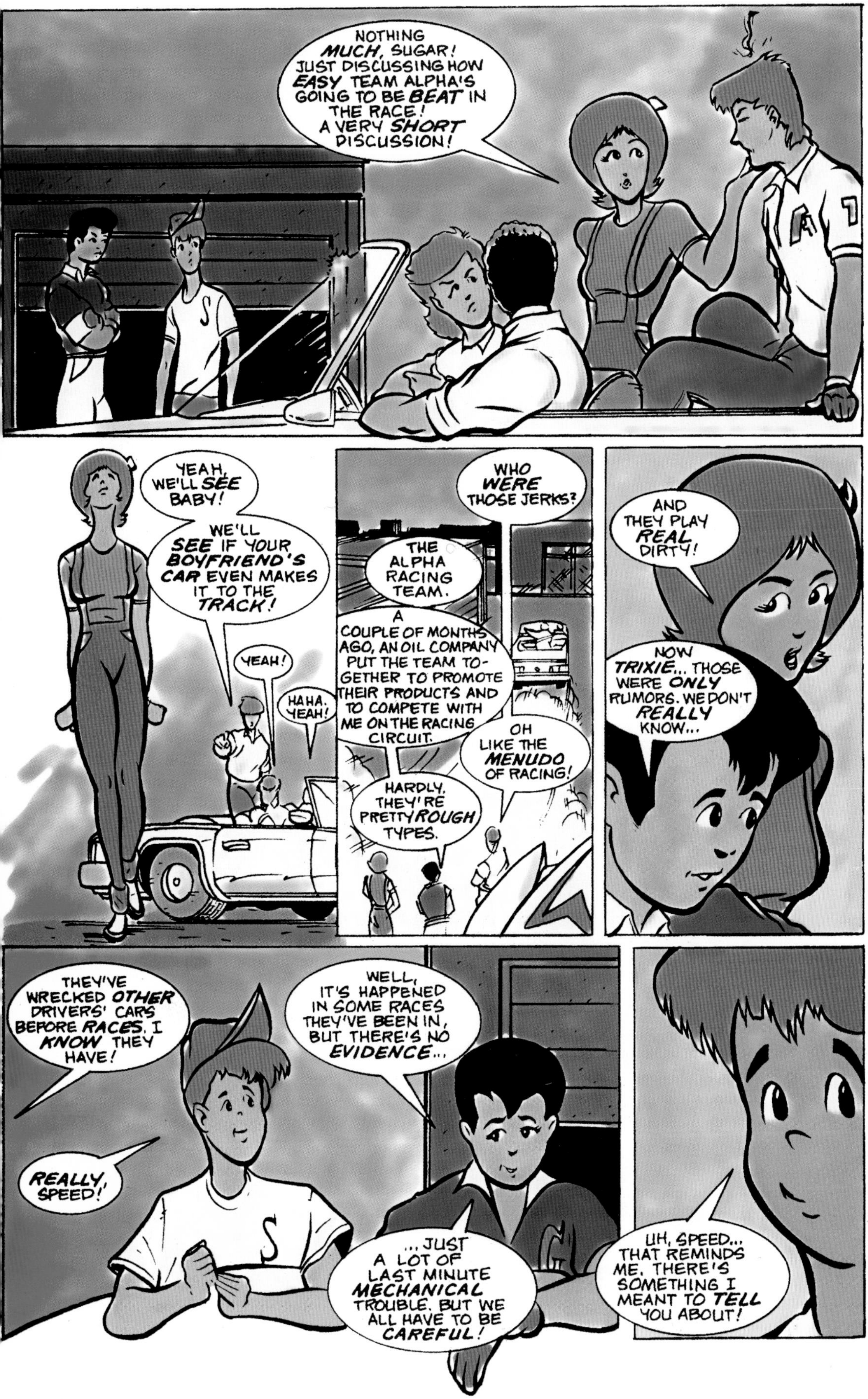
NOTHING MUCH, SUGAR! JUST DISCUSSING HOW EASY TEAM ALPHA'S GOING TO BE BEAT IN THE RACE! A VERY SHORT DISCUSSION!
YEAH, WE'LL SEE BABY!
WE'LL SEE IF YOUR BOYFRIEND'S CAR EVEN MAKES IT TO THE TRACK!
YEAH!
HAHA. YEAH!
WHO WERE THOSE JERKS?
THE ALPHA RACING TEAM.
A COUPLE OF MONTHS AGO, AN OIL COMPANY PUT THE TEAM TO-GETHER TO PROMOTE THEIR PRODUCTS AND TO COMPETE WITH ME ON THE RACING CIRCUIT.
OH LIKE THE MENUDO OF RACING!
HARDLY. THEY'RE PRETTY ROUGH TYPES.
AND THEY PLAY REAL DIRTY!
NOW TRIXIE... THOSE WERE ONLY RUMORS. WE DON'T REALLY KNOW...
THEY'VE WRECKED OTHER DRIVERS' CARS BEFORE RACES. I KNOW THEY HAVE!
REALLY, SPEED!
WELL, IT'S HAPPENED IN SOME RACES THEY'VE BEEN IN, BUT THERE'S NO EVIDENCE...
...JUST A LOT OF LAST MINUTE MECHANICAL TROUBLE. BUT WE ALL HAVE TO BE CAREFUL!
UH, SPEED... THAT REMINDS ME. THERE'S SOMETHING I MEANT TO TELL YOU ABOUT!

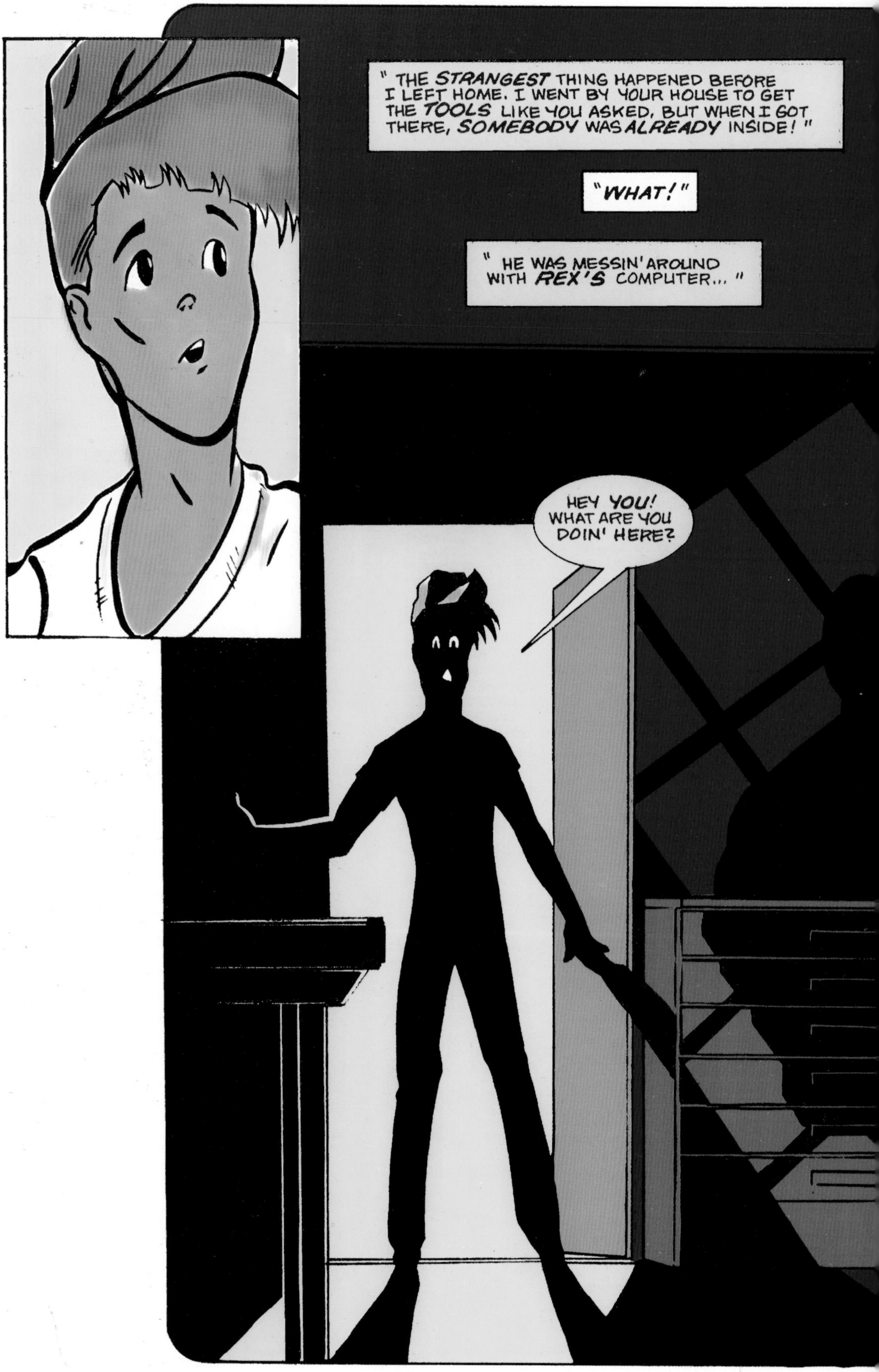
"THE STRANGEST THING HAPPENED BEFORE I LEFT HOME. I WENT BY YOUR HOUSE TO GET THE TOOLS LIKE YOU ASKED, BUT WHEN I GOT THERE, SOMEBODY WAS ALREADY INSIDE!"
"WHAT!"
"HE WAS MESSIN' AROUND WITH REX'S COMPUTER..."
HEY YOU! WHAT ARE YOU DOIN' HERE?

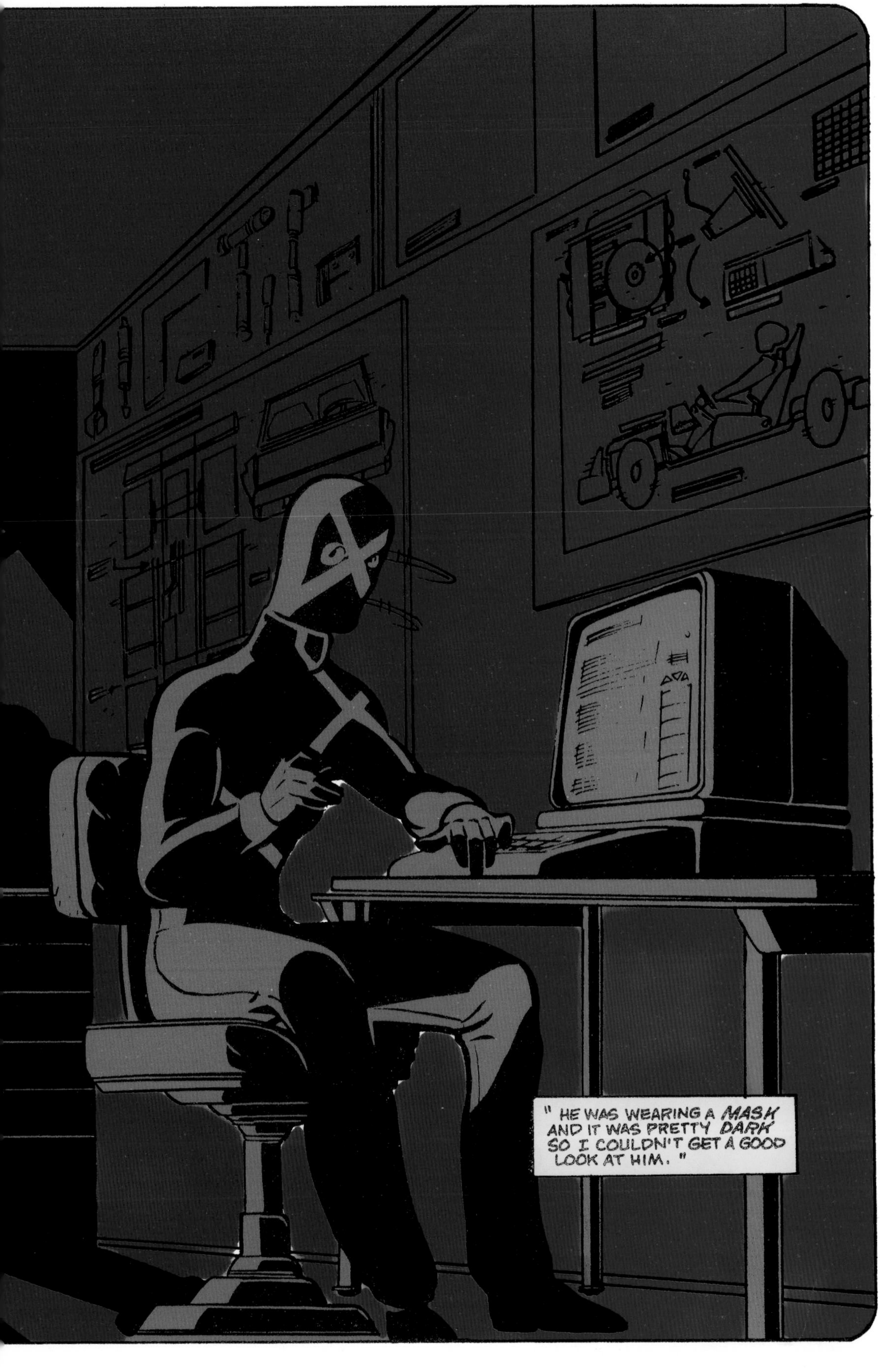
" HE WAS WEARING A *MASK* AND IT WAS PRETTY *DARK* SO I COULDN'T GET A GOOD LOOK AT HIM. "

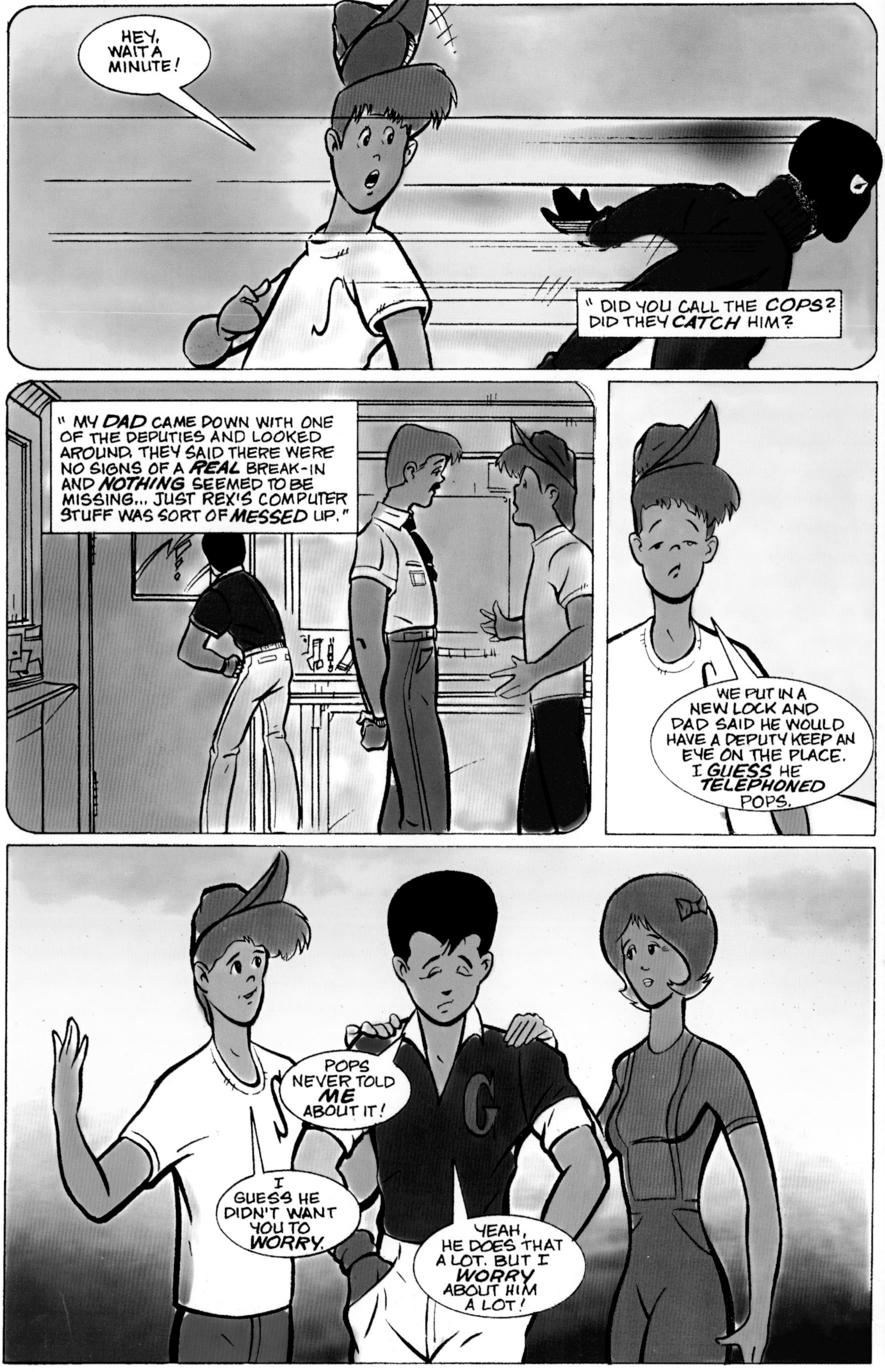

HEY, WAIT A MINUTE!
" DID YOU CALL THE COPS? DID THEY CATCH HIM?
" MY DAD CAME DOWN WITH ONE OF THE DEPUTIES AND LOOKED AROUND. THEY SAID THERE WERE NO SIGNS OF A REAL BREAK-IN AND NOTHING SEEMED TO BE MISSING... JUST REX'S COMPUTER STUFF WAS SORT OF MESSED UP."
WE PUT IN A NEW LOCK AND DAD SAID HE WOULD HAVE A DEPUTY KEEP AN EYE ON THE PLACE. I GUESS HE TELEPHONED POPS.
POPS NEVER TOLD ME ABOUT IT!
I GUESS HE DIDN'T WANT YOU TO WORRY.
YEAH, HE DOES THAT A LOT. BUT I WORRY ABOUT HIM A LOT!

AH... POPS CAN HANDLE *ANYTHING.* AFTER ALL, HE BUILT THE MACH 5, *DIDN'T HE?*

YEAH, I GUESS. BUT NOT *EVERYTHING* IS LIKE DESIGNING A RACE CAR. POPS DOESN'T ALWAYS HANDLE *PEOPLE* REAL WELL. HE MAKES *ENEMIES.*

NAH! EVERYBODY LIKES RACERS. THEY'RE *NATURALLY* LOVABLE.

C'MON, LET'S GO FOR A *RIDE!*

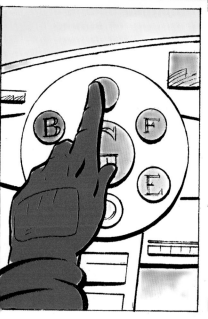

I'VE GOT TO CHANGE... PICK ME UP LATER FOR *DINNER!*

43

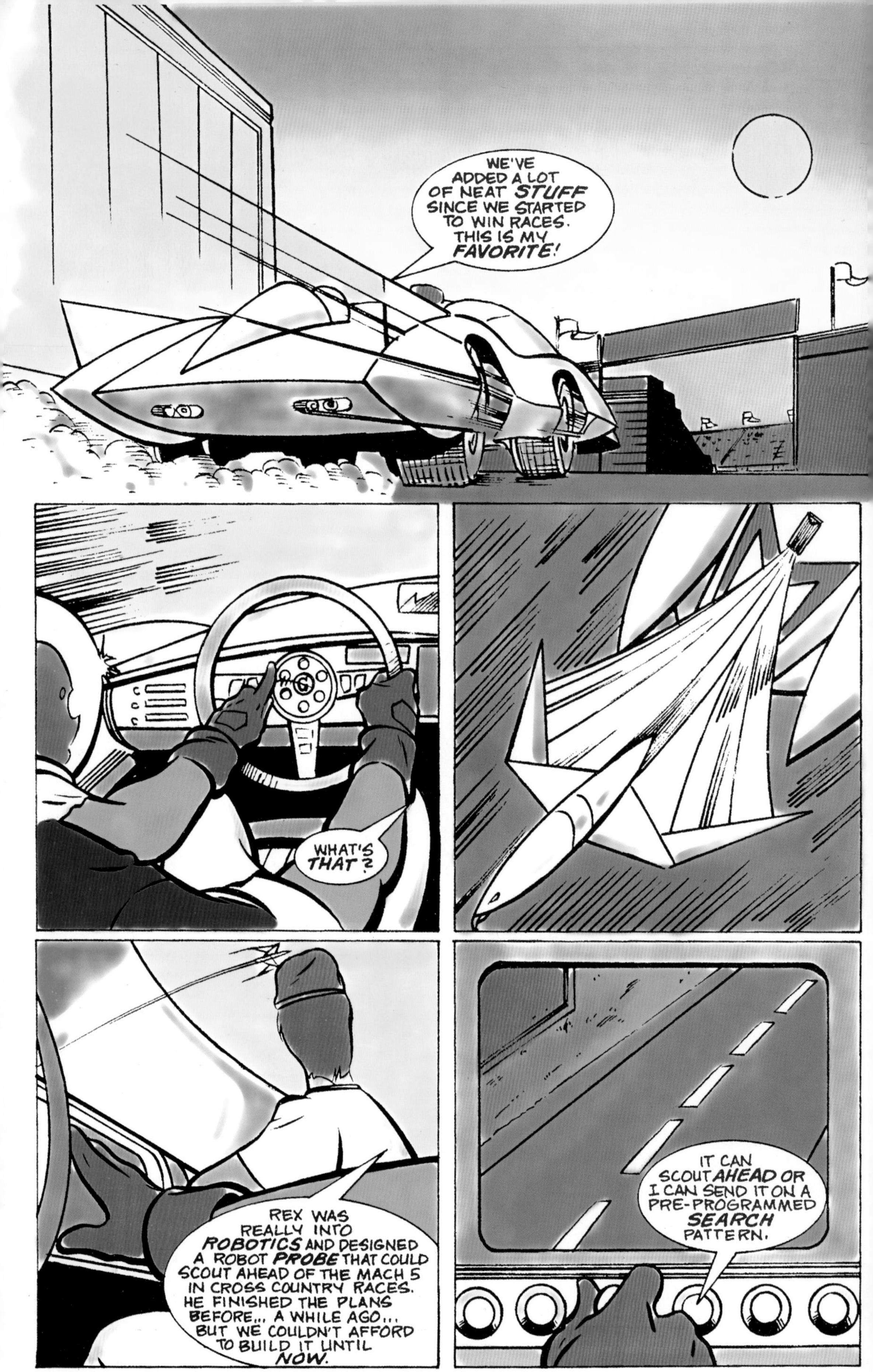
WE'VE ADDED A LOT OF NEAT STUFF SINCE WE STARTED TO WIN RACES. THIS IS MY FAVORITE!
WHAT'S THAT?
REX WAS REALLY INTO ROBOTICS AND DESIGNED A ROBOT PROBE THAT COULD SCOUT AHEAD OF THE MACH 5 IN CROSS COUNTRY RACES. HE FINISHED THE PLANS BEFORE... A WHILE AGO... BUT WE COULDN'T AFFORD TO BUILD IT UNTIL NOW.
IT CAN SCOUT AHEAD OR I CAN SEND IT ON A PRE-PROGRAMMED SEARCH PATTERN.

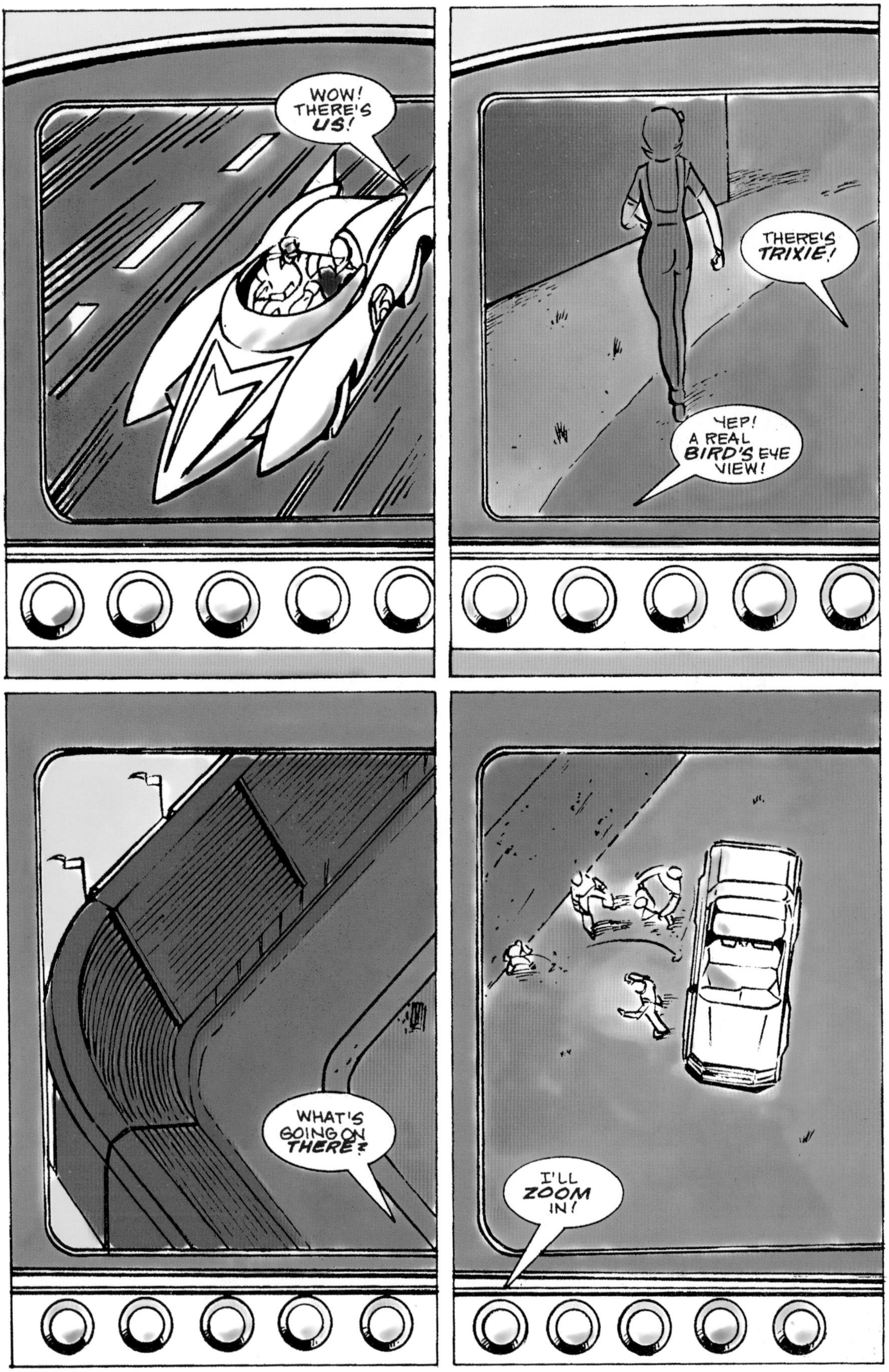

WOW! THERE'S US!
THERE'S TRIXIE!
YEP! A REAL BIRD'S EYE VIEW!
WHAT'S GOING ON THERE?
I'LL ZOOM IN!

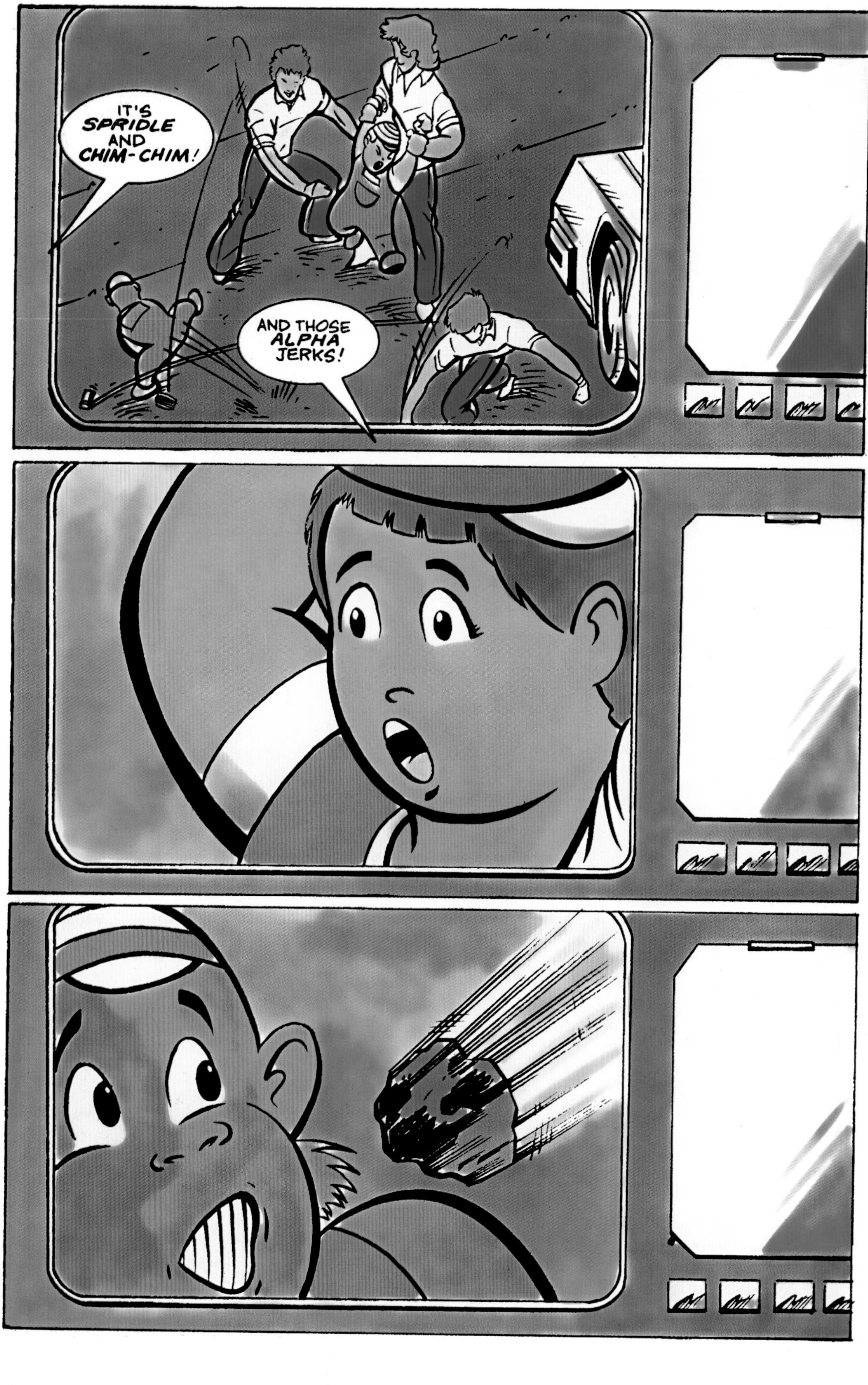
IT'S SPRIDLE AND CHIM-CHIM!
AND THOSE ALPHA JERKS!

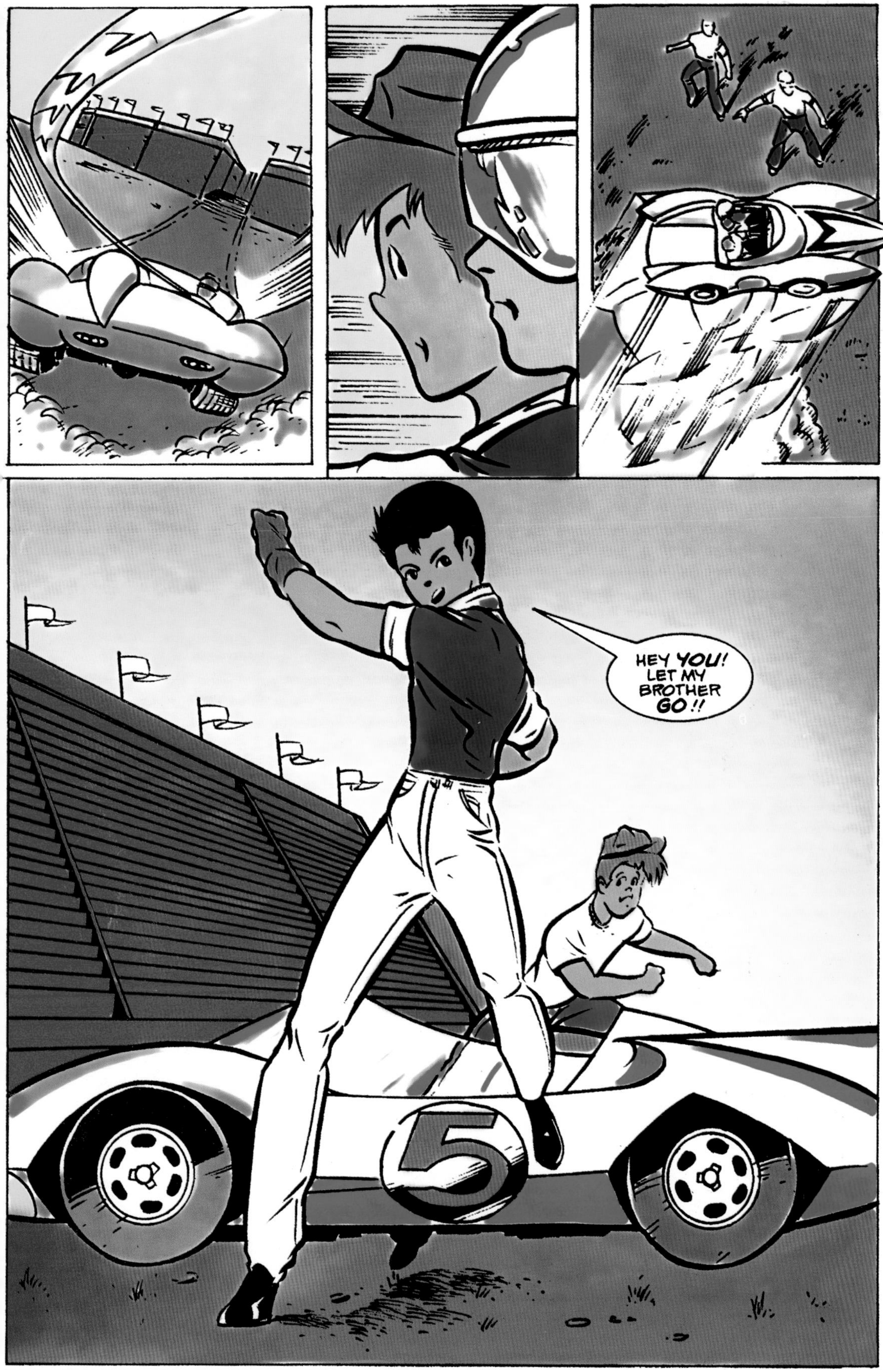
HEY YOU! LET MY BROTHER GO!!

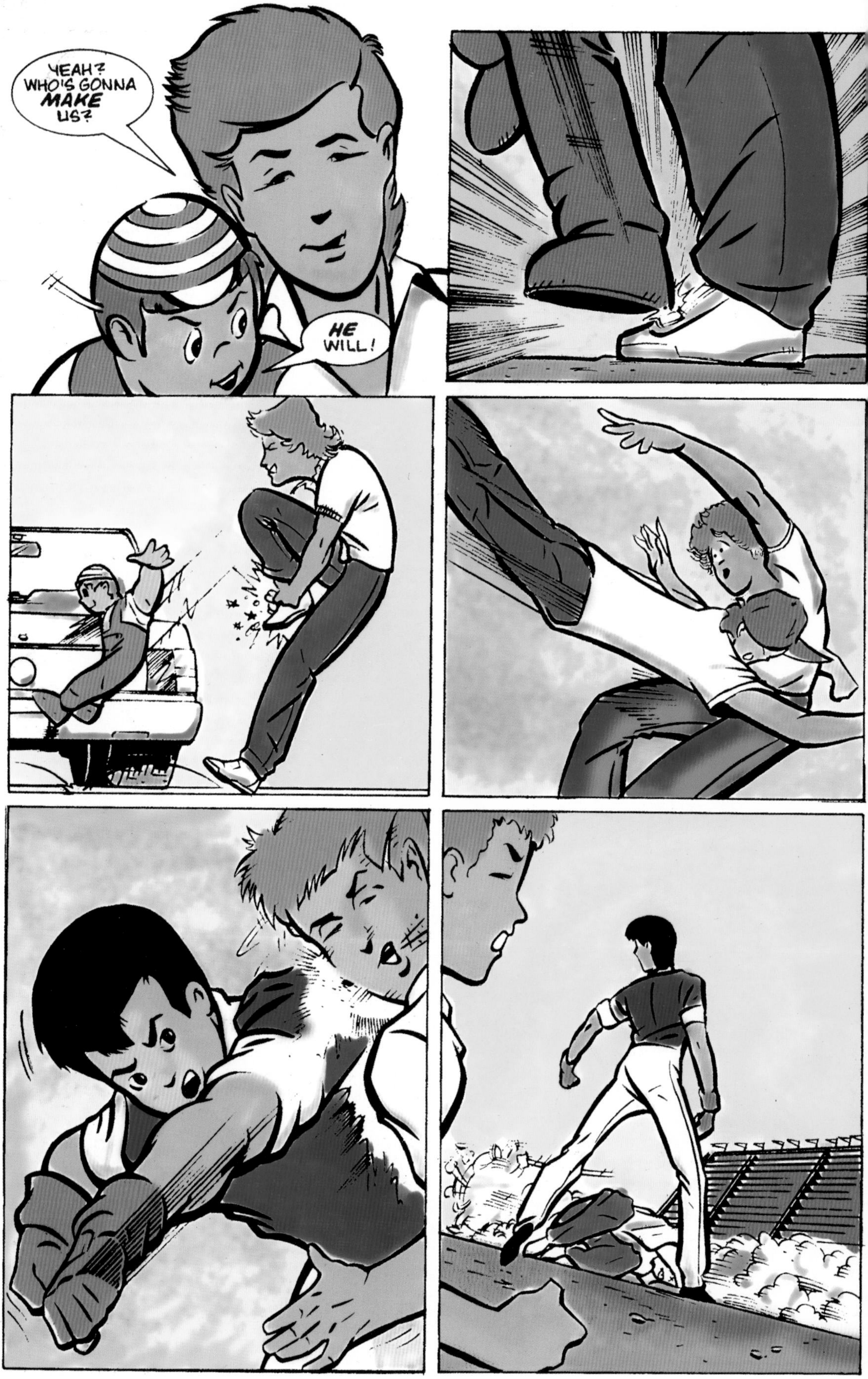
YEAH? WHO'S GONNA MAKE US?
HE WILL!

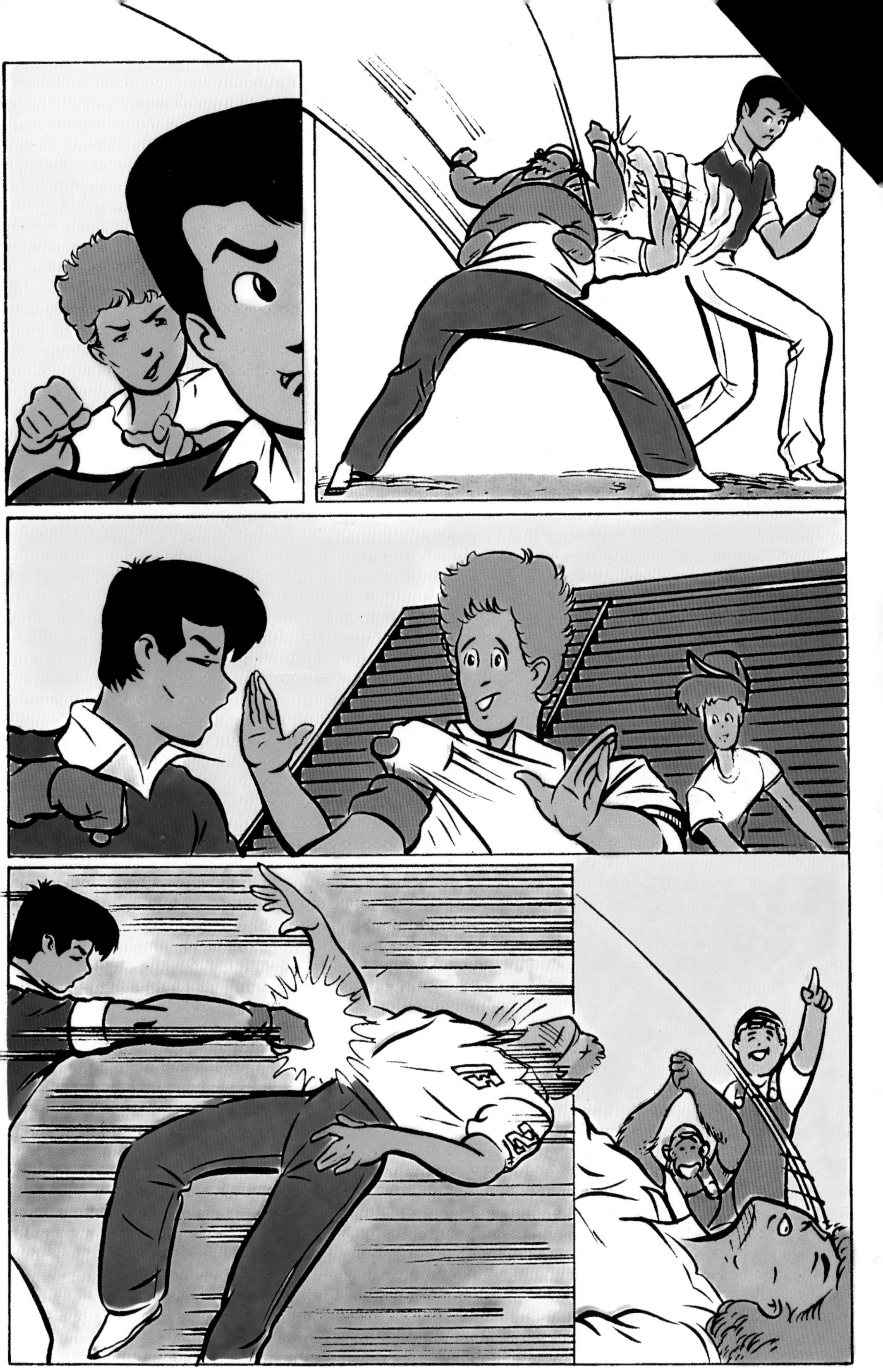

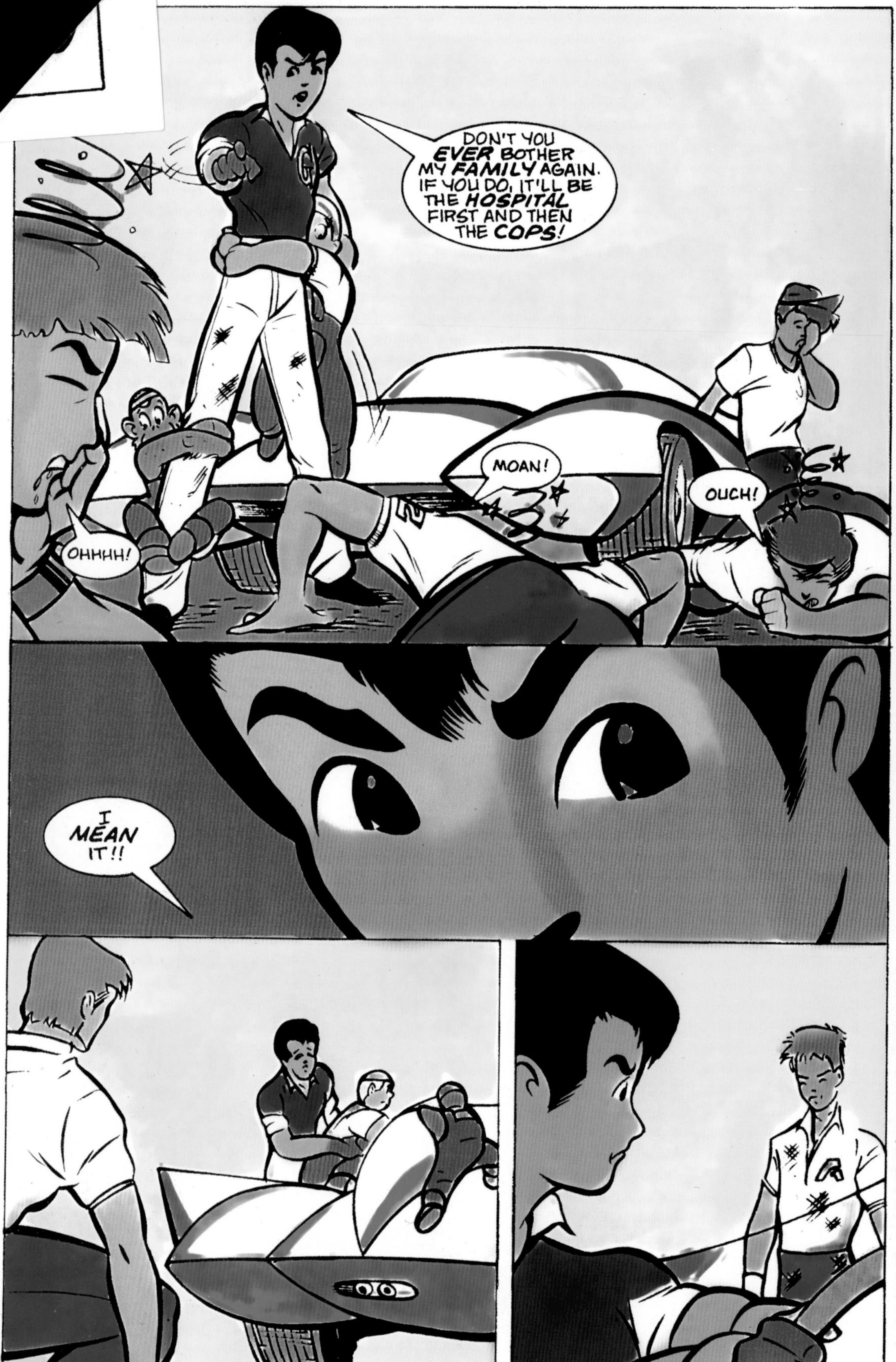
DON'T YOU EVER BOTHER MY FAMILY AGAIN. IF YOU DO, IT'LL BE THE HOSPITAL FIRST AND THEN THE COPS!
MOAN!
OUCH!
OHHHH!
I MEAN IT!!

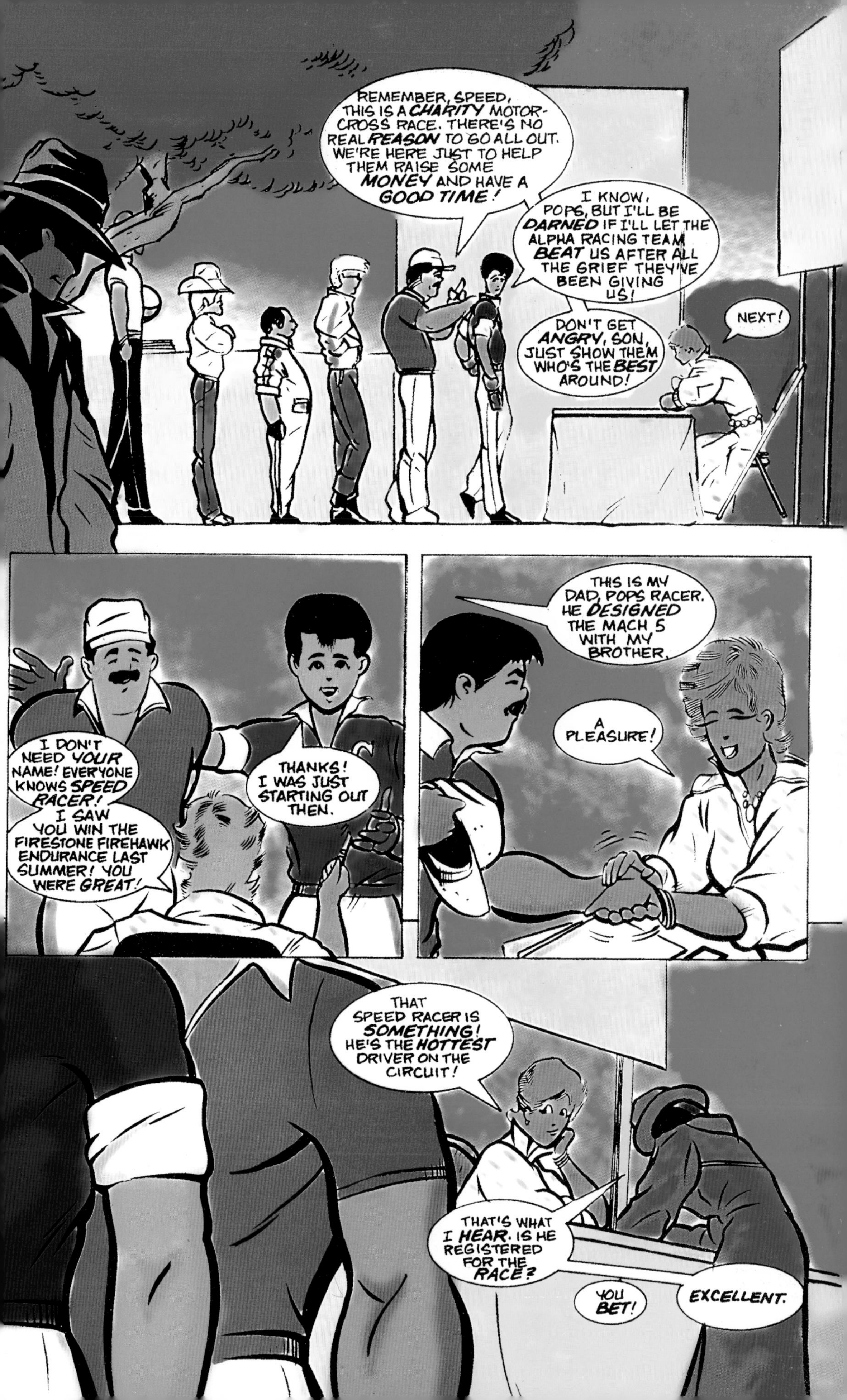
REMEMBER, SPEED, THIS IS A CHARITY MOTOR-CROSS RACE. THERE'S NO REAL REASON TO GO ALL OUT. WE'RE HERE JUST TO HELP THEM RAISE SOME MONEY AND HAVE A GOOD TIME!
I KNOW, POPS, BUT I'LL BE DARNED IF I'LL LET THE ALPHA RACING TEAM BEAT US AFTER ALL THE GRIEF THEY'VE BEEN GIVING US!
DON'T GET ANGRY, SON, JUST SHOW THEM WHO'S THE BEST AROUND!
NEXT!
I DON'T NEED YOUR NAME! EVERYONE KNOWS SPEED RACER!
I SAW YOU WIN THE FIRESTONE FIREHAWK ENDURANCE LAST SUMMER! YOU WERE GREAT!
THANKS! I WAS JUST STARTING OUT THEN.
THIS IS MY DAD, POPS RACER. HE DESIGNED THE MACH 5 WITH MY BROTHER.
A PLEASURE!
THAT SPEED RACER IS SOMETHING! HE'S THE HOTTEST DRIVER ON THE CIRCUIT!
THAT'S WHAT I HEAR. IS HE REGISTERED FOR THE RACE?
YOU BET!
EXCELLENT.

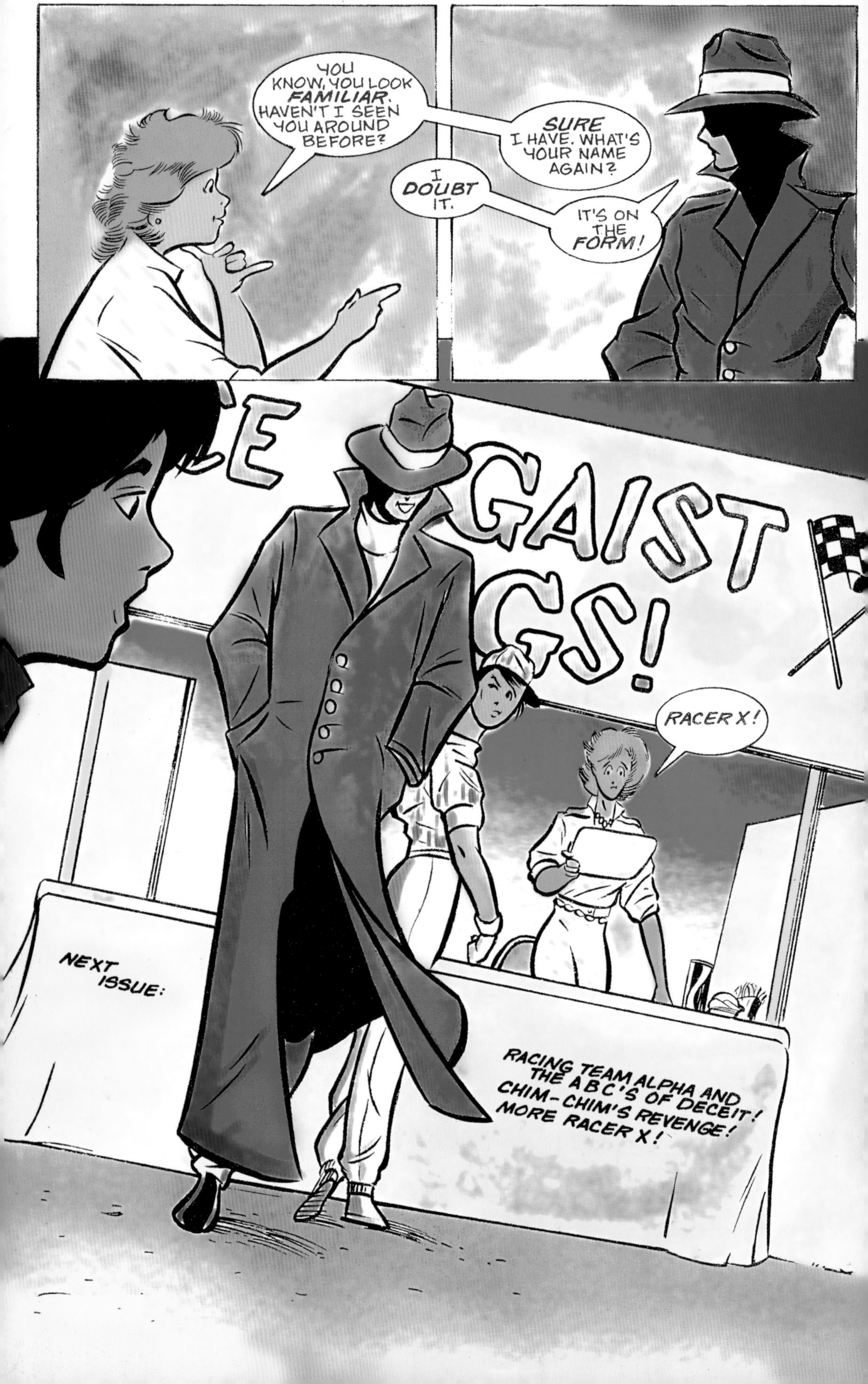
YOU KNOW, YOU LOOK FAMILIAR. HAVEN'T I SEEN YOU AROUND BEFORE?
SURE I HAVE. WHAT'S YOUR NAME AGAIN?
I DOUBT IT.
IT'S ON THE FORM!
GAIST
GS!
RACER X!
NEXT ISSUE:
RACING TEAM ALPHA AND THE A B C'S OF DECEIT! CHIM-CHIM'S REVENGE! MORE RACER X!

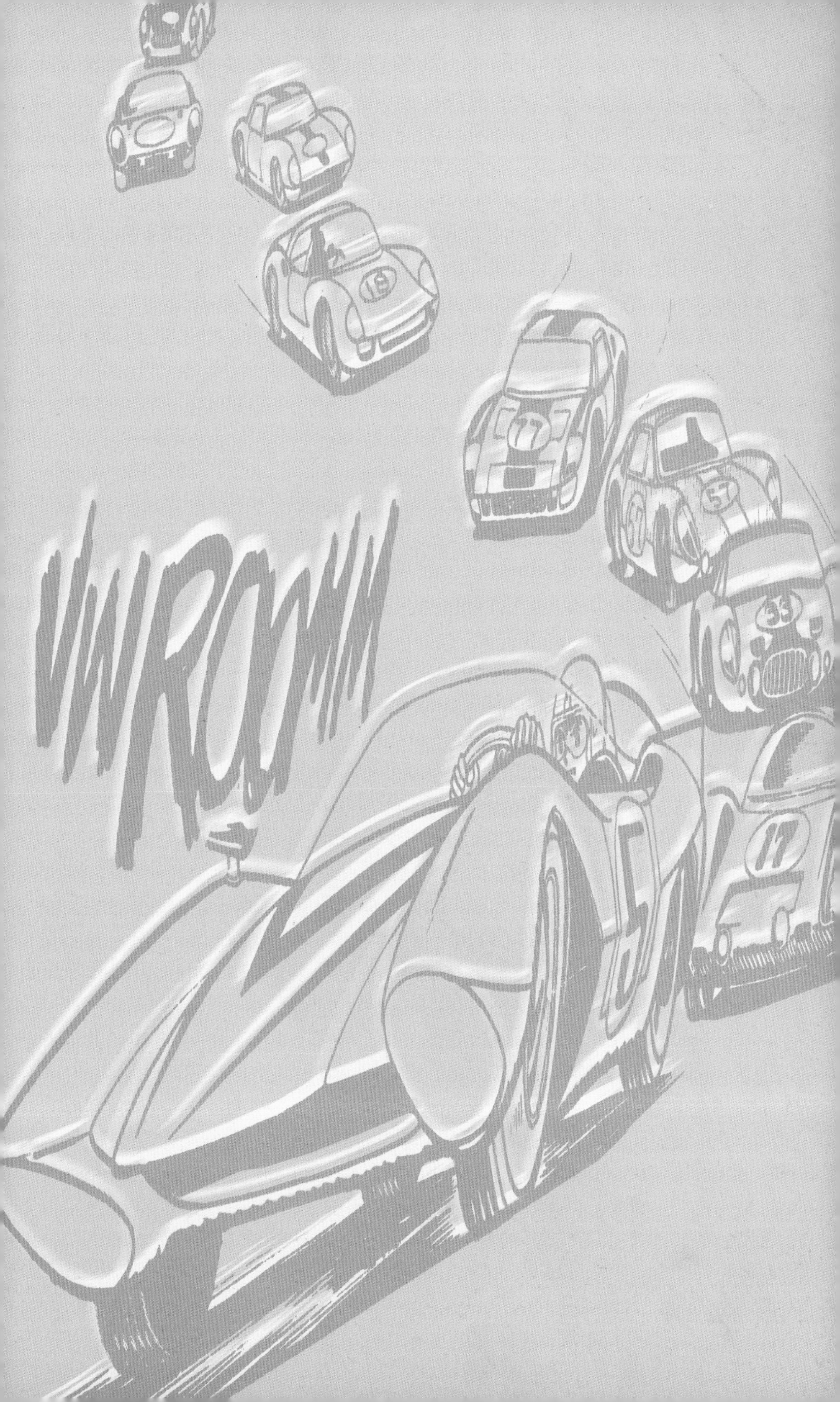
VVROOM

Speed Racer #3

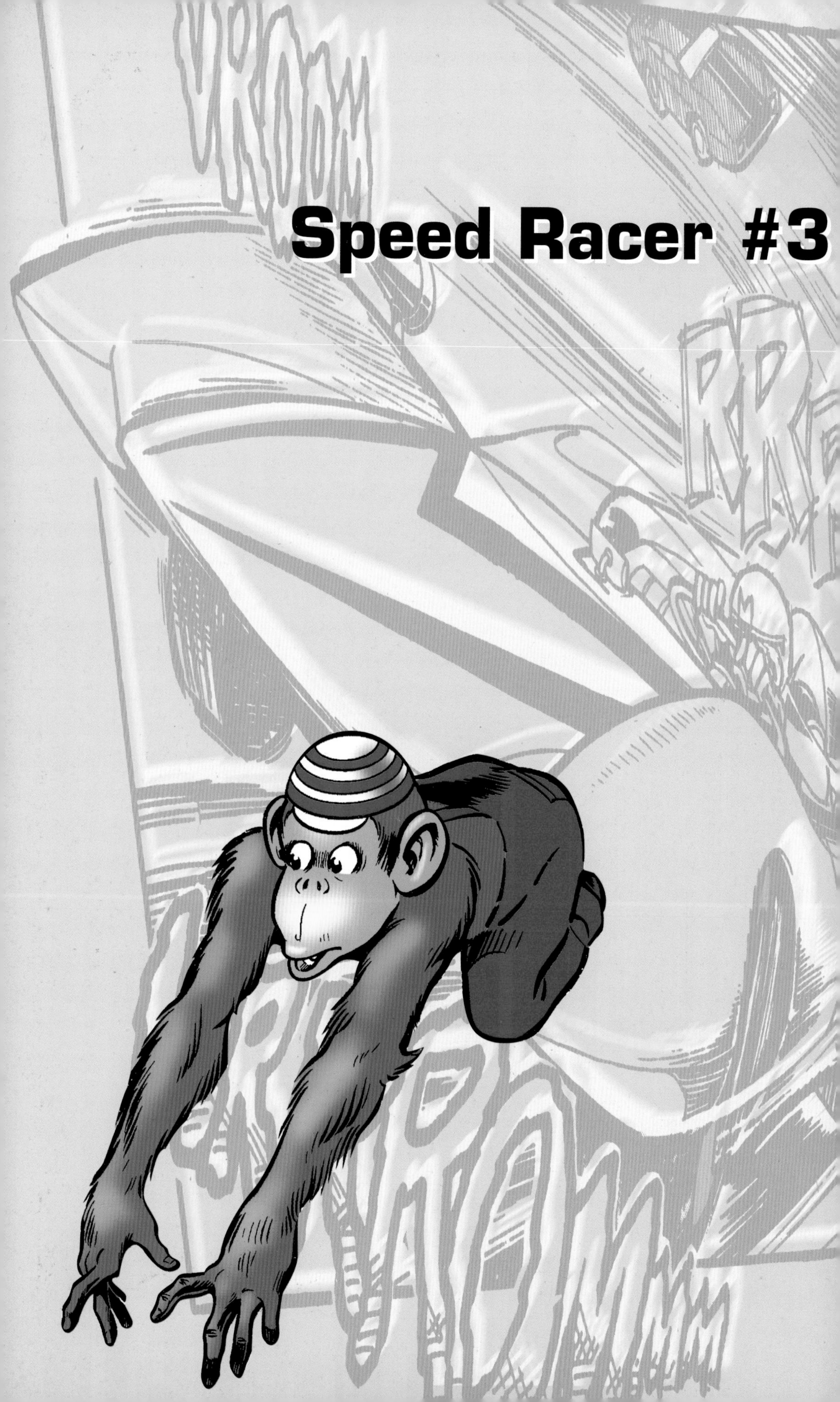

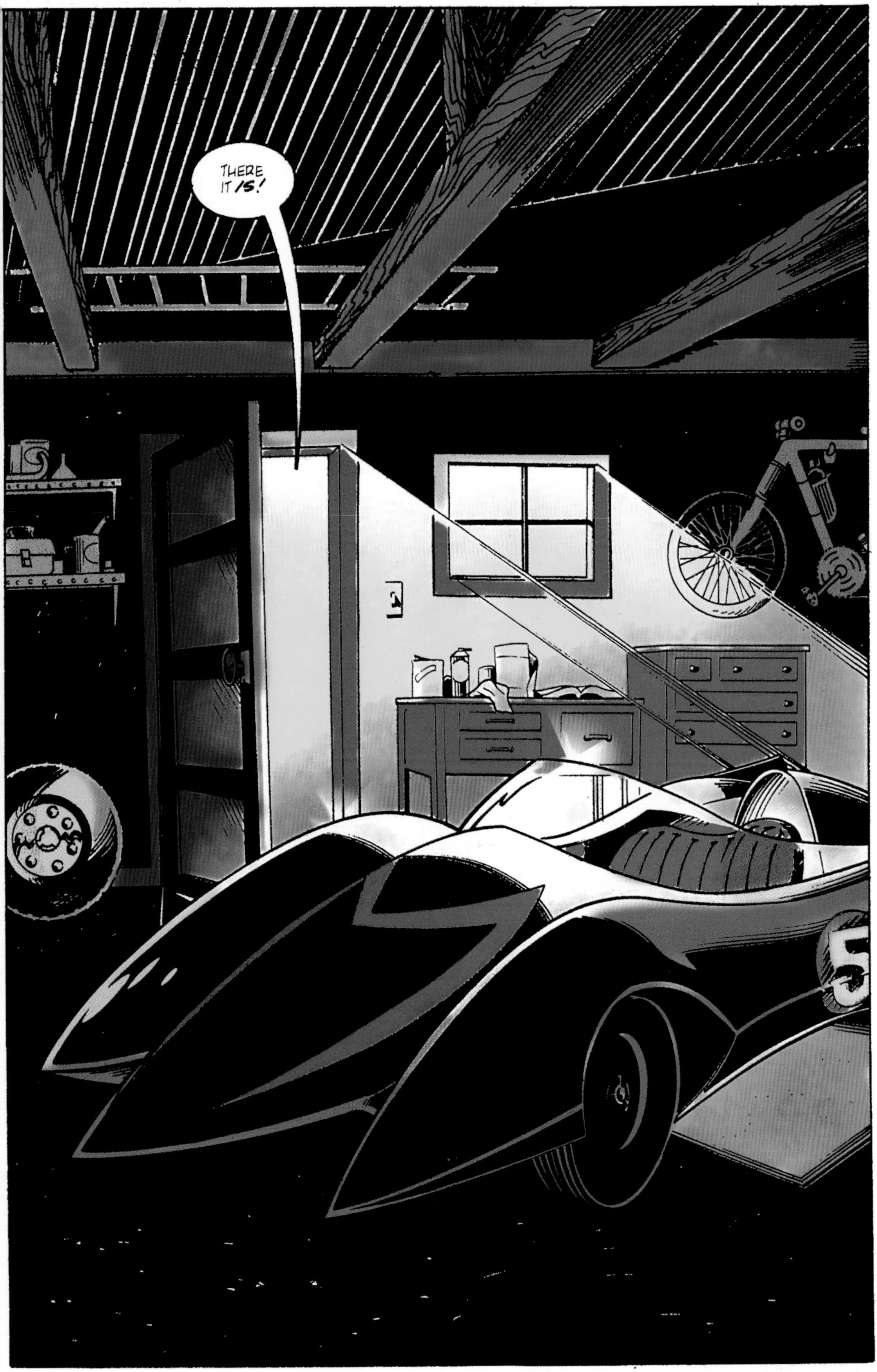
THERE IT IS!

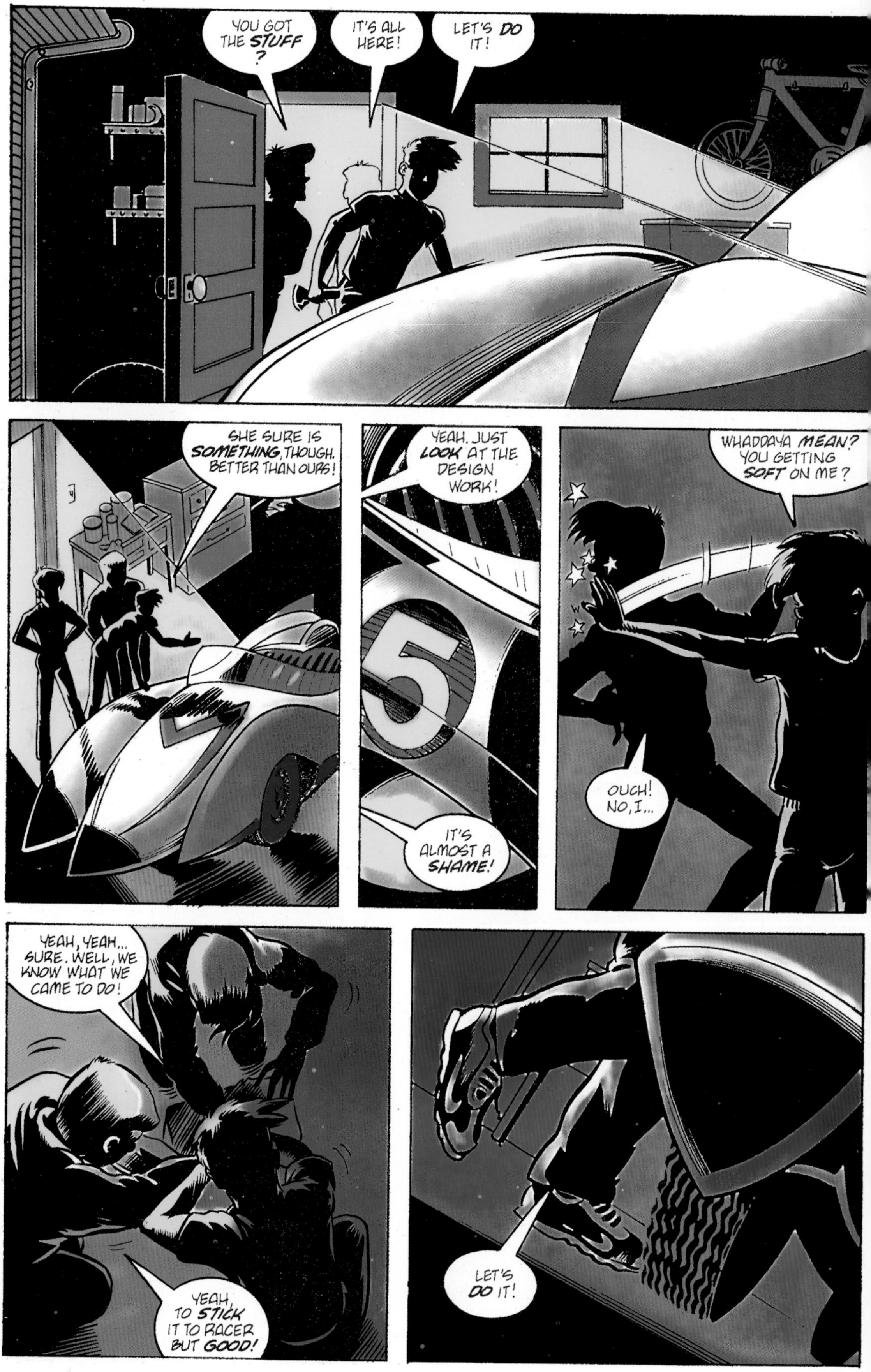

YOU GOT THE STUFF ?
IT'S ALL HERE!
LET'S DO IT!
SHE SURE IS SOMETHING, THOUGH. BETTER THAN OURS!
YEAH. JUST LOOK AT THE DESIGN WORK!
IT'S ALMOST A SHAME!
WHADDAYA MEAN? YOU GETTING SOFT ON ME?
OUCH! NO, I...
YEAH, YEAH... SURE. WELL, WE KNOW WHAT WE CAME TO DO!
YEAH, TO STICK IT TO RACER BUT GOOD!
LET'S DO IT!

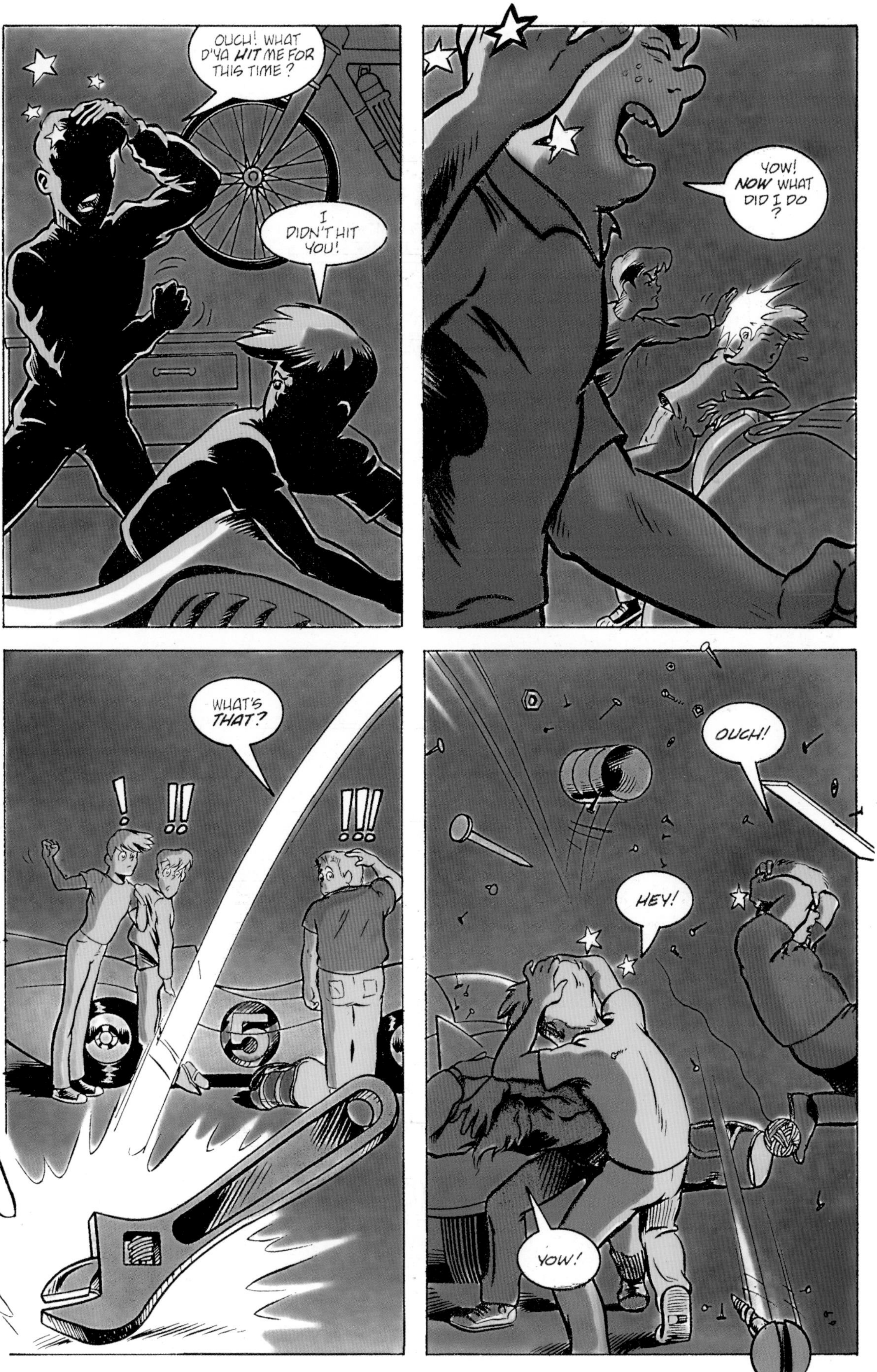
OUCH! WHAT D'YA HIT ME FOR THIS TIME?
I DIDN'T HIT YOU!
YOW! NOW WHAT DID I DO?
WHAT'S THAT?
!
!!
!!!
OUCH!
HEY!
YOW!

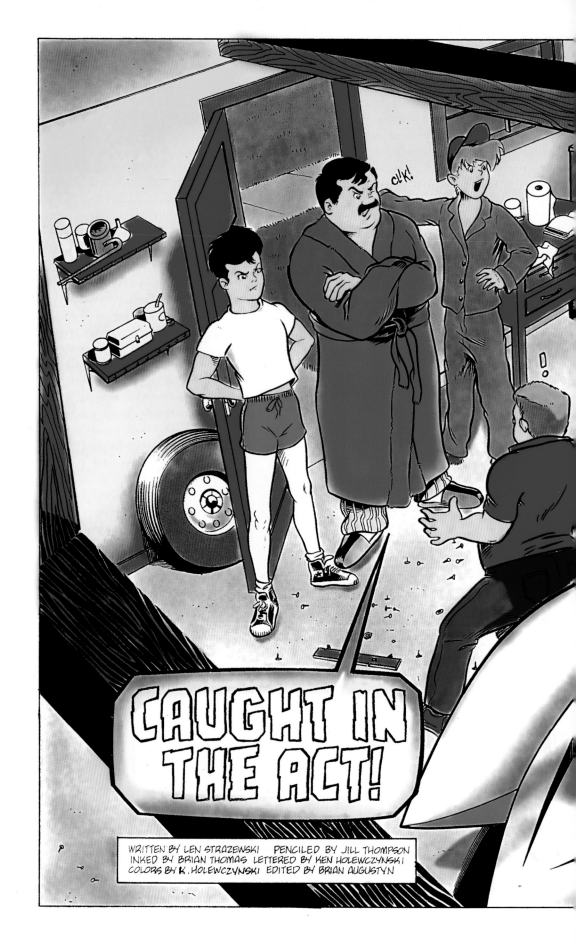

CAUGHT IN THE ACT!

WRITTEN BY LEN STRAZEWSKI   PENCILED BY JILL THOMPSON
INKED BY BRIAN THOMAS LETTERED BY KEN HOLEWCZYNSKI
COLORS BY K.HOLEWCZYNSKI EDITED BY BRIAN AUGUSTYN

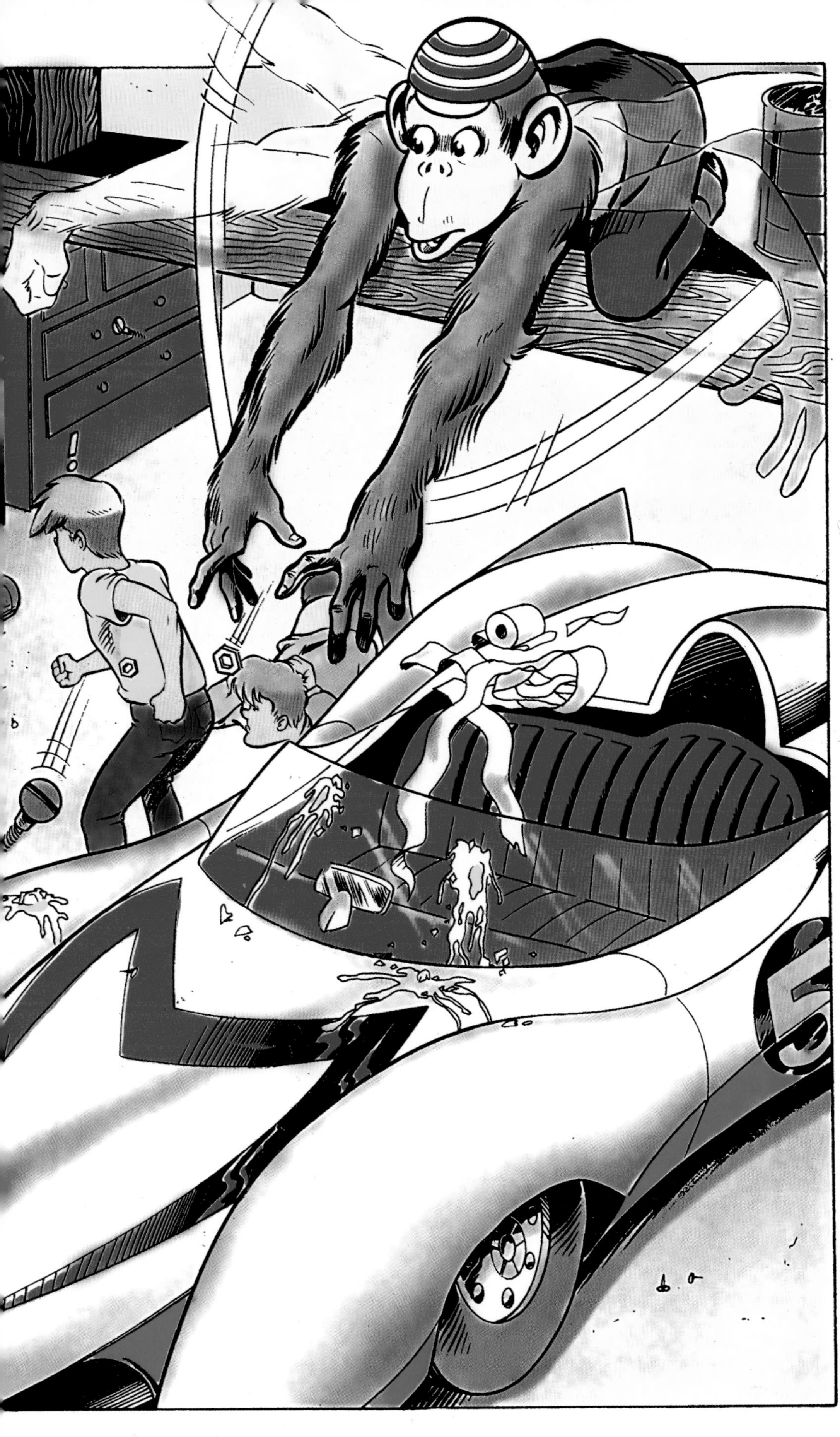

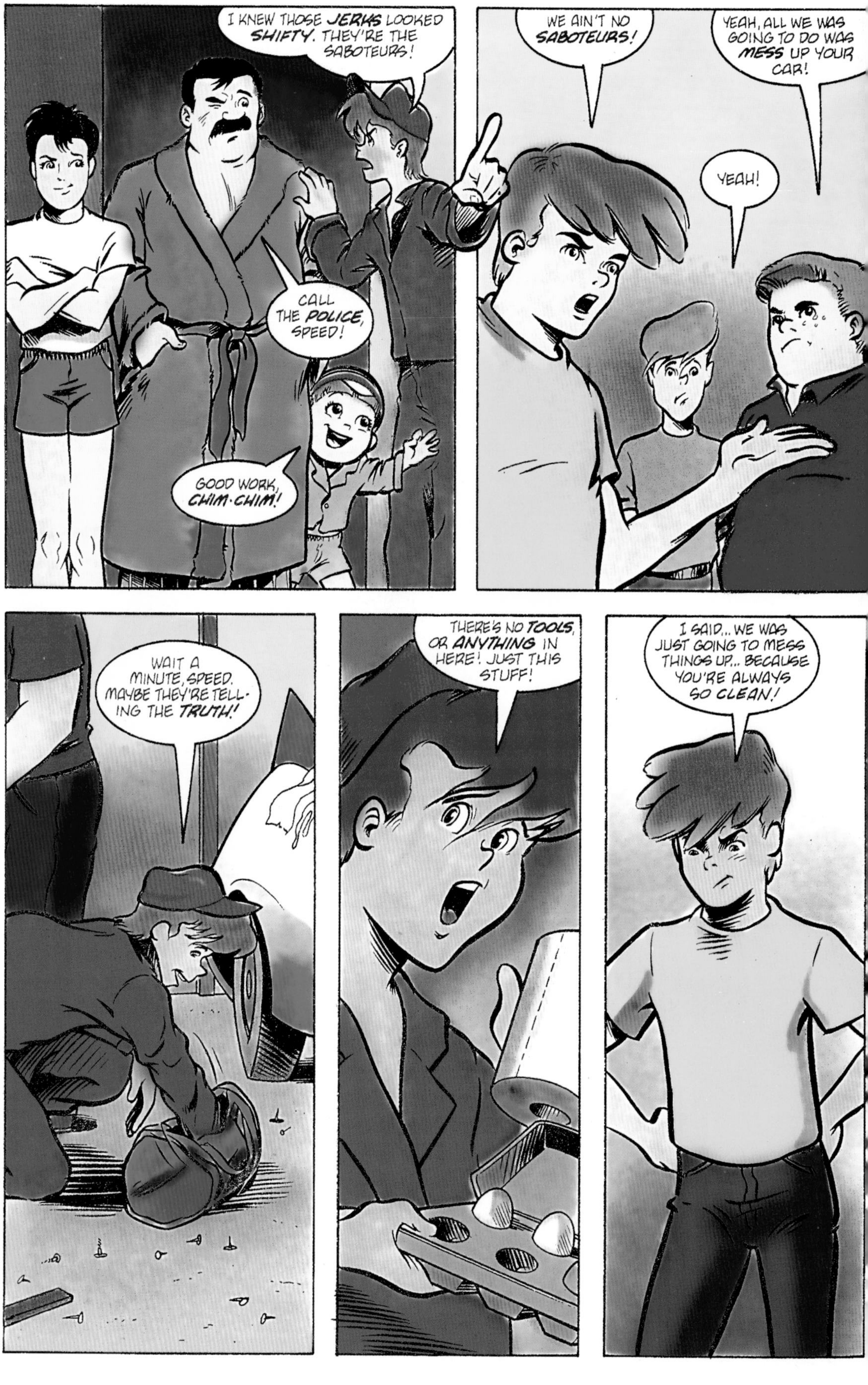
I KNEW THOSE JERKS LOOKED SHIFTY. THEY'RE THE SABOTEURS!
CALL THE POLICE, SPEED!
GOOD WORK, CHIM-CHIM!
WE AIN'T NO SABOTEURS!
YEAH, ALL WE WAS GOING TO DO WAS MESS UP YOUR CAR!
YEAH!
WAIT A MINUTE, SPEED. MAYBE THEY'RE TELLING THE TRUTH!
THERE'S NO TOOLS, OR ANYTHING IN HERE! JUST THIS STUFF!
I SAID... WE WAS JUST GOING TO MESS THINGS UP... BECAUSE YOU'RE ALWAYS SO CLEAN!

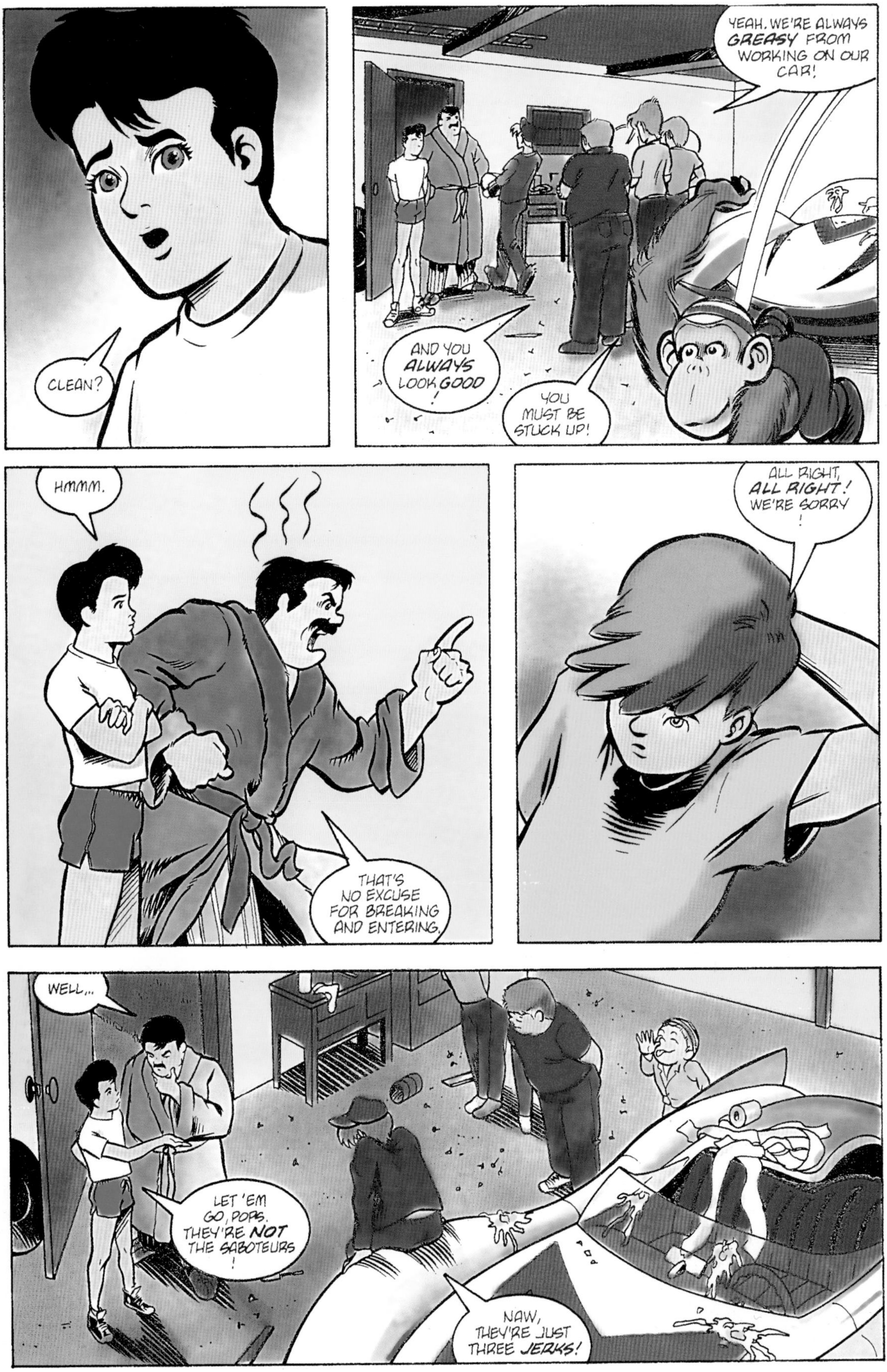
CLEAN?
YEAH. WE'RE ALWAYS GREASY FROM WORKING ON OUR CAR!
AND YOU ALWAYS LOOK GOOD!
YOU MUST BE STUCK UP!
HMMM.
THAT'S NO EXCUSE FOR BREAKING AND ENTERING.
ALL RIGHT, ALL RIGHT! WE'RE SORRY!
WELL...
LET 'EM GO, POPS. THEY'RE NOT THE SABOTEURS!
NAW, THEY'RE JUST THREE JERKS!

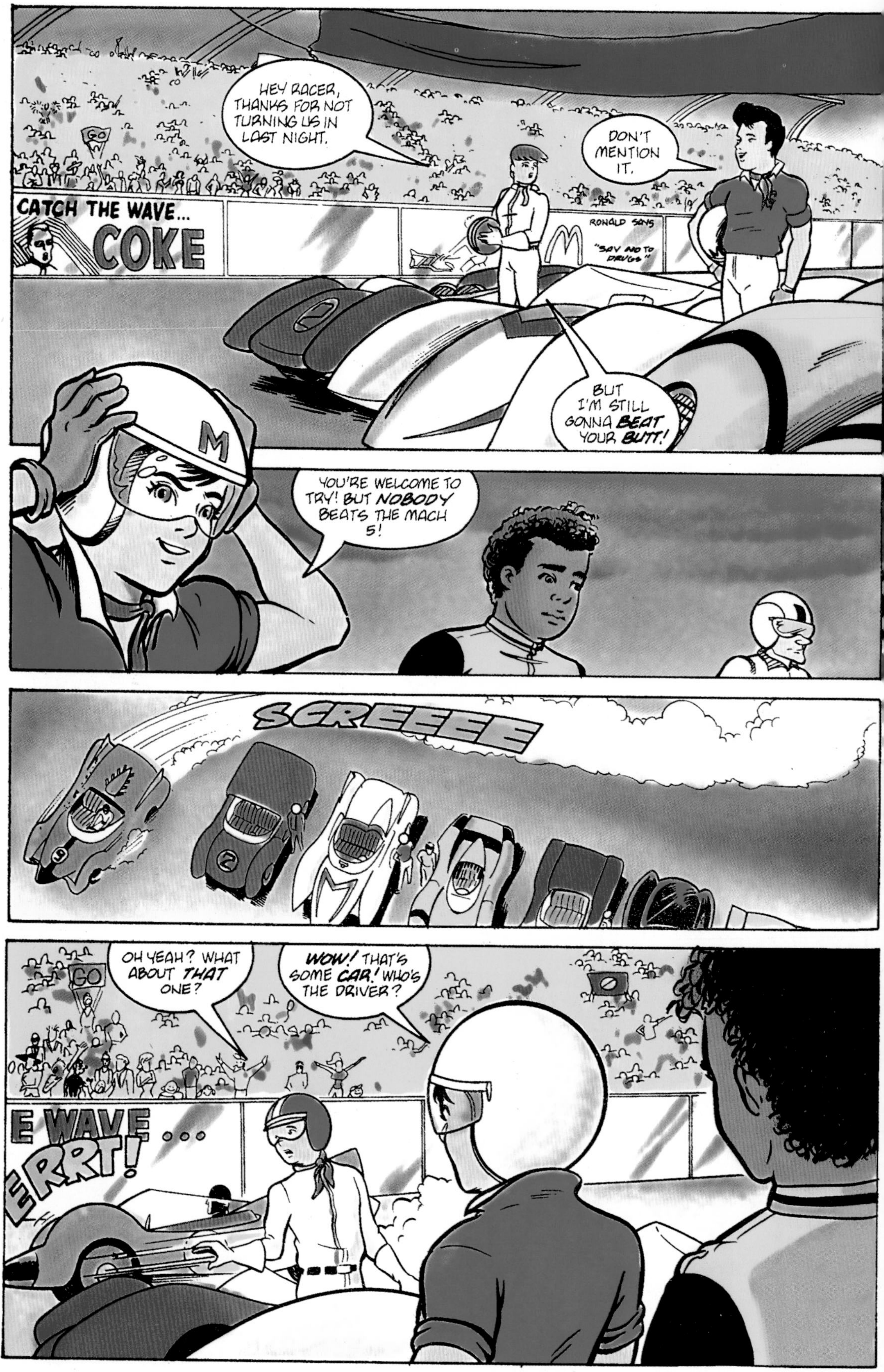
HEY RACER, THANKS FOR NOT TURNING US IN LAST NIGHT.
DON'T MENTION IT.
CATCH THE WAVE... COKE
RONALD SAYS "SAY NO TO DRUGS"
BUT I'M STILL GONNA BEAT YOUR BUTT!
YOU'RE WELCOME TO TRY! BUT NOBODY BEATS THE MACH 5!
SCREEEE
OH YEAH? WHAT ABOUT THAT ONE?
WOW! THAT'S SOME CAR! WHO'S THE DRIVER?
E WAVE ...
ERRT!

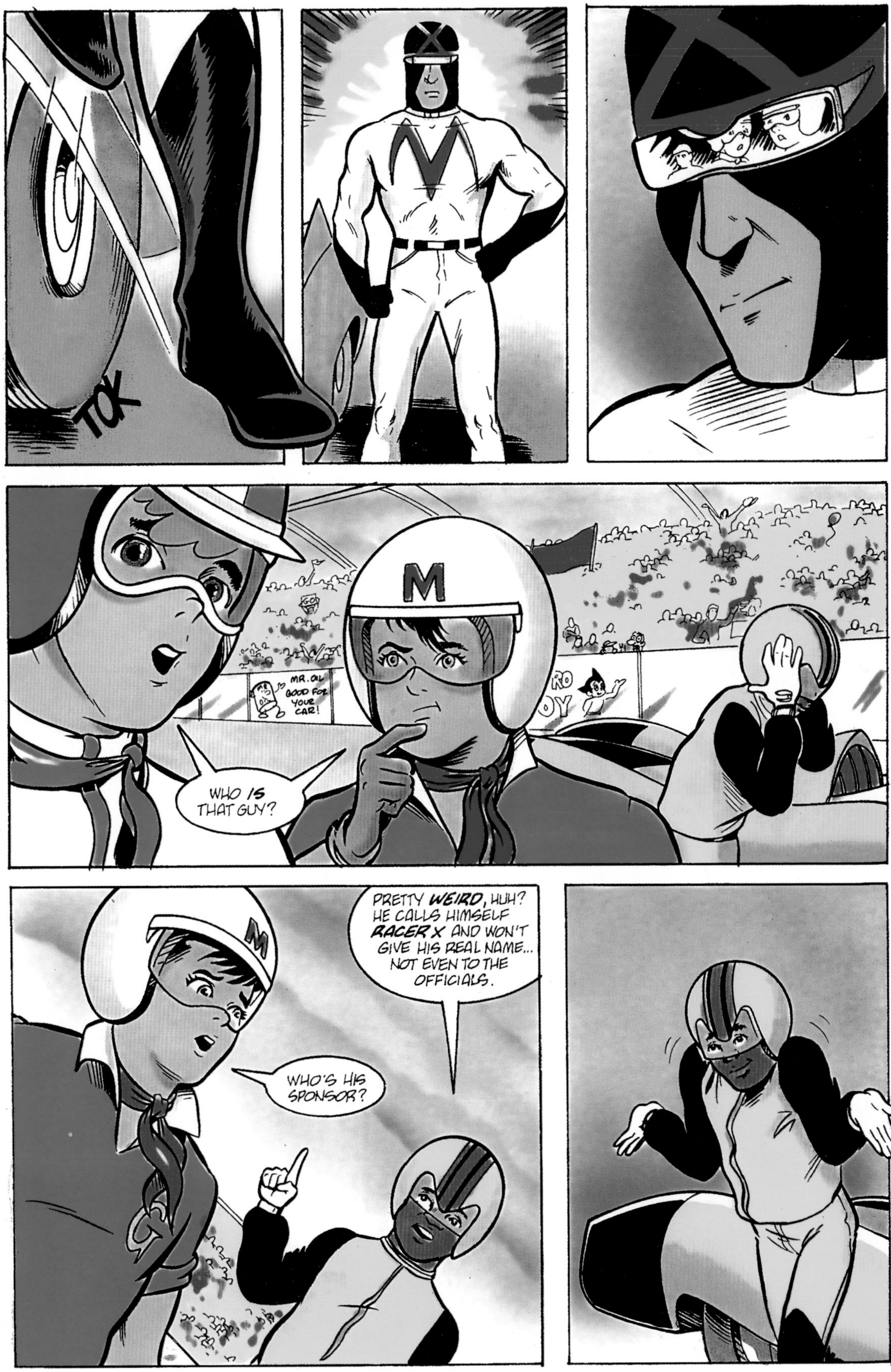
TOK
MR. OIL
GOOD FOR YOUR CAR!
WHO IS THAT GUY?
PRETTY WEIRD, HUH? HE CALLS HIMSELF RACER X AND WON'T GIVE HIS REAL NAME... NOT EVEN TO THE OFFICIALS.
WHO'S HIS SPONSOR?

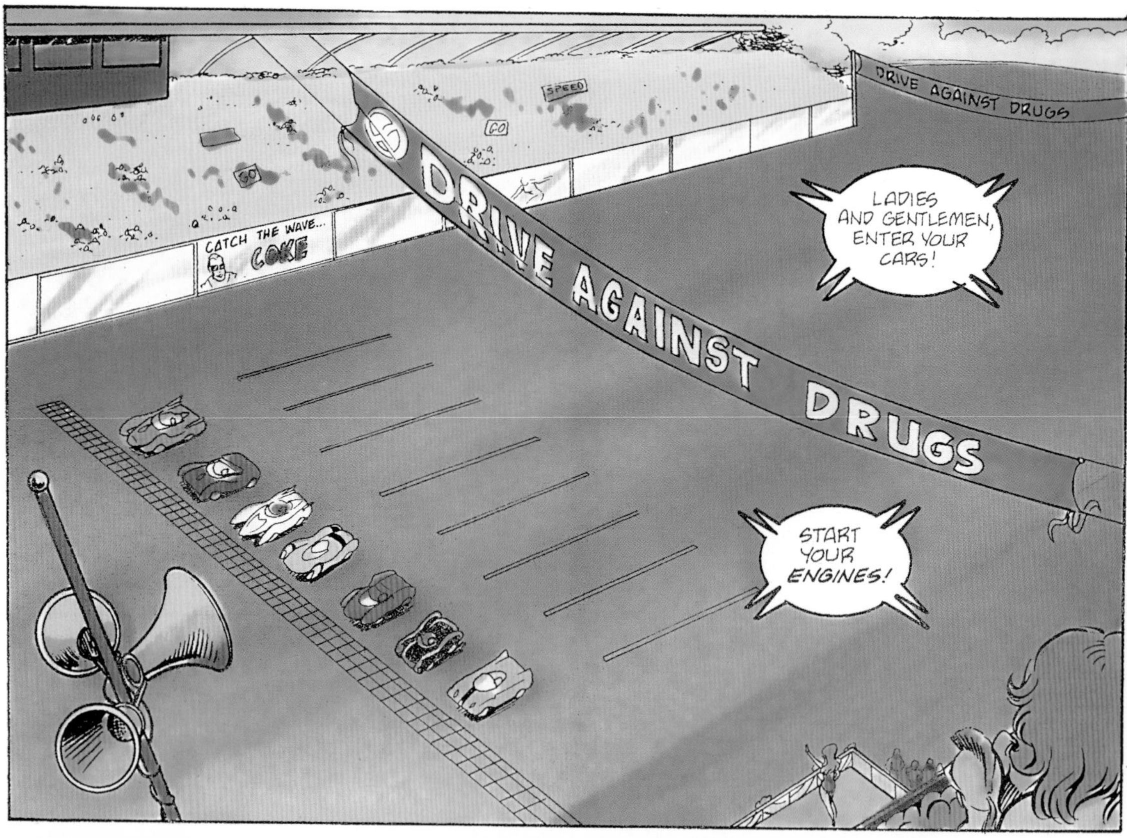
DRIVE AGAINST DRUGS
CATCH THE WAVE...
COKE
SPEED
GO
DRIVE AGAINST DRUGS
LADIES AND GENTLEMEN, ENTER YOUR CARS!
START YOUR ENGINES!

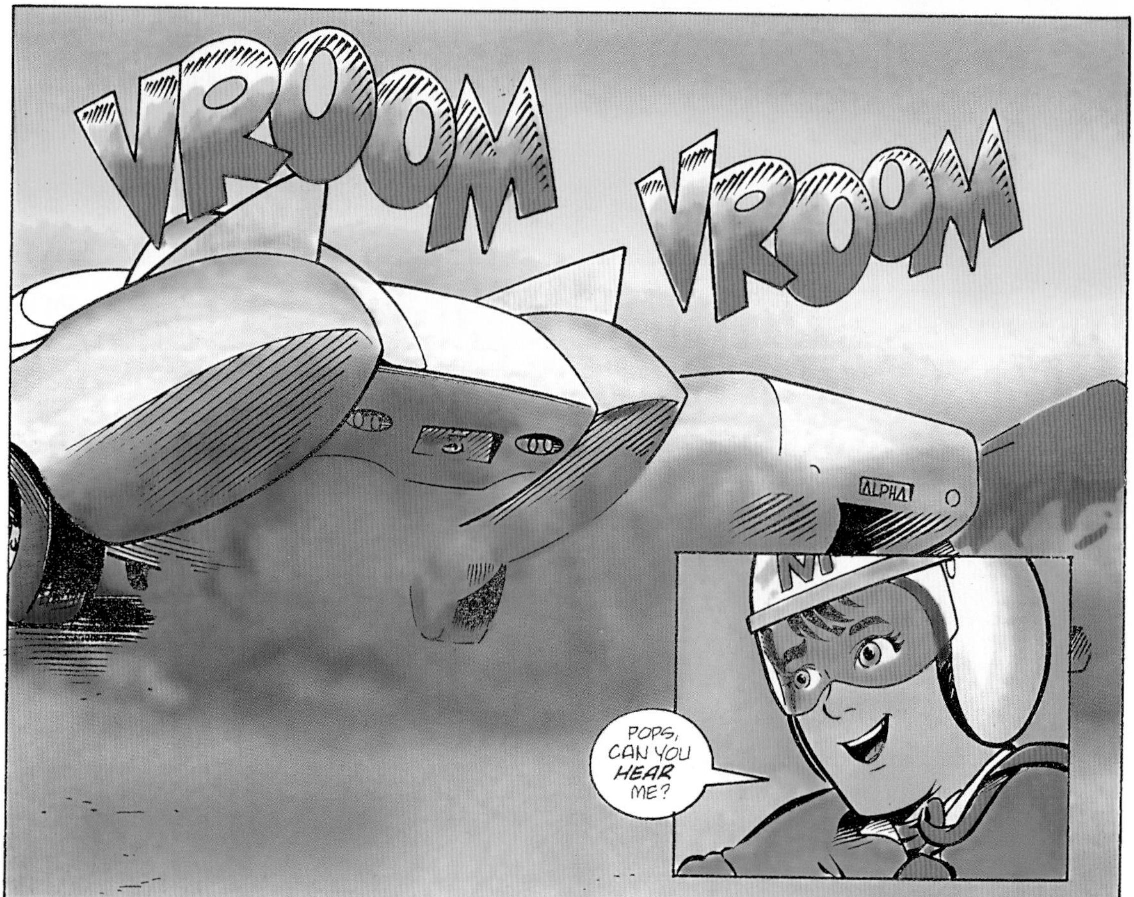
VROOM
VROOM
ALPHA
POPS, CAN YOU *HEAR* ME?

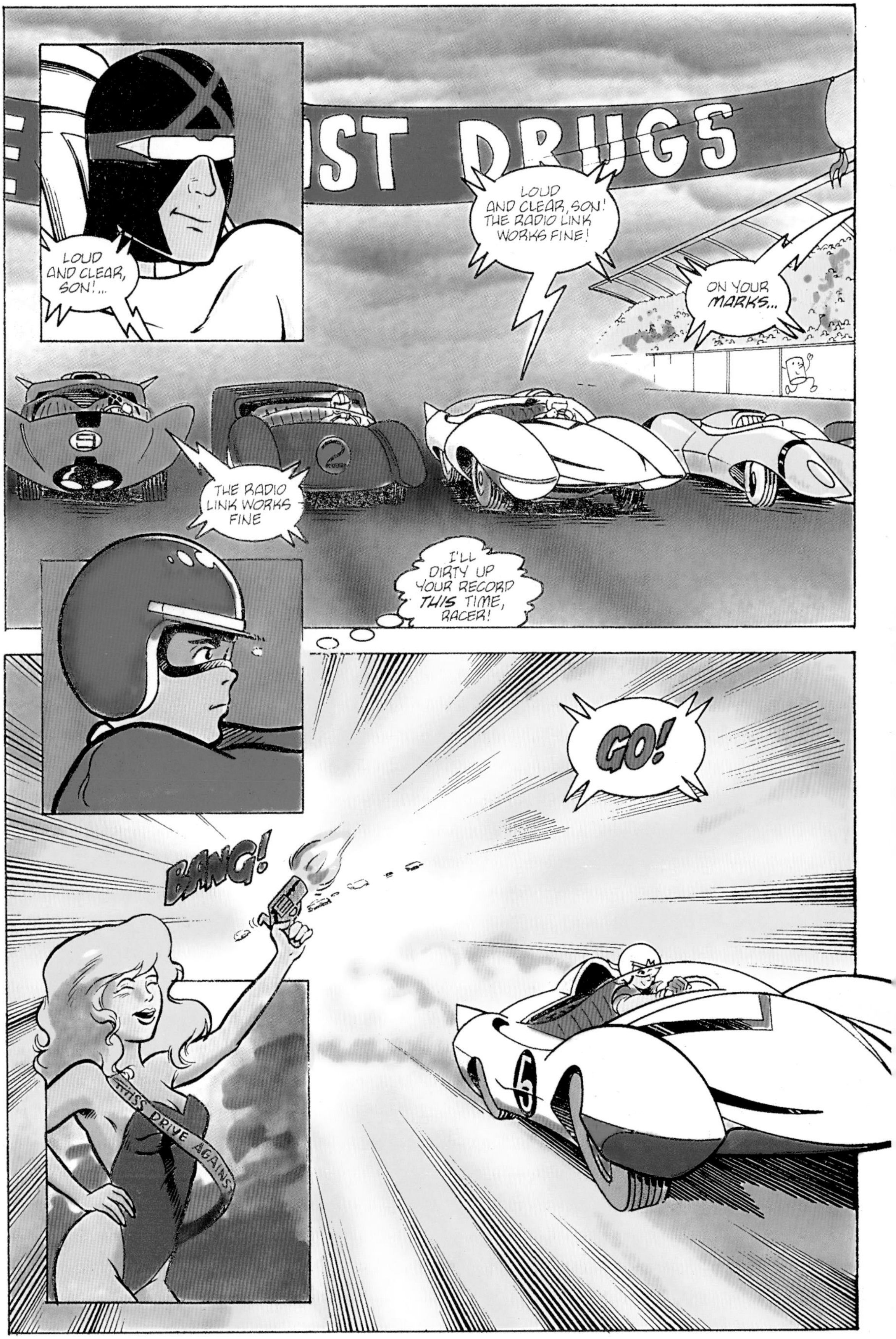

...OST DRUGS
LOUD AND CLEAR, SON!...
LOUD AND CLEAR, SON! THE RADIO LINK WORKS FINE!
ON YOUR MARKS...
THE RADIO LINK WORKS FINE
I'LL DIRTY UP YOUR RECORD THIS TIME, RACER!
GO!
BANG!
MISS DRIVE AGAINS...

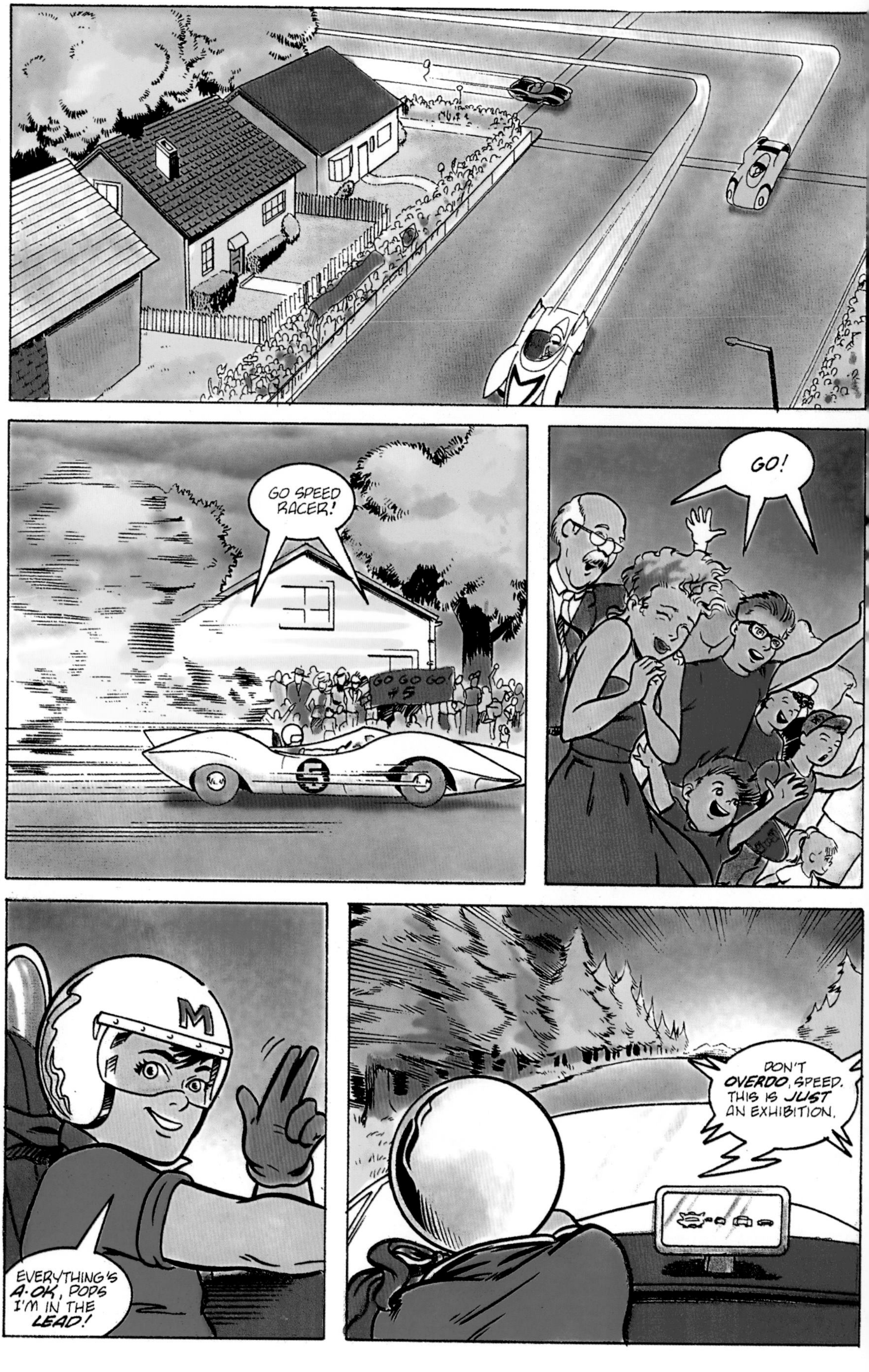
GO SPEED RACER!
GO GO GO! #5
GO!
EVERYTHING'S A-OK, POPS I'M IN THE LEAD!
DON'T OVERDO, SPEED. THIS IS JUST AN EXHIBITION.

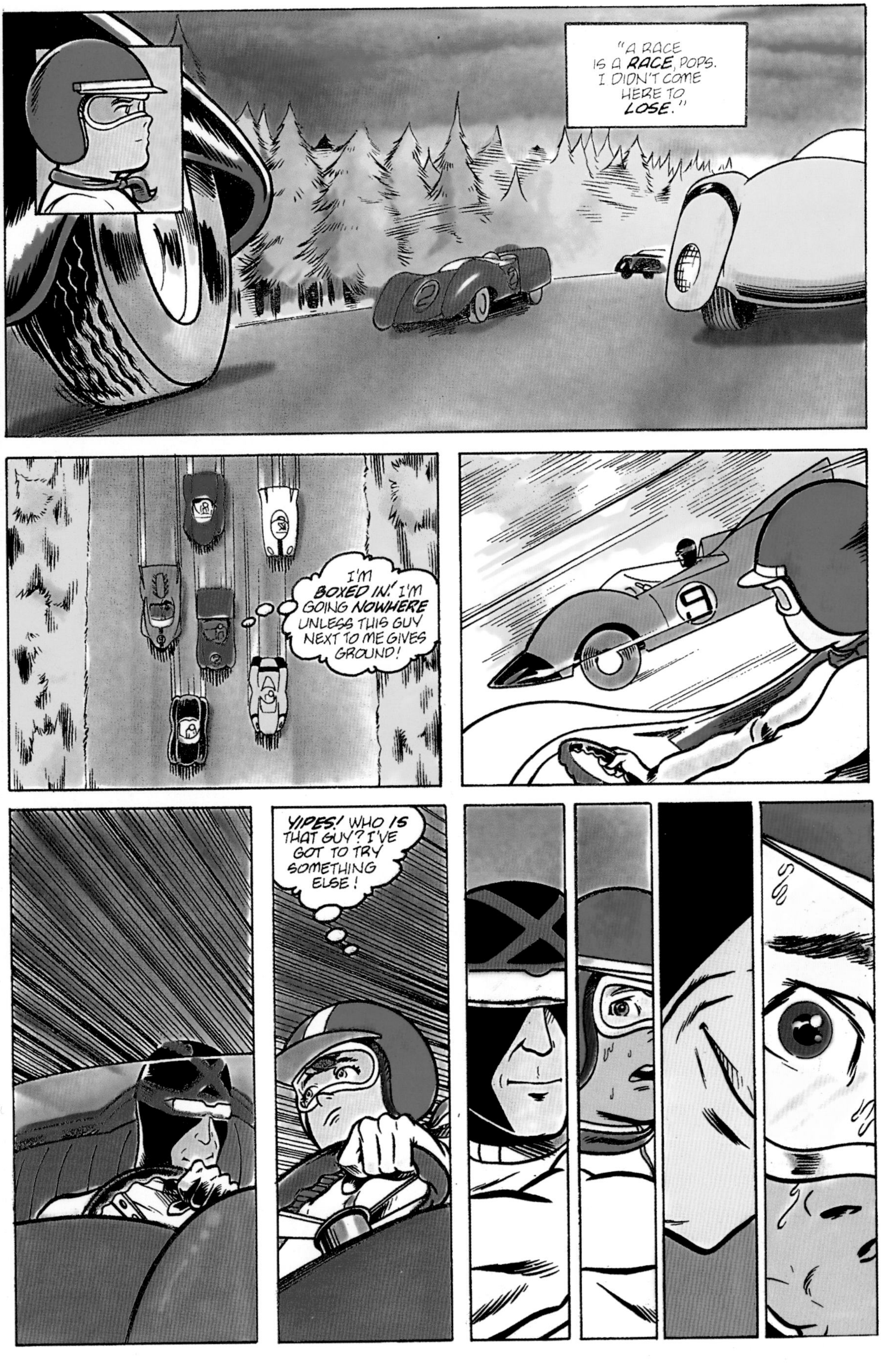
"A RACE IS A RACE, POPS. I DIDN'T COME HERE TO LOSE."
I'M BOXED IN! I'M GOING NOWHERE UNLESS THIS GUY NEXT TO ME GIVES GROUND!
YIPES! WHO IS THAT GUY? I'VE GOT TO TRY SOMETHING ELSE!

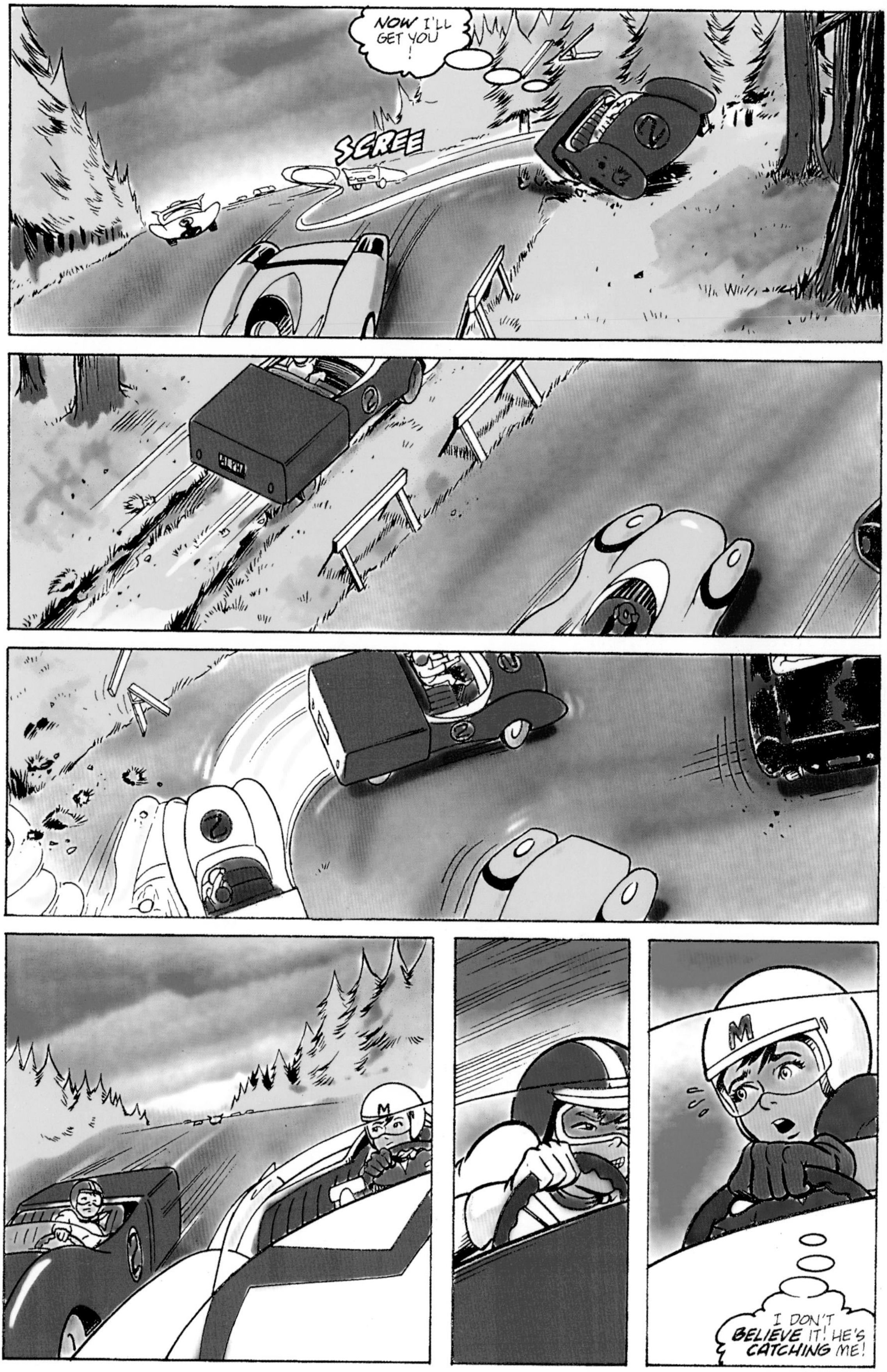
NOW I'LL GET YOU!
SCREE
I DON'T BELIEVE IT! HE'S CATCHING ME!

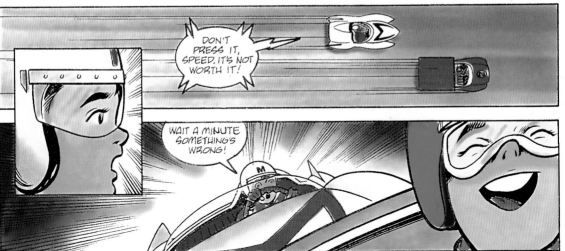

I GOT YOU *BEAT*, RACER!

POPS, ALPHA'S PULLING AHEAD. THEIR CAR IS BETTER THAN WE *THOUGHT!*

DON'T PRESS IT, SPEED, IT'S NOT WORTH IT!

WAIT A MINUTE SOMETHING'S WRONG!

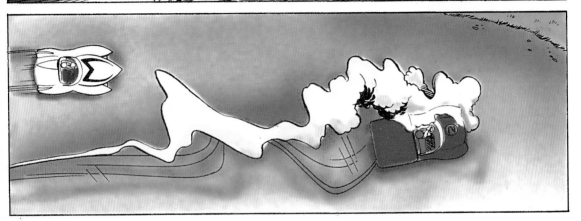

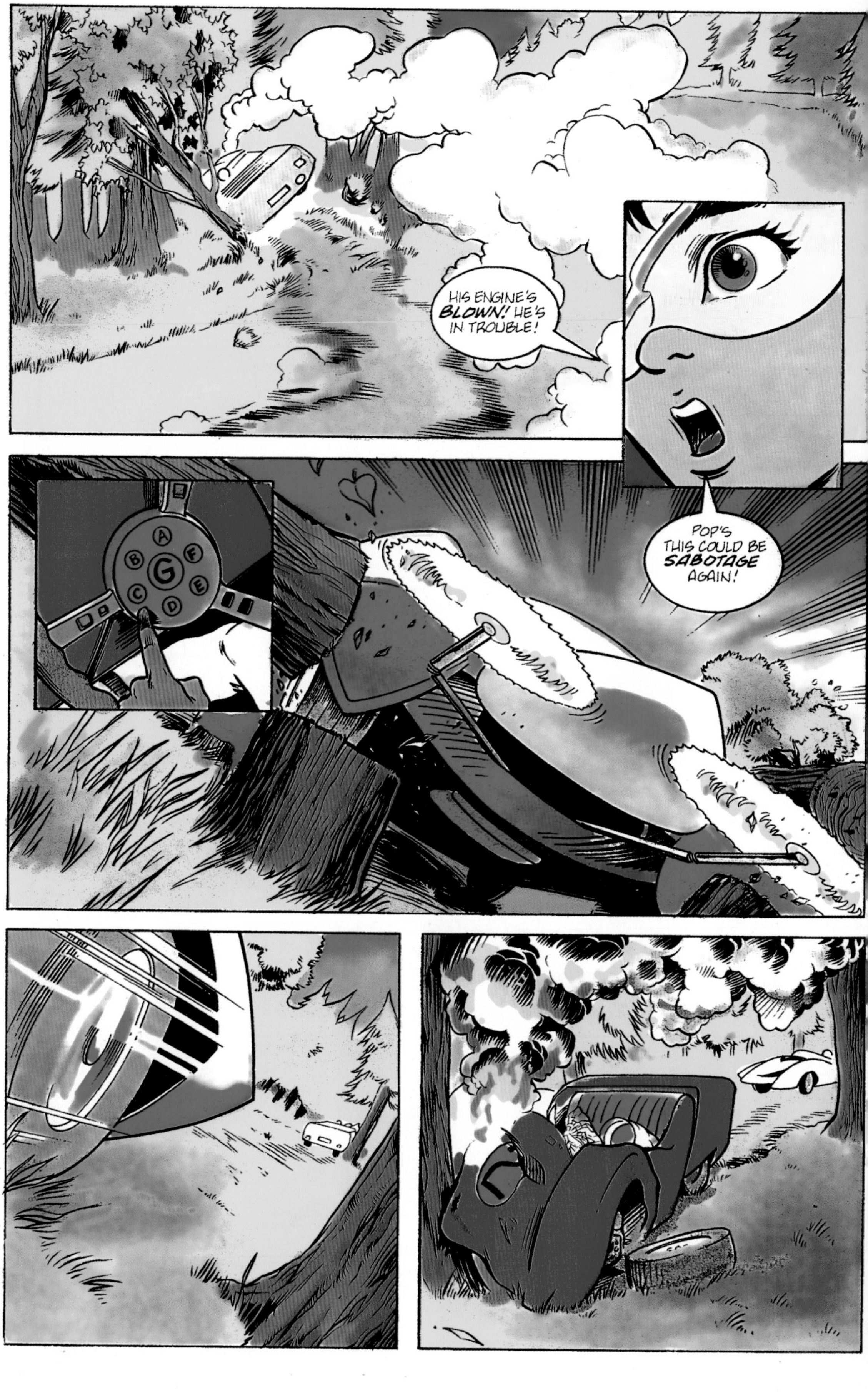
HIS ENGINE'S BLOWN! HE'S IN TROUBLE!
POP'S THIS COULD BE SABOTAGE AGAIN!
A
B
F
G
C
E
D

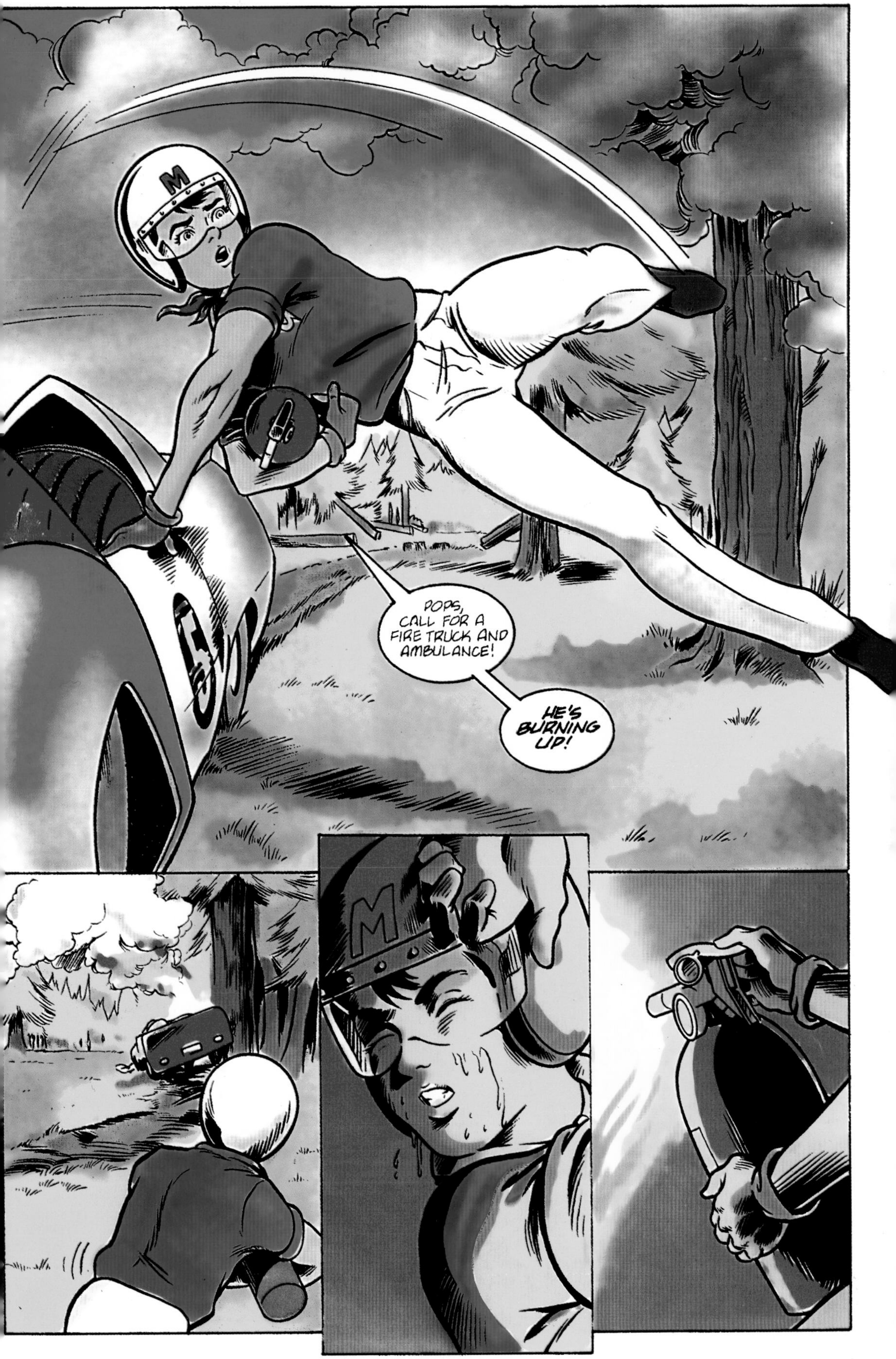
POPS, CALL FOR A FIRE TRUCK AND AMBULANCE!
HE'S BURNING UP!

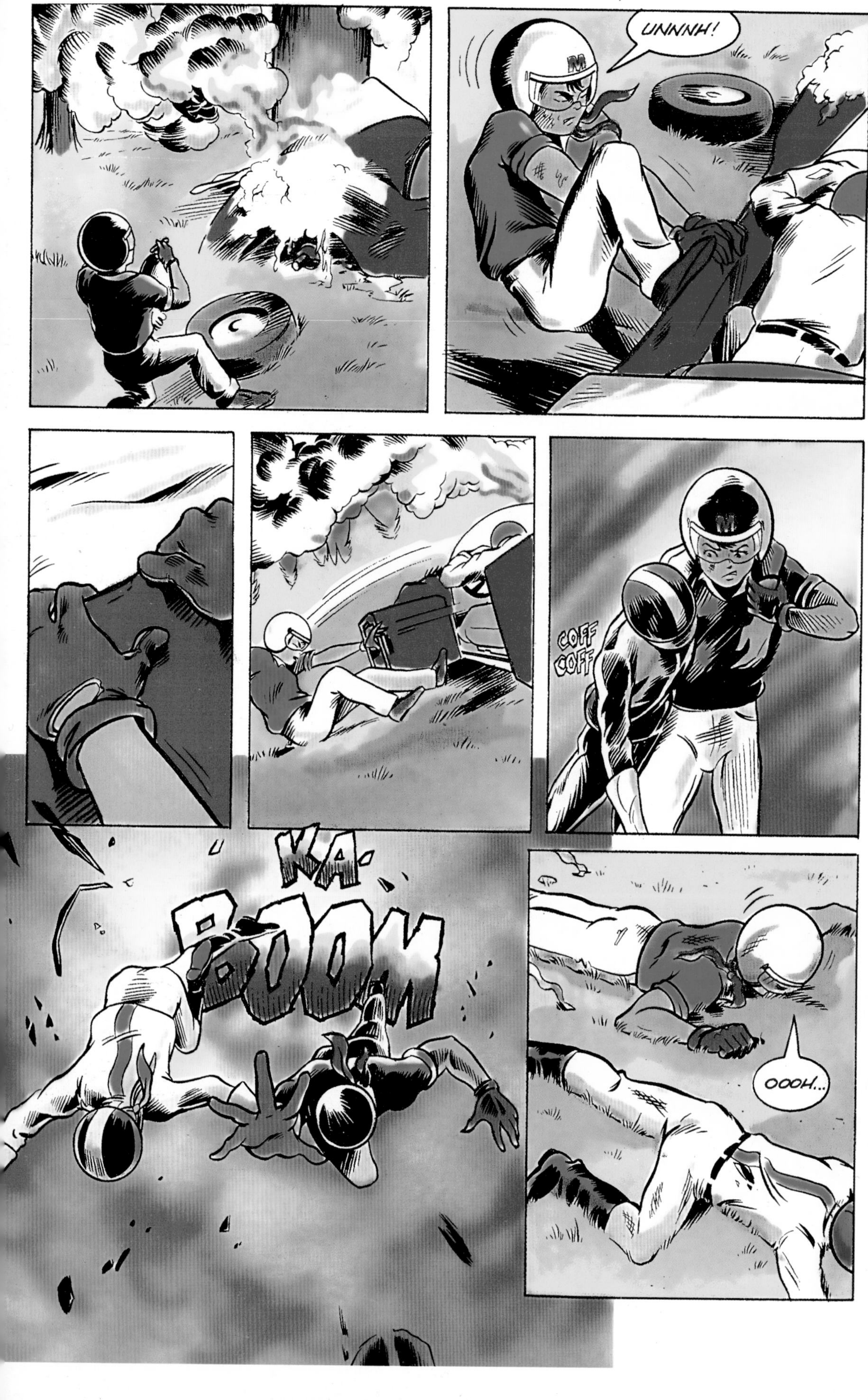
UNNNH!
COFF
COFF
KA-
BOOM
OOOH...

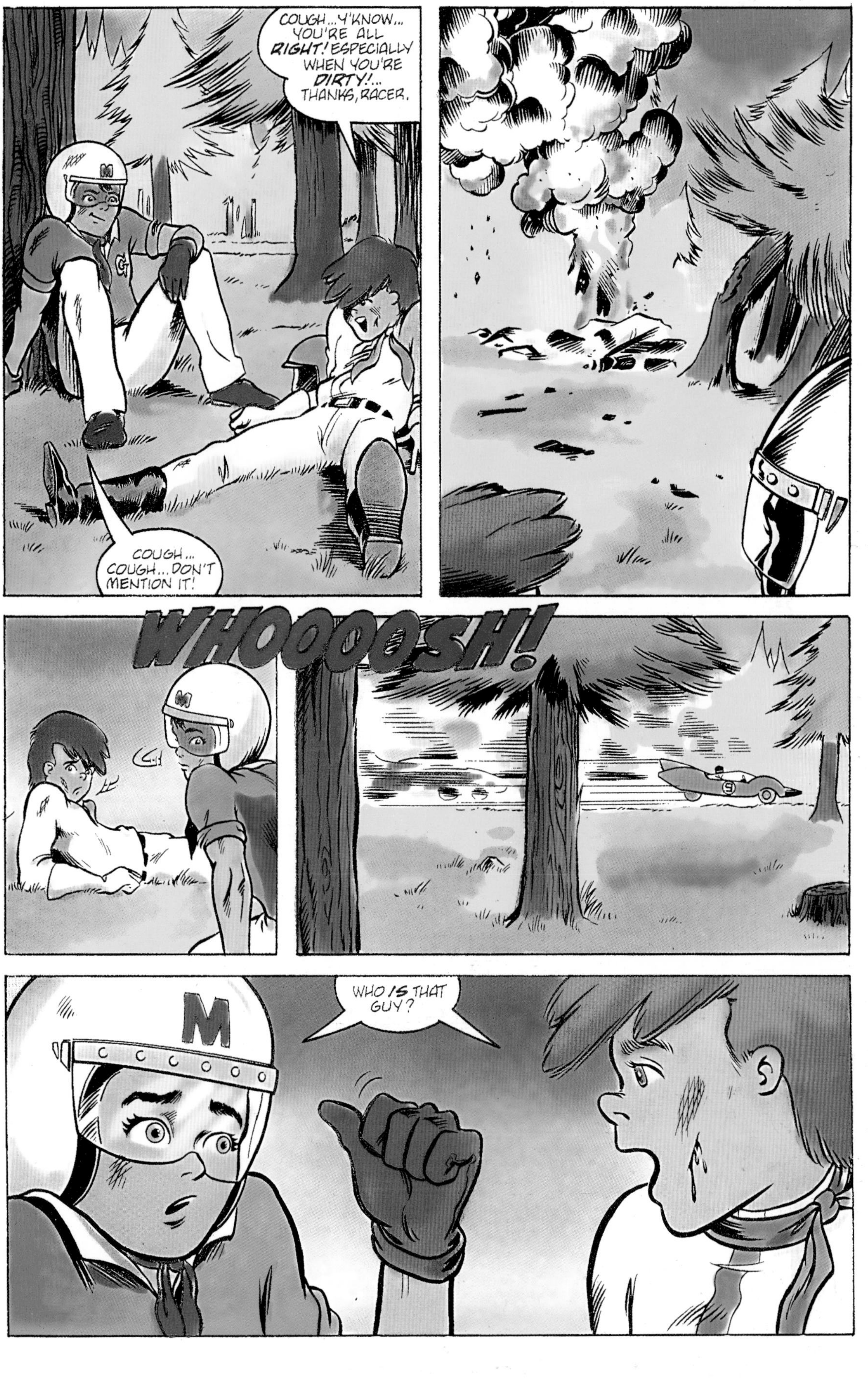
COUGH...Y'KNOW... YOU'RE ALL RIGHT! ESPECIALLY WHEN YOU'RE DIRTY!... THANKS, RACER.
COUGH... COUGH... DON'T MENTION IT!
WHOOOOSH!
WHO IS THAT GUY?

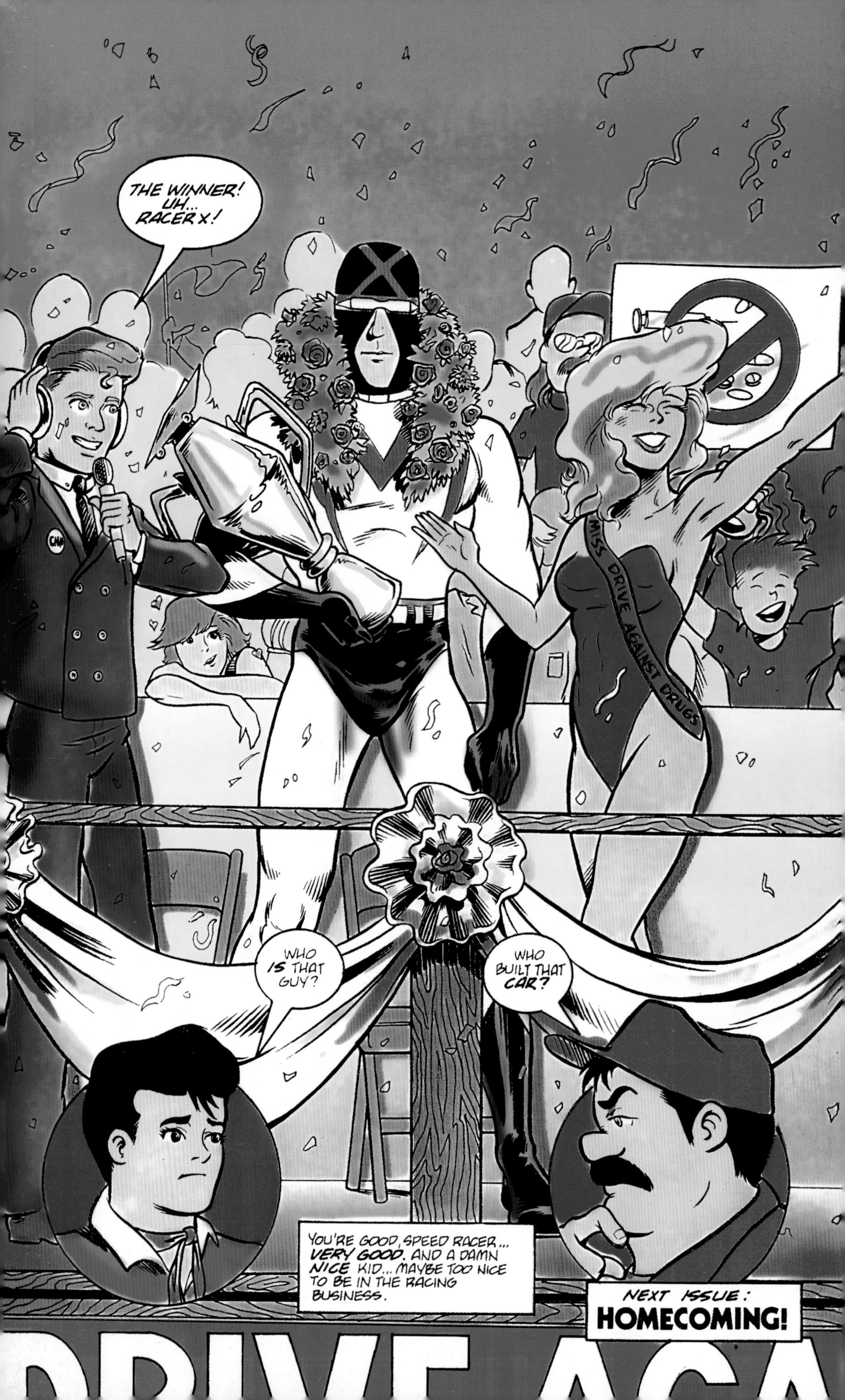
THE WINNER! UH... RACER X!
MISS DRIVE AGAINST DRUGS
WHO IS THAT GUY?
WHO BUILT THAT CAR?
YOU'RE GOOD, SPEED RACER... VERY GOOD. AND A DAMN NICE KID... MAYBE TOO NICE TO BE IN THE RACING BUSINESS.
NEXT ISSUE: HOMECOMING!

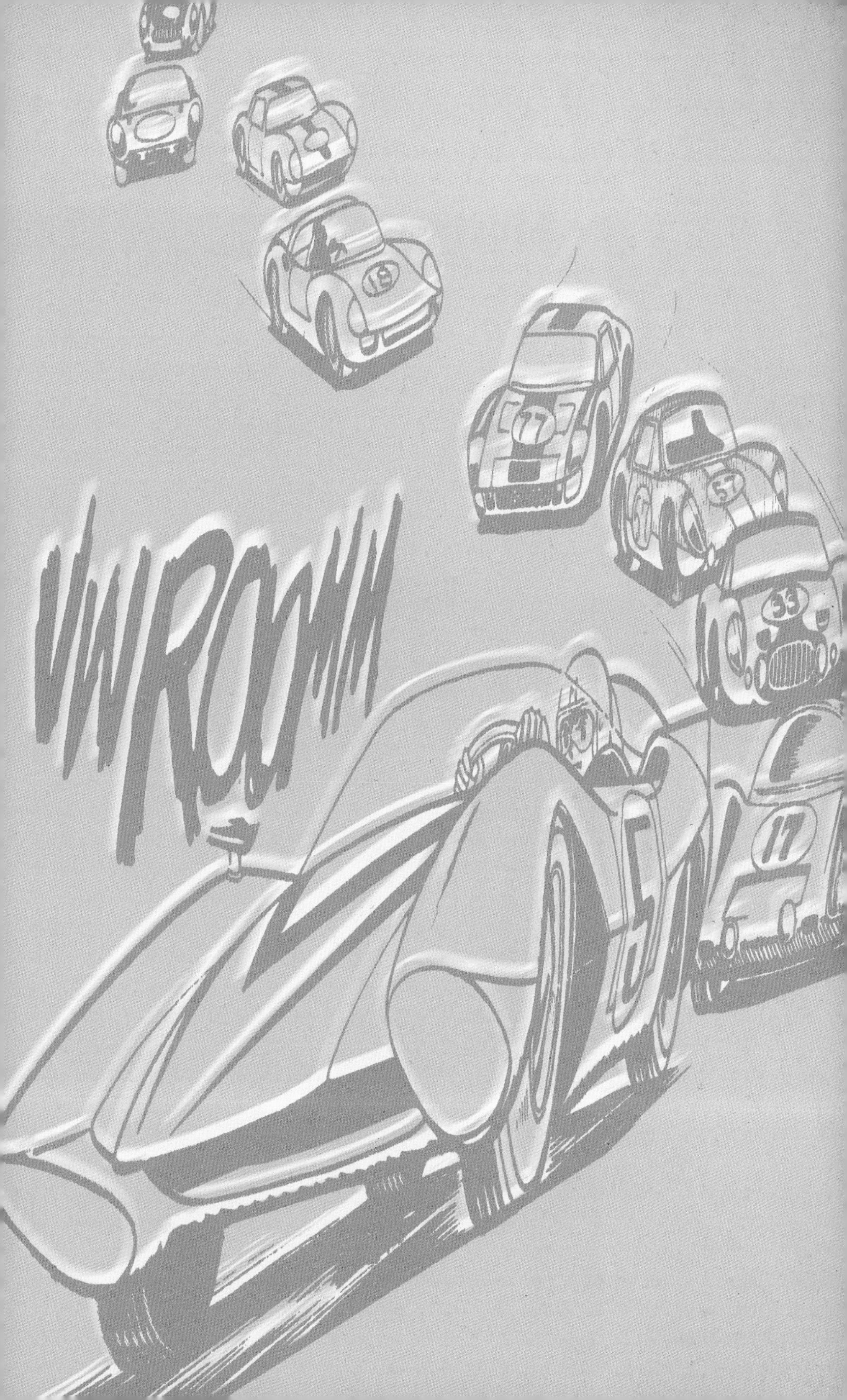
VWROOM

Speed Racer #4

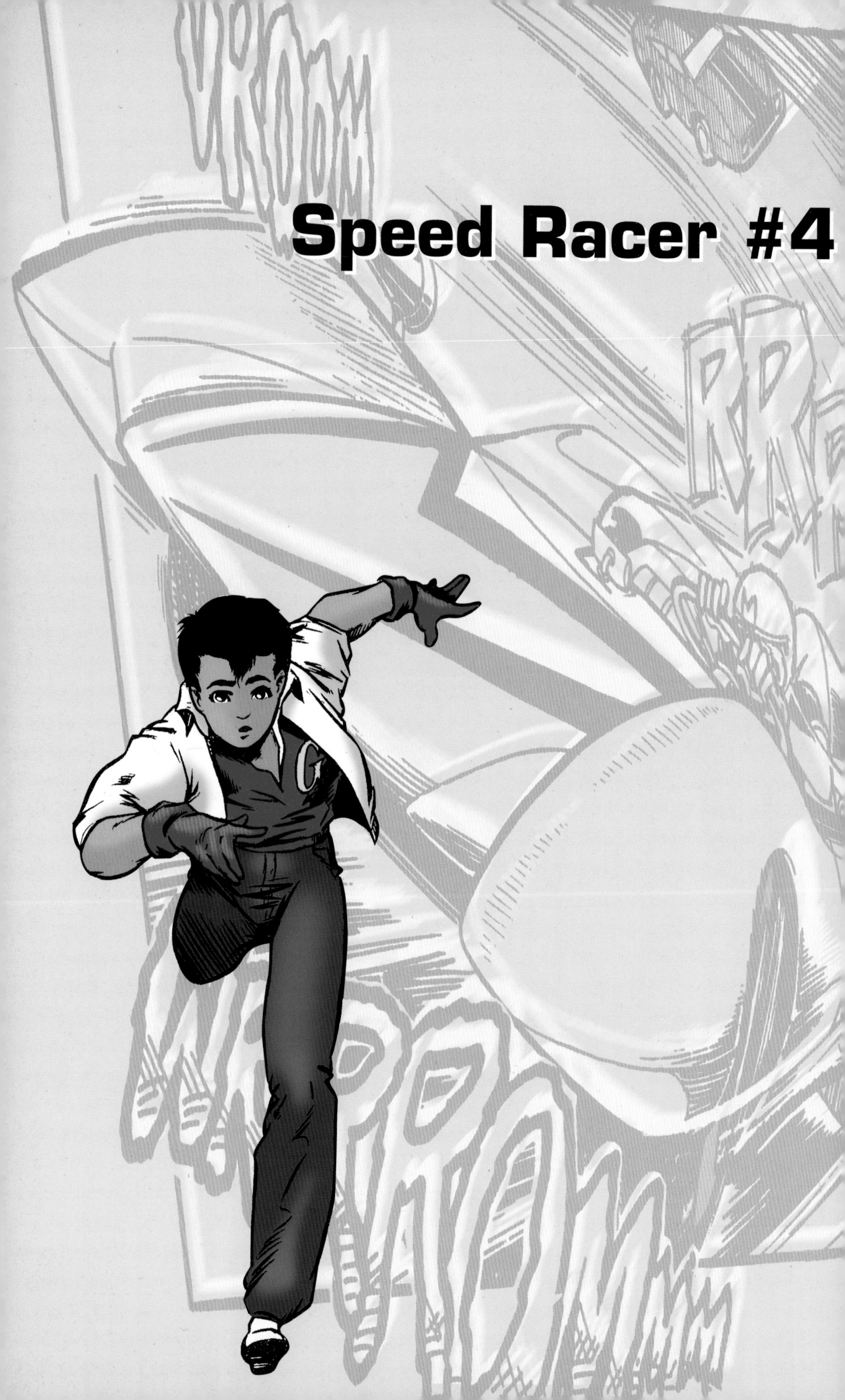

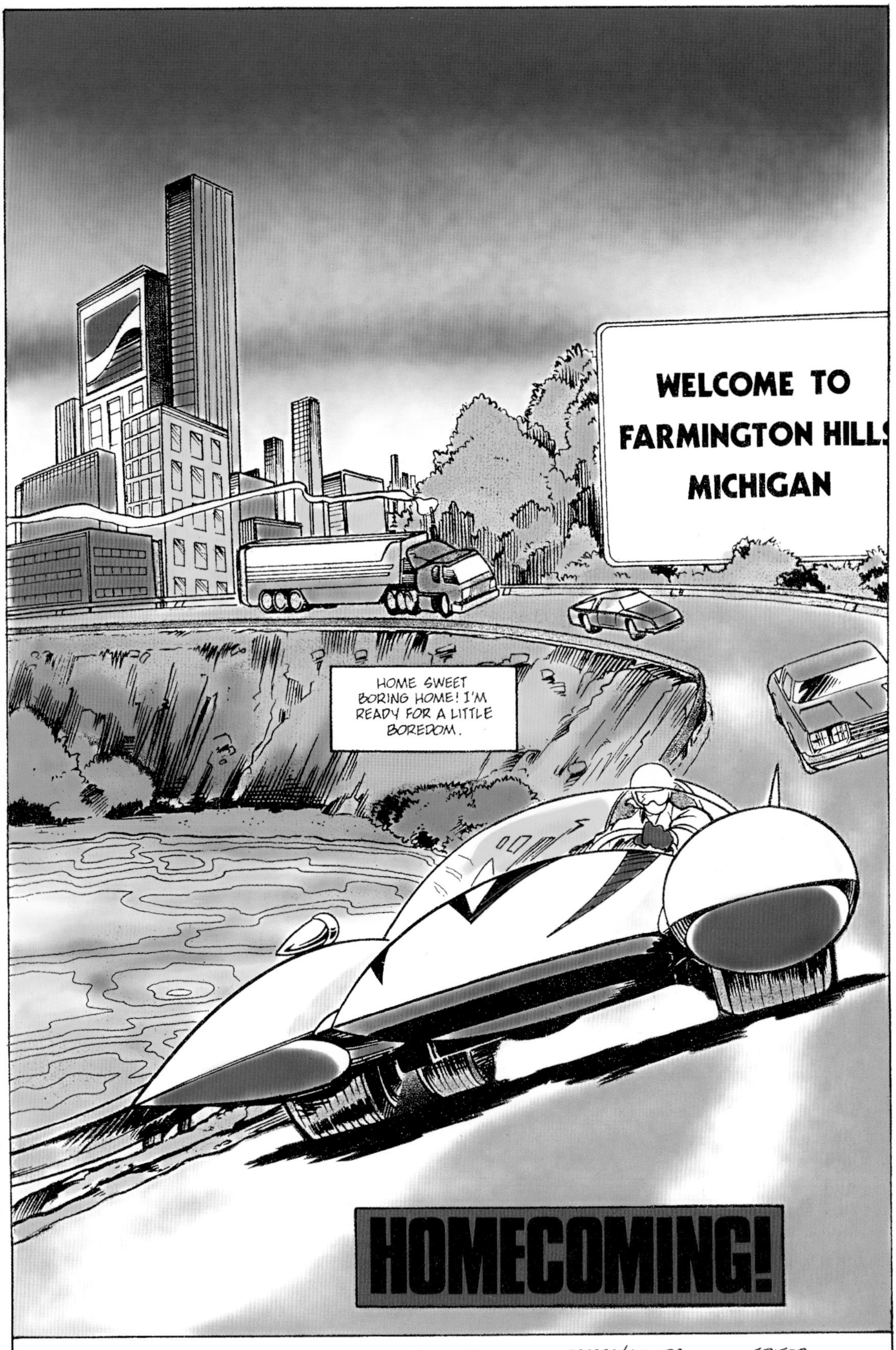
WELCOME TO
FARMINGTON HILLS
MICHIGAN
HOME SWEET BORING HOME! I'M READY FOR A LITTLE BOREDOM.
HOMECOMING!

STORY	PENCILS	INKS	LETTERS/COLORS	EDITOR
LEN STRAZEWSKI	GARY THOMAS WASHINGTON	BRIAN THOMAS	KEN HOLEWCZYNSKI	BRIAN AUGUSTYN

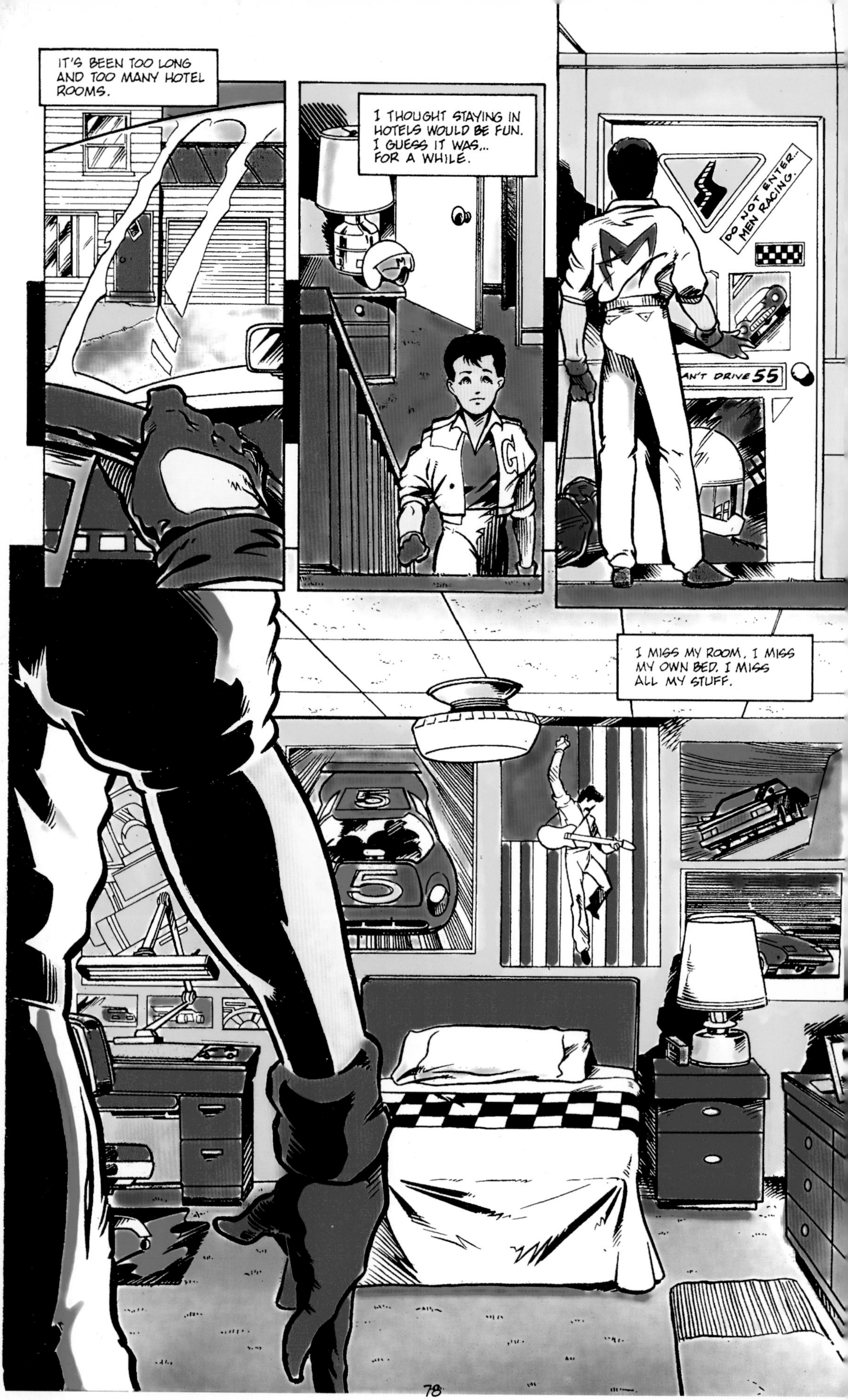
IT'S BEEN TOO LONG AND TOO MANY HOTEL ROOMS.
I THOUGHT STAYING IN HOTELS WOULD BE FUN. I GUESS IT WAS... FOR A WHILE.
DO NOT ENTER... MEN RACING.
AN'T DRIVE 55
I MISS MY ROOM. I MISS MY OWN BED. I MISS ALL MY STUFF.

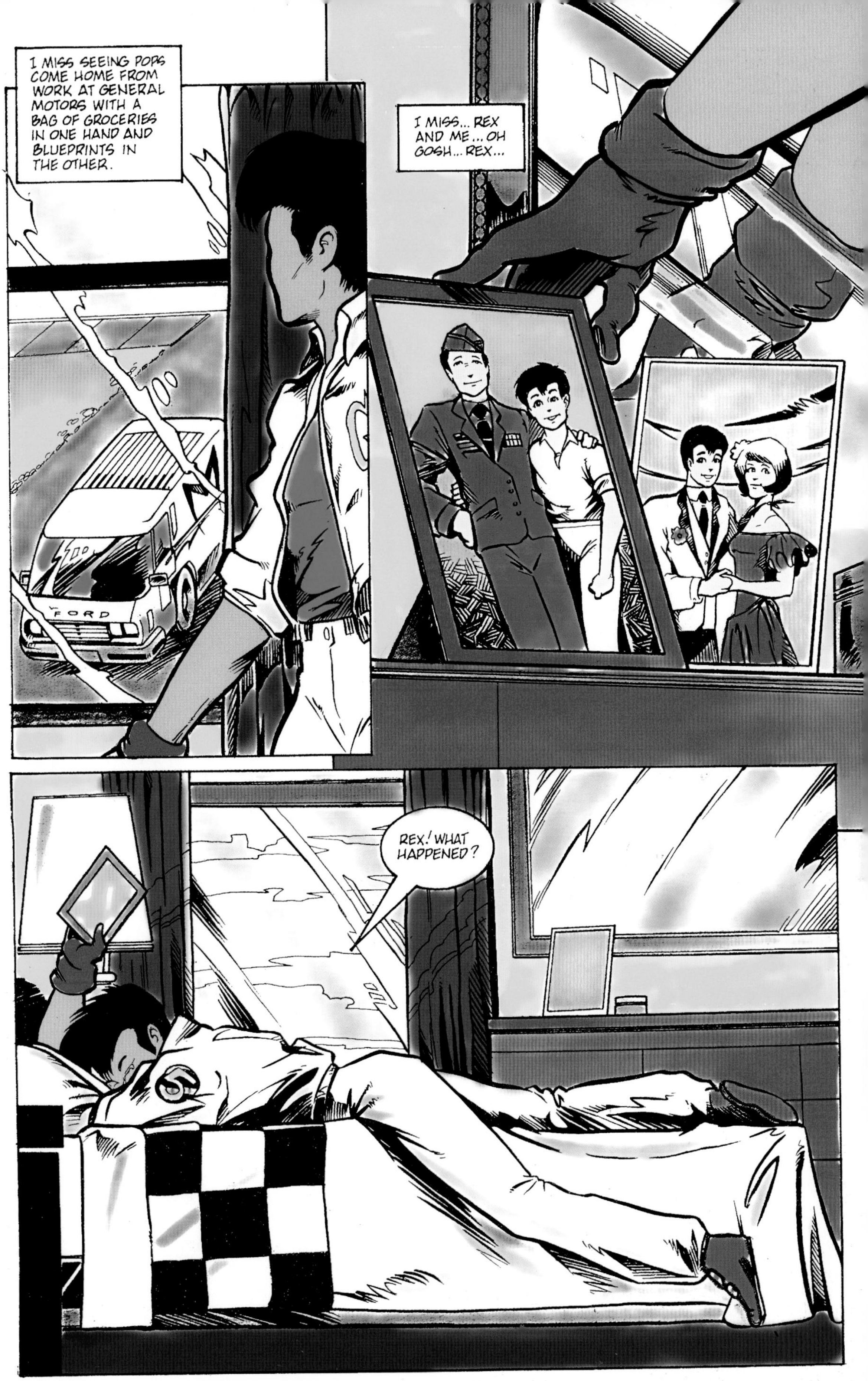
I MISS SEEING POPS COME HOME FROM WORK AT GENERAL MOTORS WITH A BAG OF GROCERIES IN ONE HAND AND BLUEPRINTS IN THE OTHER.
I MISS... REX AND ME... OH GOSH... REX...
FORD
REX! WHAT HAPPENED?

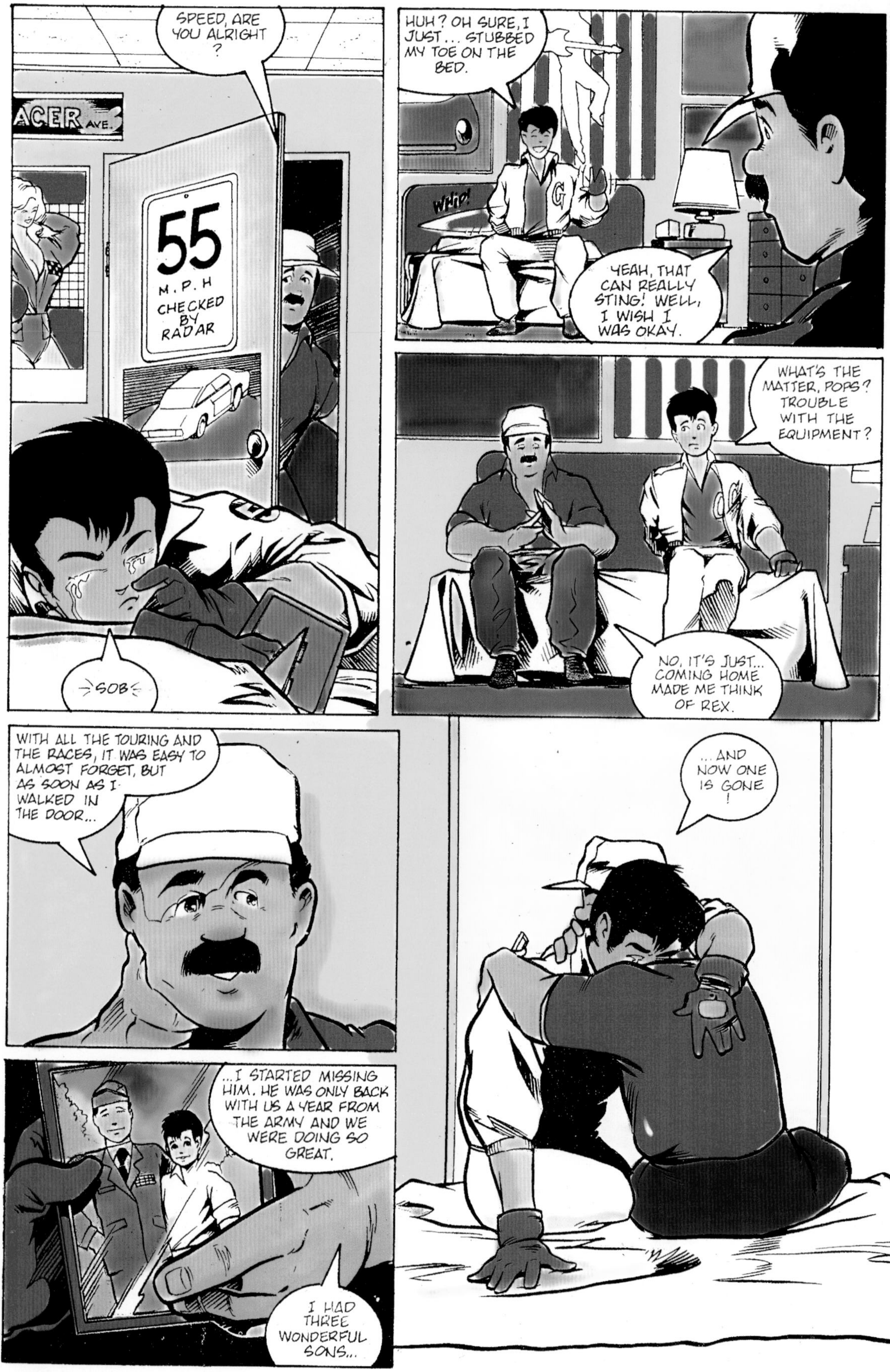
SPEED, ARE YOU ALRIGHT ?
ACER AVE.
55 M.P.H CHECKED BY RADAR
SOB
HUH? OH SURE, I JUST... STUBBED MY TOE ON THE BED.
WHIP!
YEAH, THAT CAN REALLY STING! WELL, I WISH I WAS OKAY.
WHAT'S THE MATTER, POPS? TROUBLE WITH THE EQUIPMENT?
NO, IT'S JUST... COMING HOME MADE ME THINK OF REX.
WITH ALL THE TOURING AND THE RACES, IT WAS EASY TO ALMOST FORGET, BUT AS SOON AS I WALKED IN THE DOOR...
...I STARTED MISSING HIM. HE WAS ONLY BACK WITH US A YEAR FROM THE ARMY AND WE WERE DOING SO GREAT.
I HAD THREE WONDERFUL SONS...
...AND NOW ONE IS GONE !

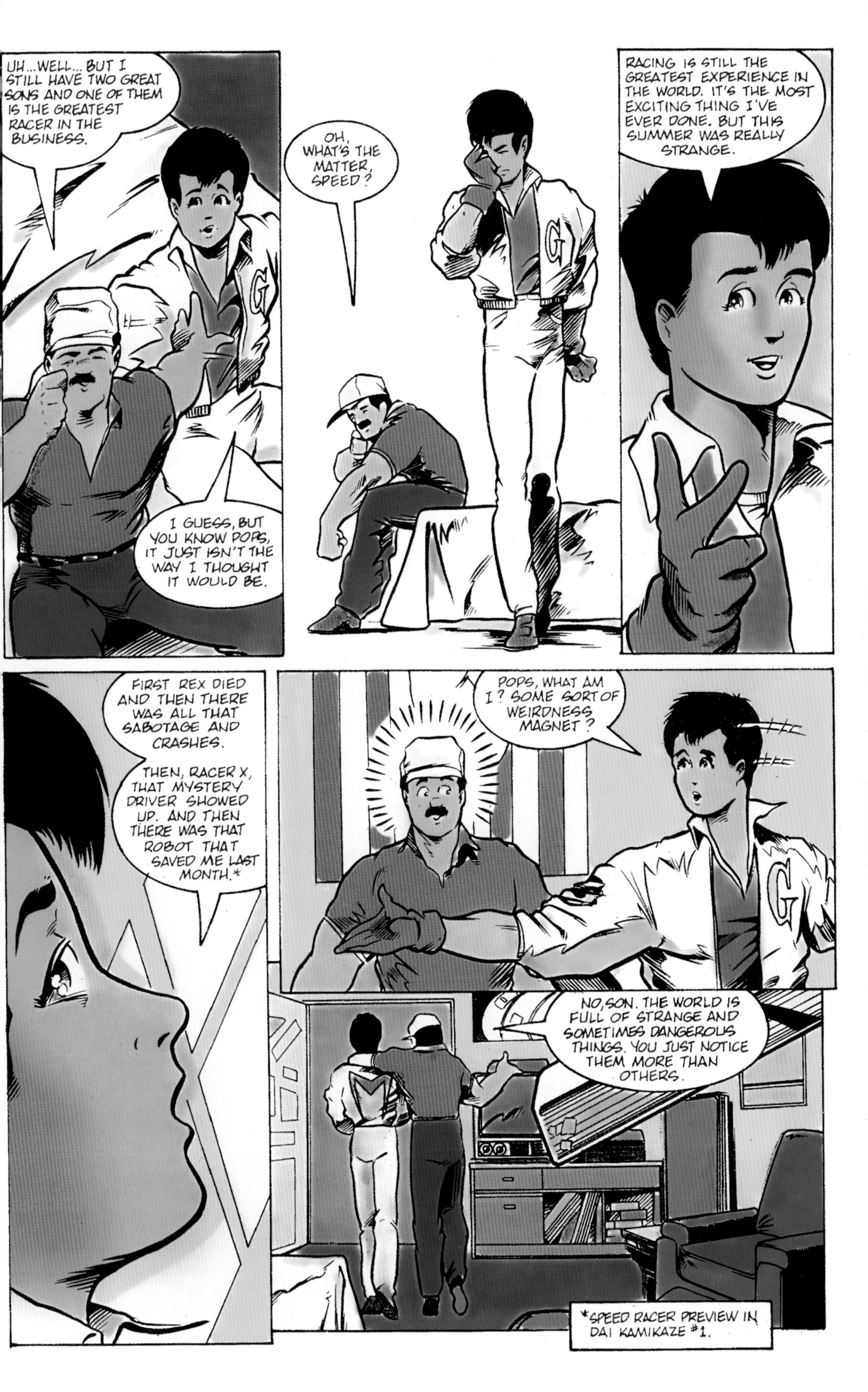
UH...WELL... BUT I STILL HAVE TWO GREAT SONS AND ONE OF THEM IS THE GREATEST RACER IN THE BUSINESS.
I GUESS, BUT YOU KNOW POPS, IT JUST ISN'T THE WAY I THOUGHT IT WOULD BE.
OH, WHAT'S THE MATTER, SPEED?
RACING IS STILL THE GREATEST EXPERIENCE IN THE WORLD. IT'S THE MOST EXCITING THING I'VE EVER DONE. BUT THIS SUMMER WAS REALLY STRANGE.
FIRST REX DIED AND THEN THERE WAS ALL THAT SABOTAGE AND CRASHES.
THEN, RACER X, THAT MYSTERY DRIVER SHOWED UP. AND THEN THERE WAS THAT ROBOT THAT SAVED ME LAST MONTH.*
POPS, WHAT AM I? SOME SORT OF WEIRDNESS MAGNET?
NO, SON. THE WORLD IS FULL OF STRANGE AND SOMETIMES DANGEROUS THINGS. YOU JUST NOTICE THEM MORE THAN OTHERS.
*SPEED RACER PREVIEW IN DAI KAMIKAZE #1.

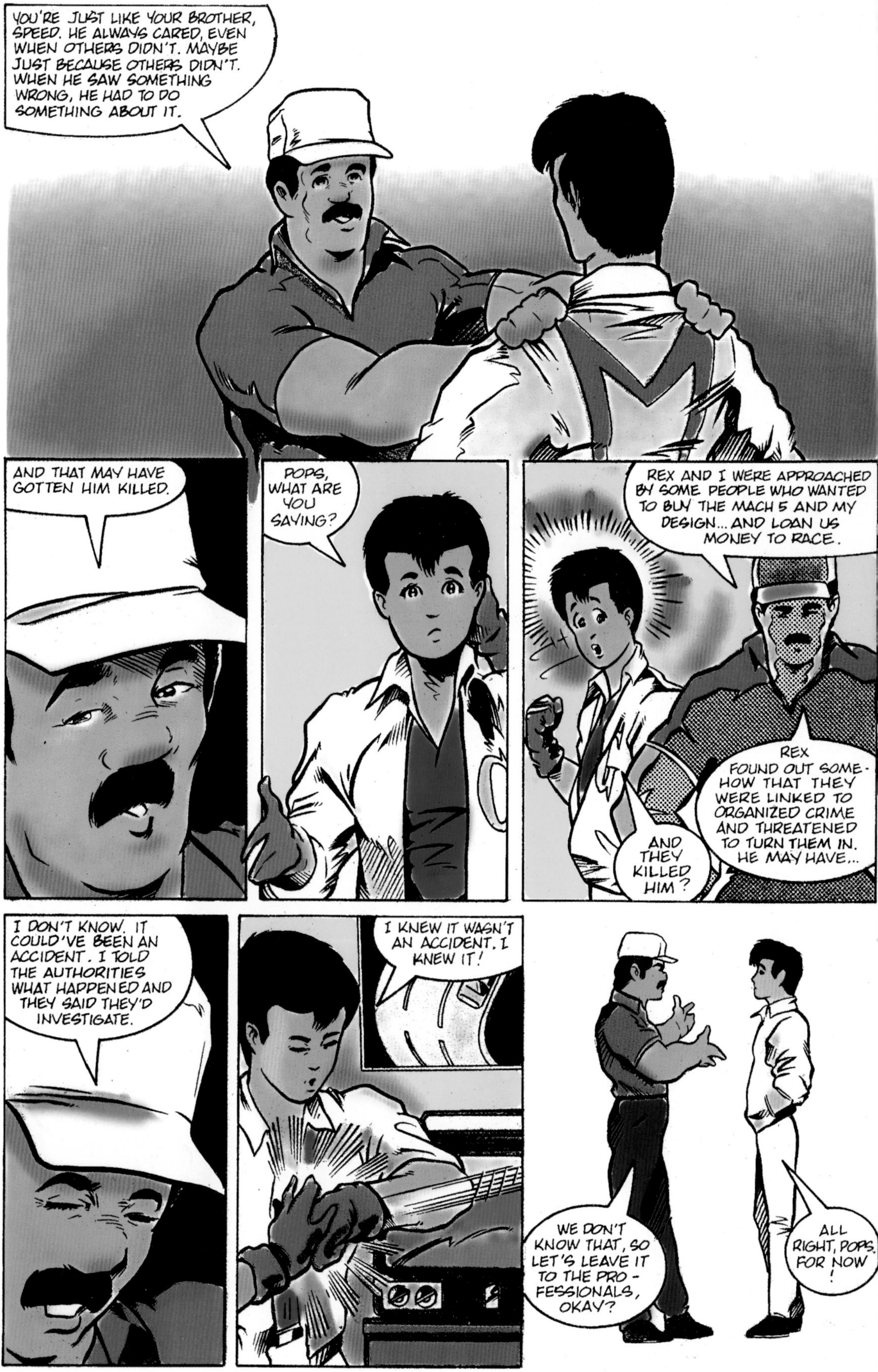
YOU'RE JUST LIKE YOUR BROTHER, SPEED. HE ALWAYS CARED, EVEN WHEN OTHERS DIDN'T. MAYBE JUST BECAUSE OTHERS DIDN'T. WHEN HE SAW SOMETHING WRONG, HE HAD TO DO SOMETHING ABOUT IT.
AND THAT MAY HAVE GOTTEN HIM KILLED.
POPS, WHAT ARE YOU SAYING?
REX AND I WERE APPROACHED BY SOME PEOPLE WHO WANTED TO BUY THE MACH 5 AND MY DESIGN... AND LOAN US MONEY TO RACE.
REX FOUND OUT SOME-HOW THAT THEY WERE LINKED TO ORGANIZED CRIME AND THREATENED TO TURN THEM IN. HE MAY HAVE...
AND THEY KILLED HIM?
I DON'T KNOW. IT COULD'VE BEEN AN ACCIDENT. I TOLD THE AUTHORITIES WHAT HAPPENED AND THEY SAID THEY'D INVESTIGATE.
I KNEW IT WASN'T AN ACCIDENT. I KNEW IT!
WE DON'T KNOW THAT, SO LET'S LEAVE IT TO THE PRO-FESSIONALS, OKAY?
ALL RIGHT, POPS. FOR NOW!

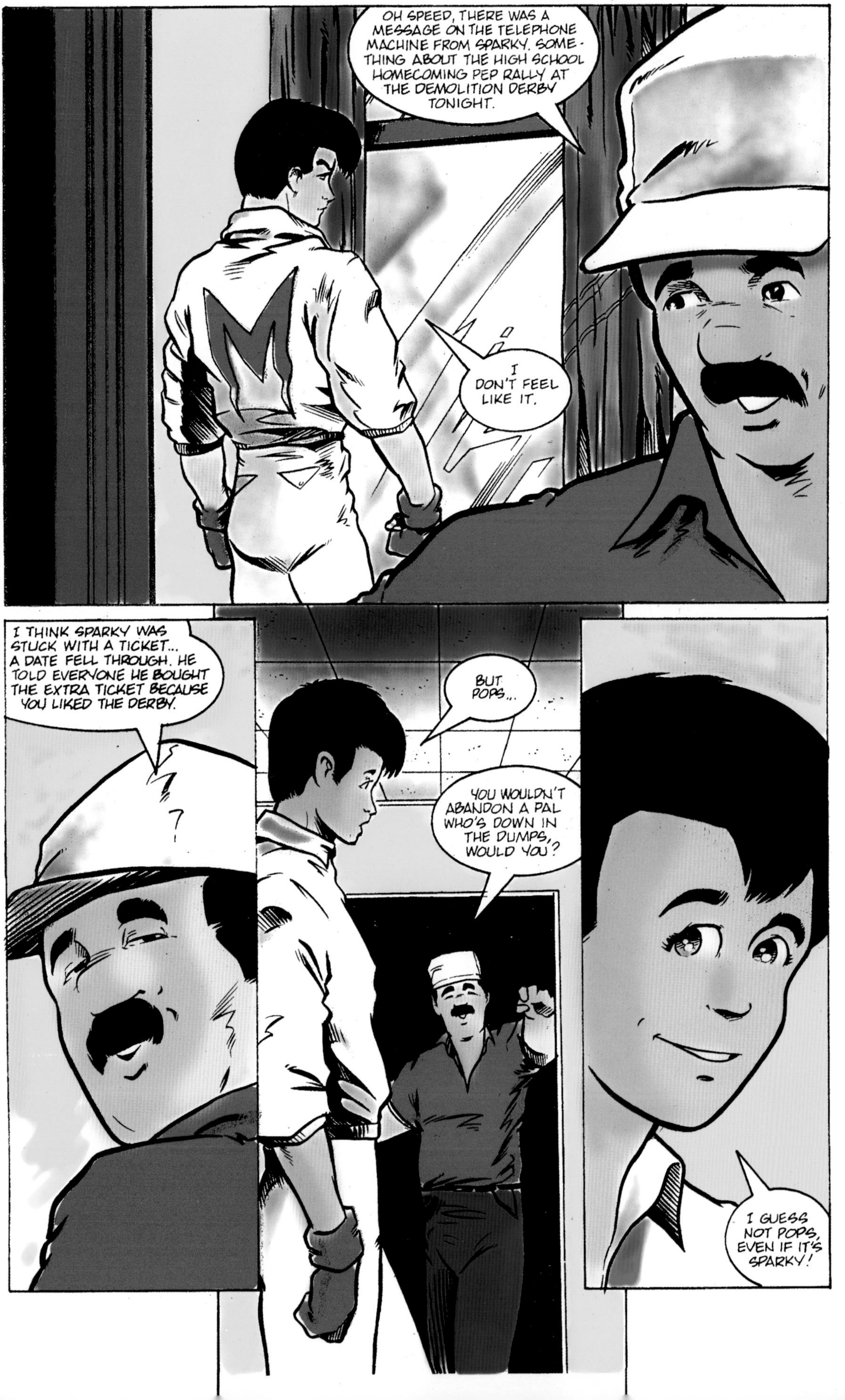
OH SPEED, THERE WAS A MESSAGE ON THE TELEPHONE MACHINE FROM SPARKY. SOMETHING ABOUT THE HIGH SCHOOL HOMECOMING PEP RALLY AT THE DEMOLITION DERBY TONIGHT.
I DON'T FEEL LIKE IT.
I THINK SPARKY WAS STUCK WITH A TICKET... A DATE FELL THROUGH. HE TOLD EVERYONE HE BOUGHT THE EXTRA TICKET BECAUSE YOU LIKED THE DERBY.
BUT POPS...
YOU WOULDN'T ABANDON A PAL WHO'S DOWN IN THE DUMPS, WOULD YOU?
I GUESS NOT POPS, EVEN IF IT'S SPARKY!

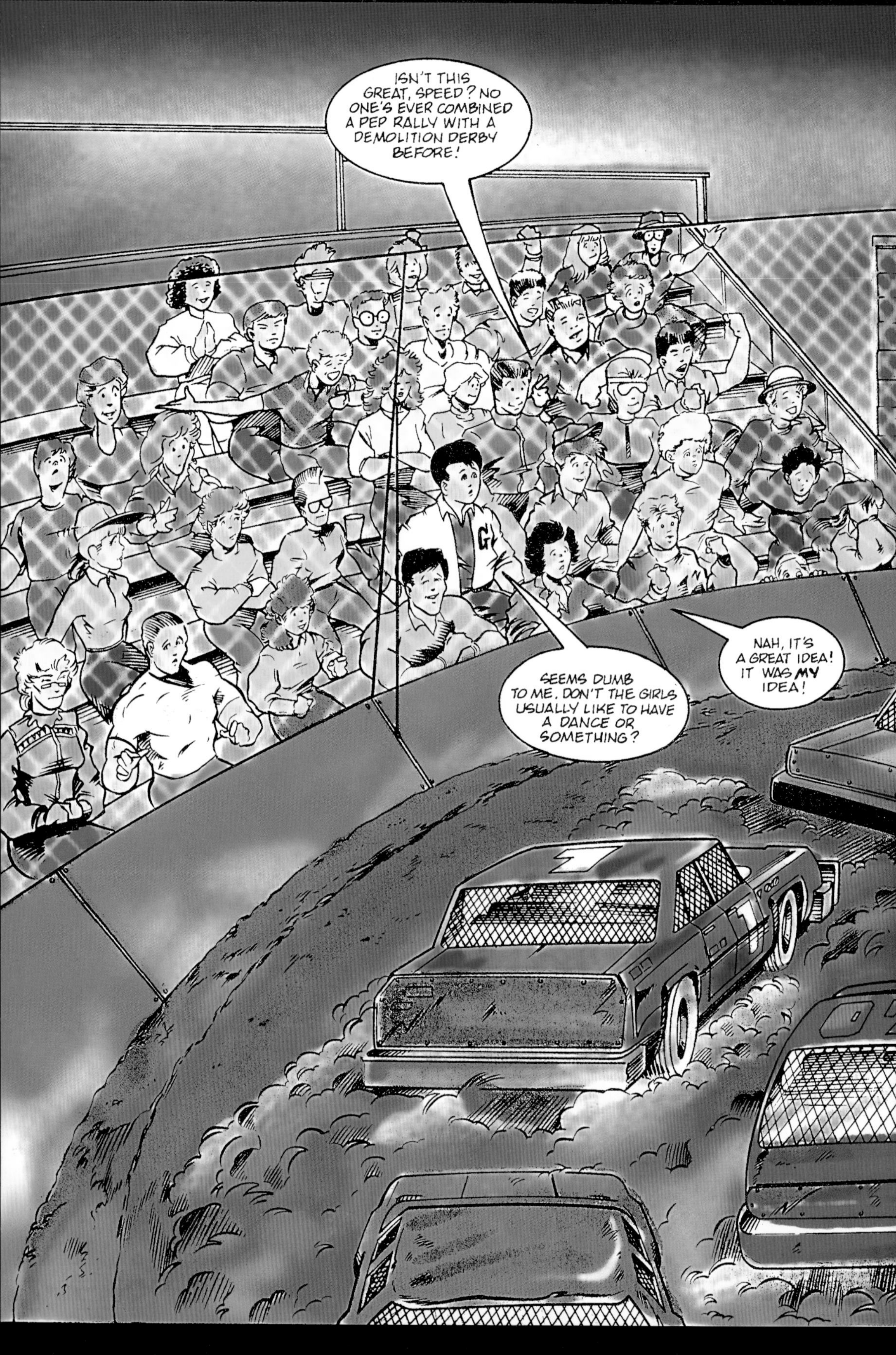
ISN'T THIS GREAT, SPEED? NO ONE'S EVER COMBINED A PEP RALLY WITH A DEMOLITION DERBY BEFORE!
SEEMS DUMB TO ME. DON'T THE GIRLS USUALLY LIKE TO HAVE A DANCE OR SOMETHING?
NAH, IT'S A GREAT IDEA! IT WAS **MY** IDEA!

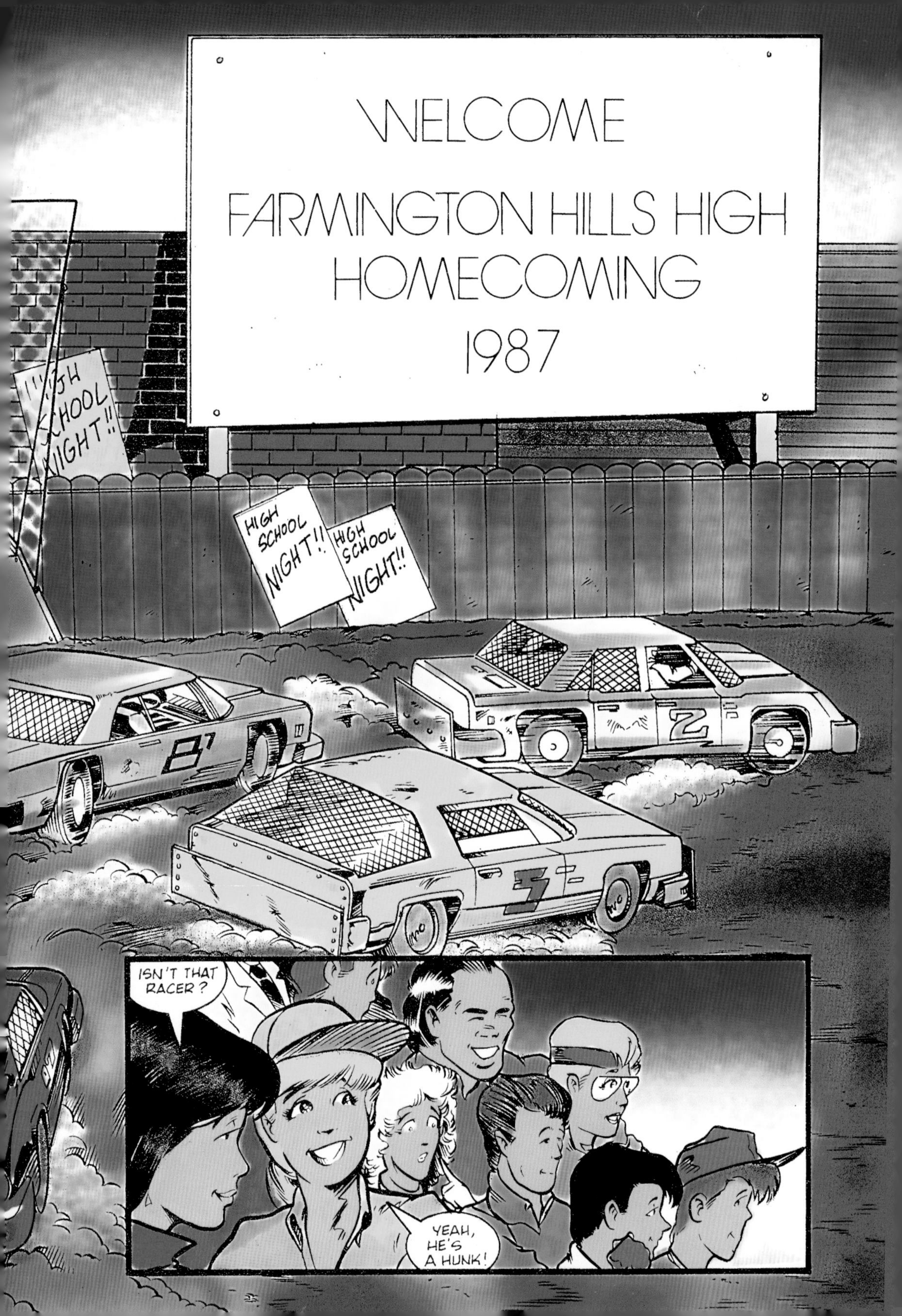
WELCOME
FARMINGTON HILLS HIGH
HOMECOMING
1987
HIGH SCHOOL NIGHT!!
HIGH SCHOOL NIGHT!!
ISN'T THAT RACER?
YEAH, HE'S A HUNK!

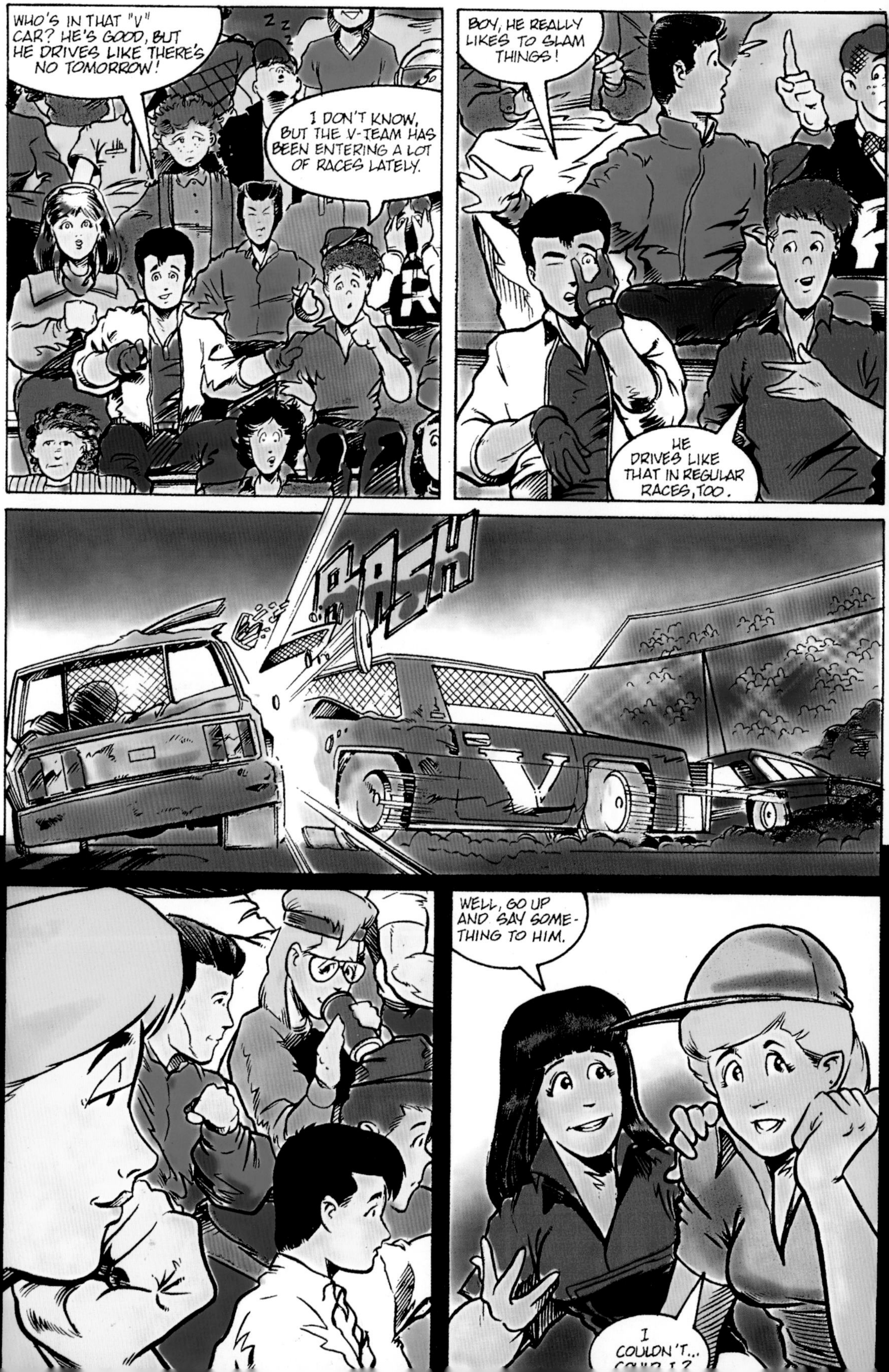
WHO'S IN THAT "V" CAR? HE'S GOOD, BUT HE DRIVES LIKE THERE'S NO TOMORROW!
I DON'T KNOW, BUT THE V-TEAM HAS BEEN ENTERING A LOT OF RACES LATELY.
BOY, HE REALLY LIKES TO SLAM THINGS!
HE DRIVES LIKE THAT IN REGULAR RACES, TOO.
WELL, GO UP AND SAY SOMETHING TO HIM.
I COULDN'T...

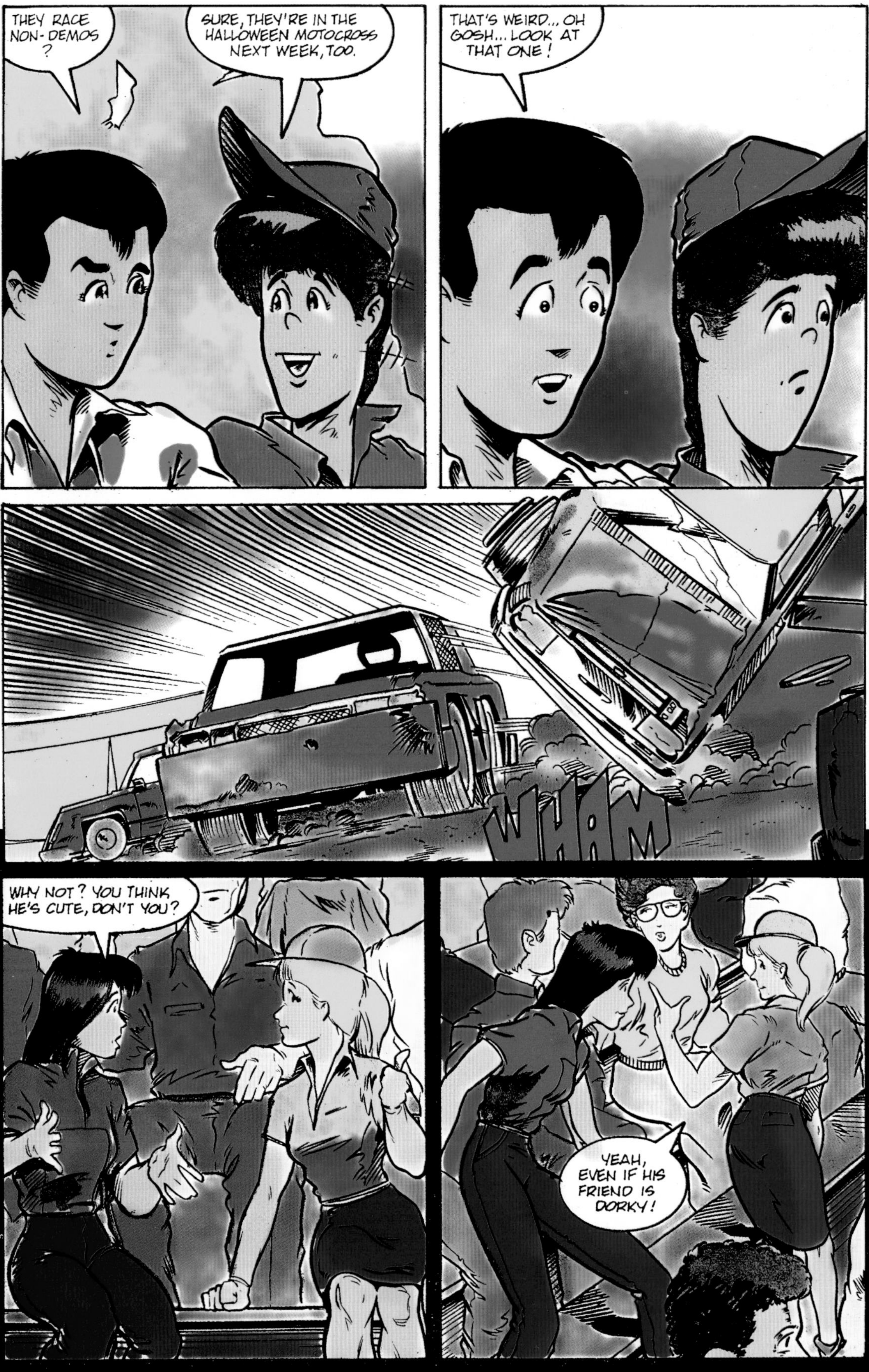
THEY RACE NON-DEMOS ?
SURE, THEY'RE IN THE HALLOWEEN MOTOCROSS NEXT WEEK, TOO.
THAT'S WEIRD... OH GOSH... LOOK AT THAT ONE!
WHAM
WHY NOT? YOU THINK HE'S CUTE, DON'T YOU?
YEAH, EVEN IF HIS FRIEND IS DORKY!

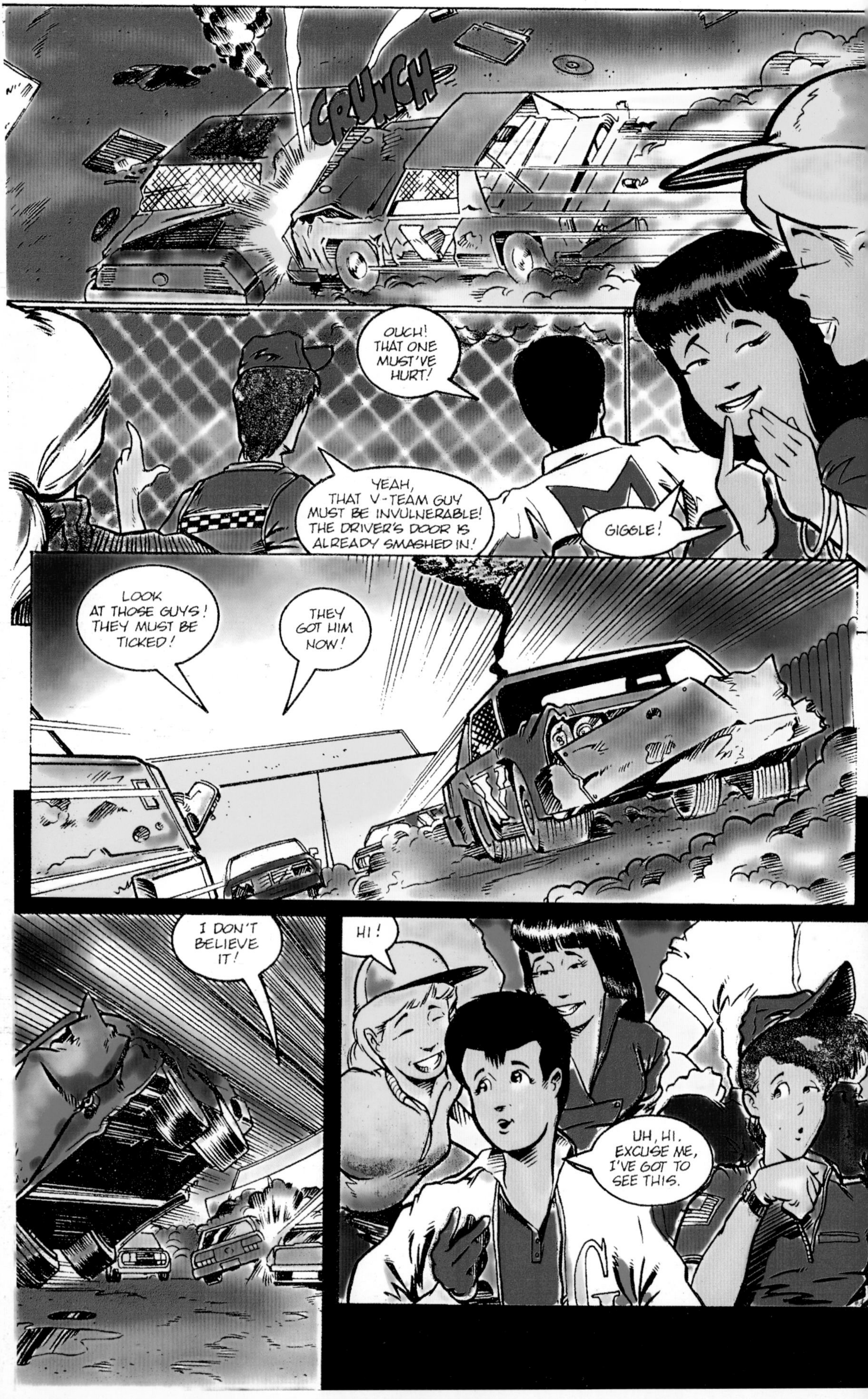
CRUNCH
OUCH! THAT ONE MUST'VE HURT!
YEAH, THAT V-TEAM GUY MUST BE INVULNERABLE! THE DRIVER'S DOOR IS ALREADY SMASHED IN!
GIGGLE!
LOOK AT THOSE GUYS! THEY MUST BE TICKED!
THEY GOT HIM NOW!
I DON'T BELIEVE IT!
HI!
UH, HI. EXCUSE ME, I'VE GOT TO SEE THIS.

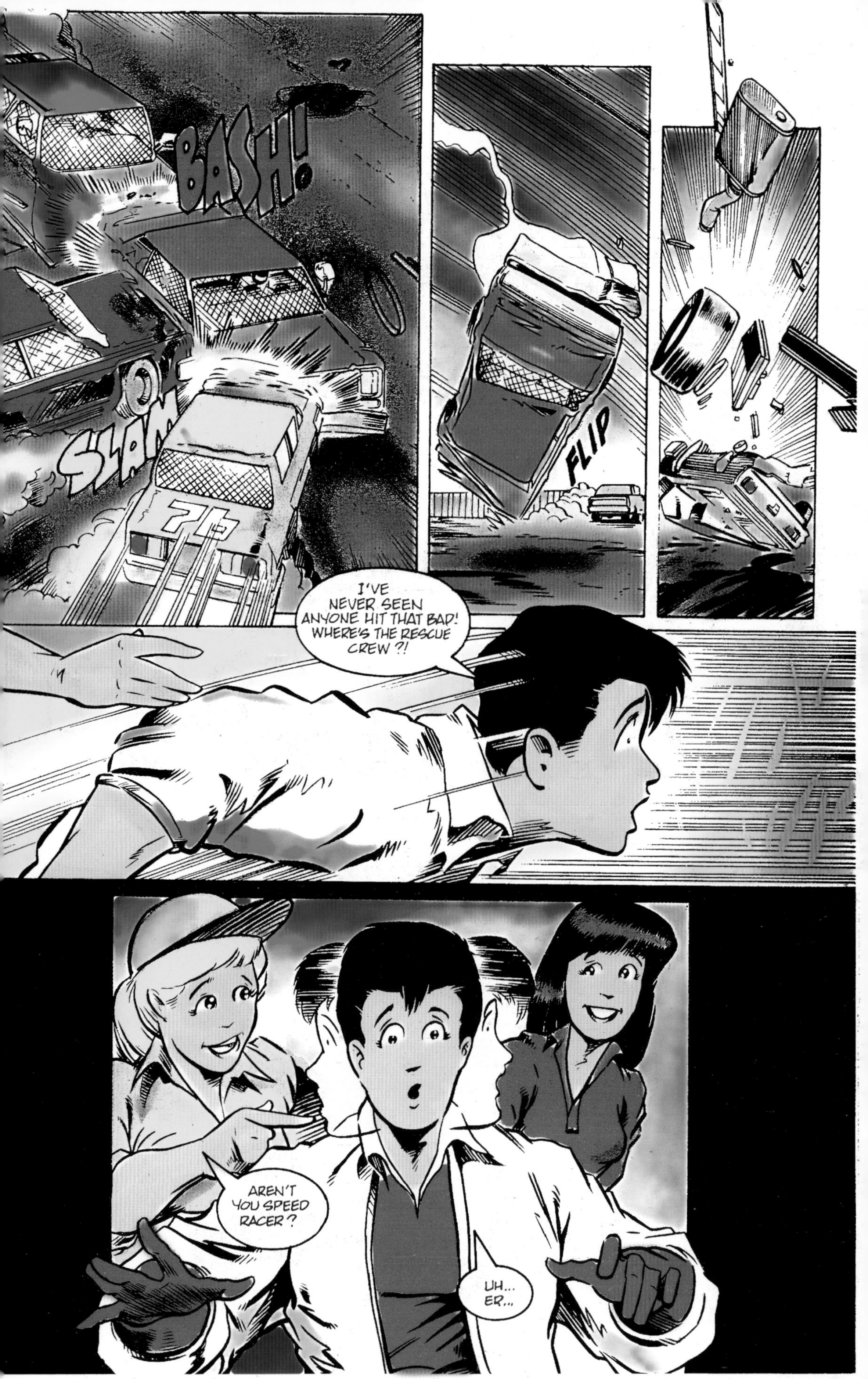
BASH!
SLAM
FLIP
I'VE NEVER SEEN ANYONE HIT THAT BAD! WHERE'S THE RESCUE CREW ?!
AREN'T YOU SPEED RACER?
UH... ER...

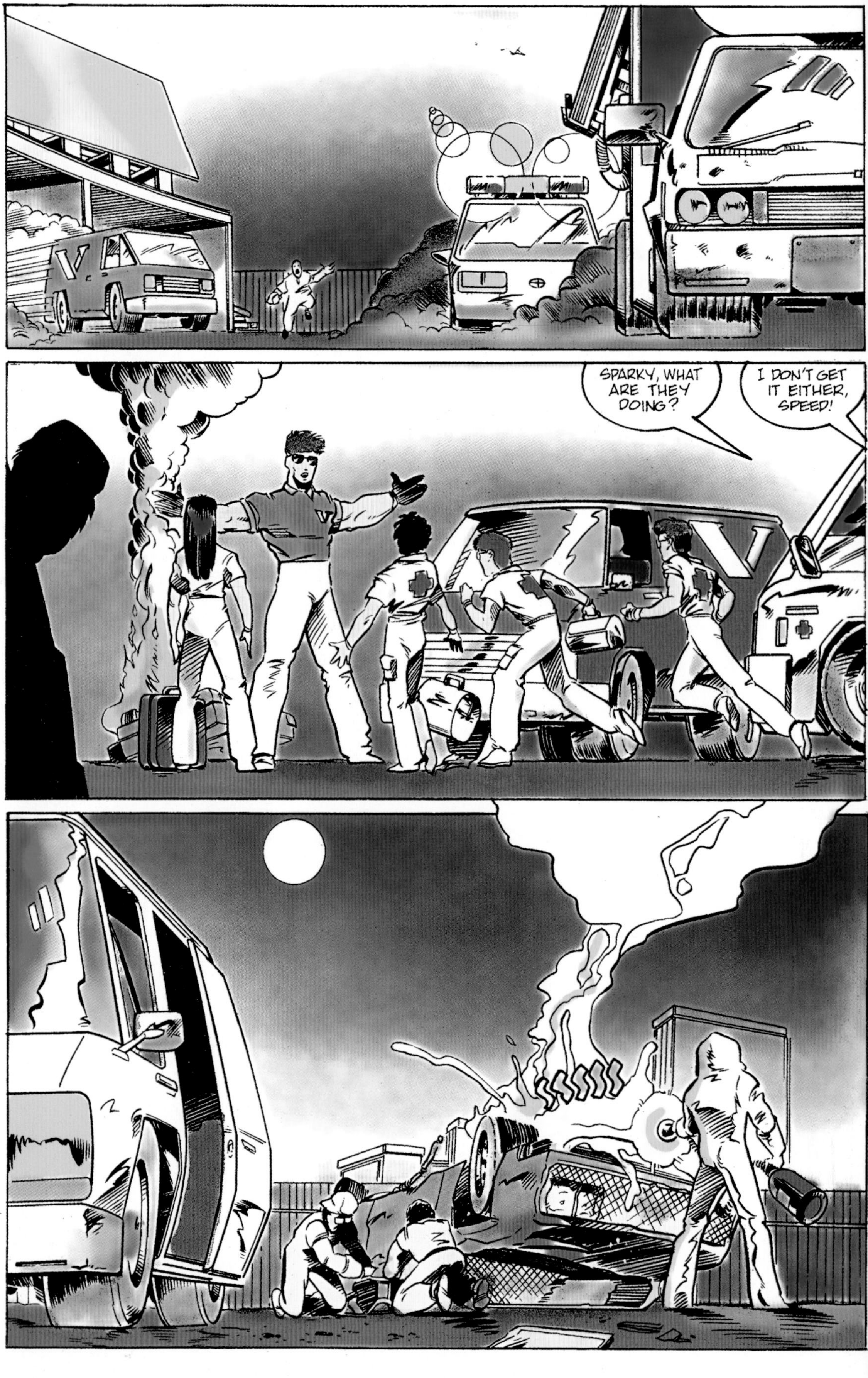
SPARKY, WHAT ARE THEY DOING?
I DON'T GET IT EITHER, SPEED!

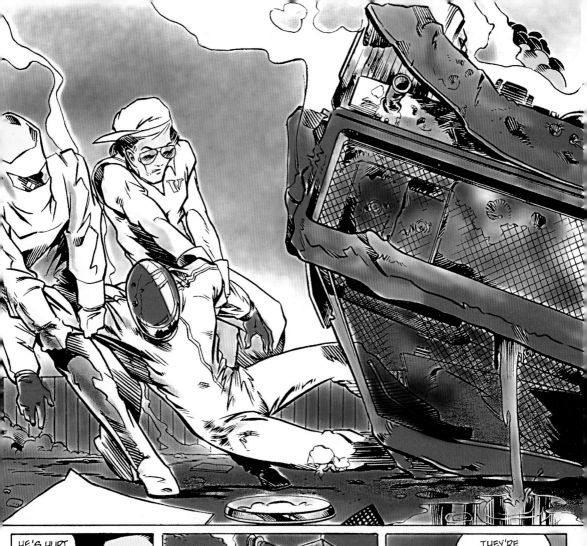

HE'S HURT BAD!

THEY'RE NOT EVEN HEADING TOWARDS FIRST-AID!

HE'S INJURED. THEY CAN'T HANDLE HIM LIKE THAT!

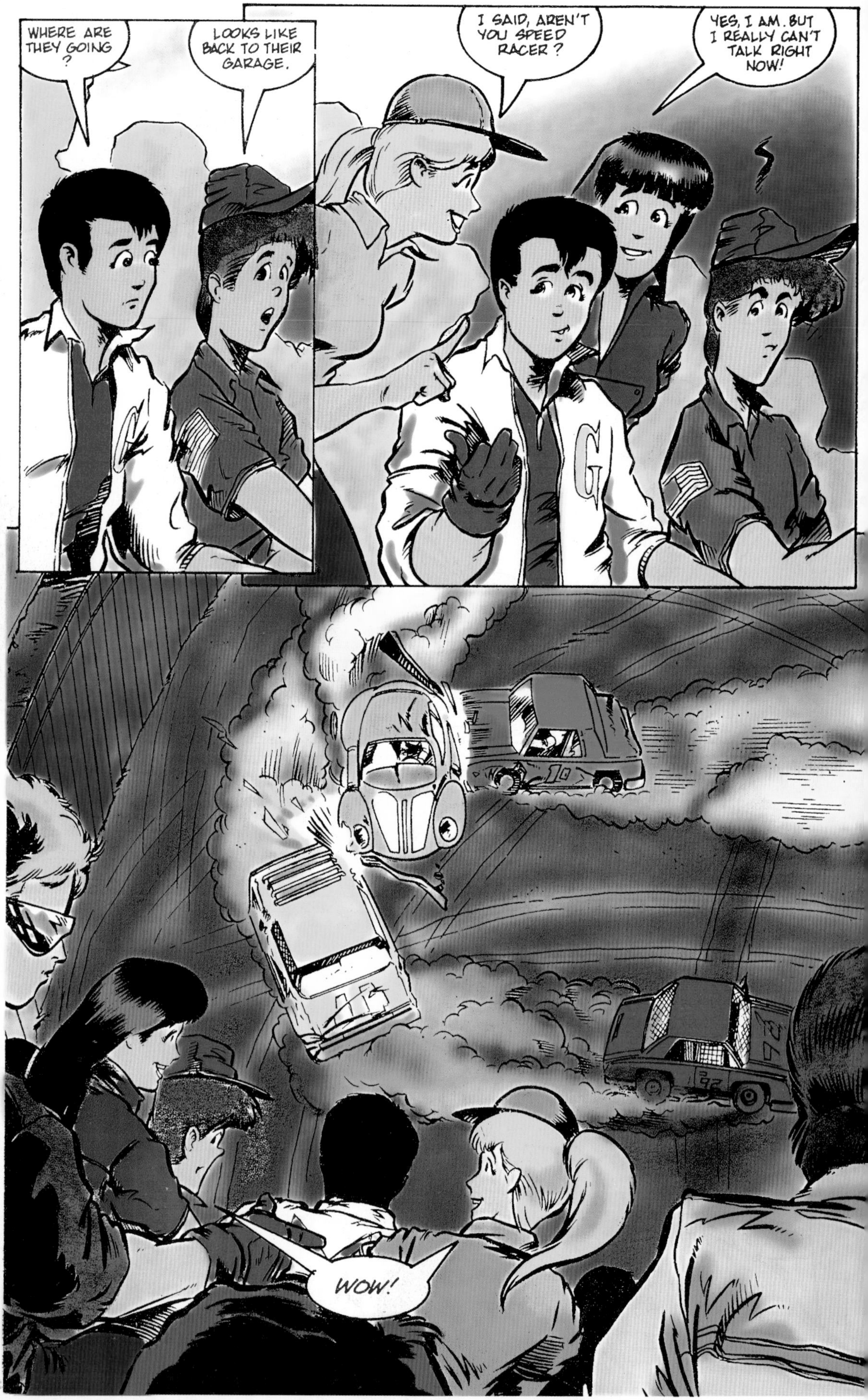
WHERE ARE THEY GOING ?
LOOKS LIKE BACK TO THEIR GARAGE.
I SAID, AREN'T YOU SPEED RACER ?
YES, I AM. BUT I REALLY CAN'T TALK RIGHT NOW!
WOW!

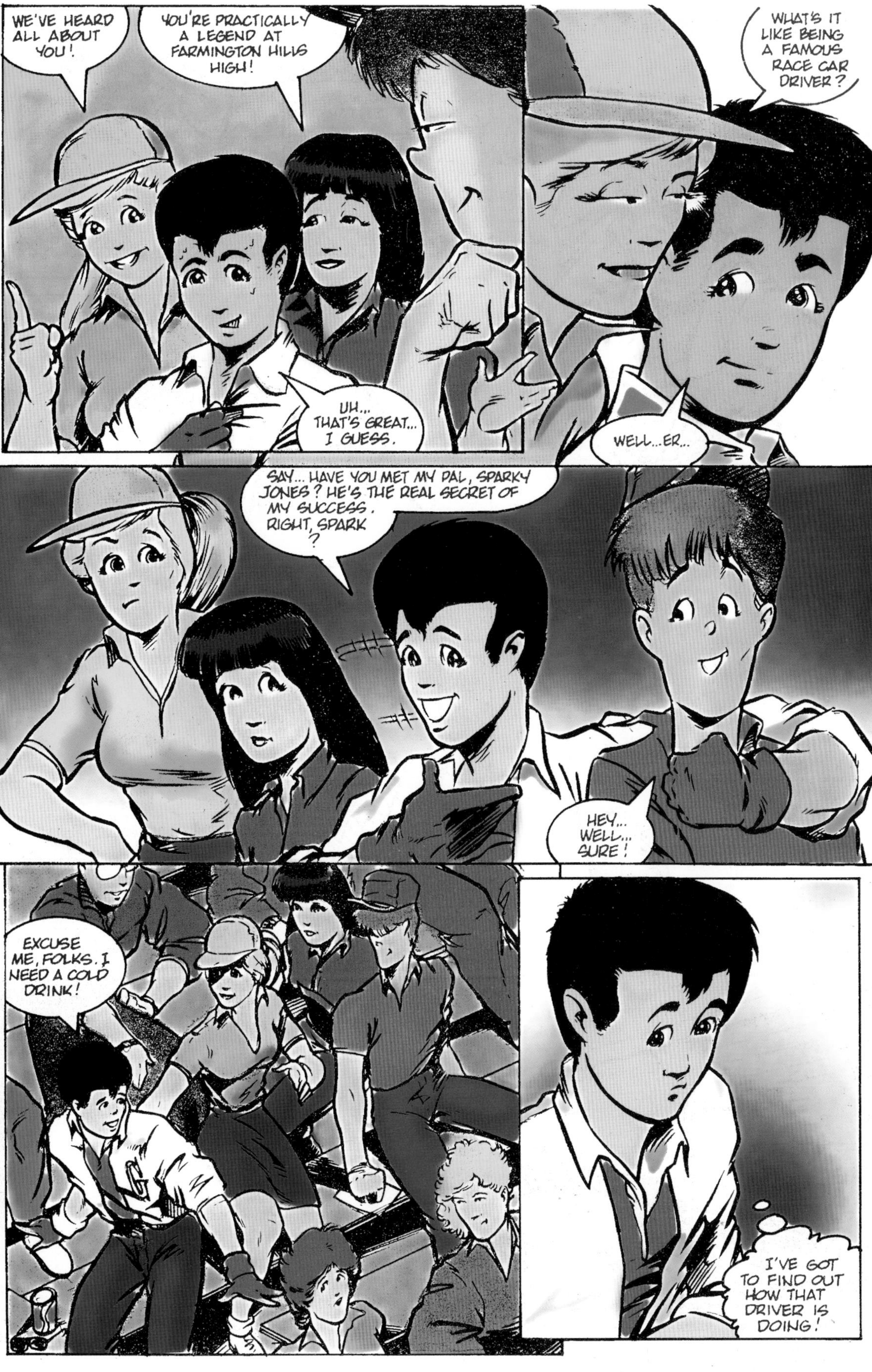
WE'VE HEARD ALL ABOUT YOU!
YOU'RE PRACTICALLY A LEGEND AT FARMINGTON HILLS HIGH!
UH... THAT'S GREAT... I GUESS.
WHAT'S IT LIKE BEING A FAMOUS RACE CAR DRIVER?
WELL...ER...
SAY... HAVE YOU MET MY PAL, SPARKY JONES? HE'S THE REAL SECRET OF MY SUCCESS. RIGHT, SPARK?
HEY... WELL... SURE!
EXCUSE ME, FOLKS. I NEED A COLD DRINK!
I'VE GOT TO FIND OUT HOW THAT DRIVER IS DOING!

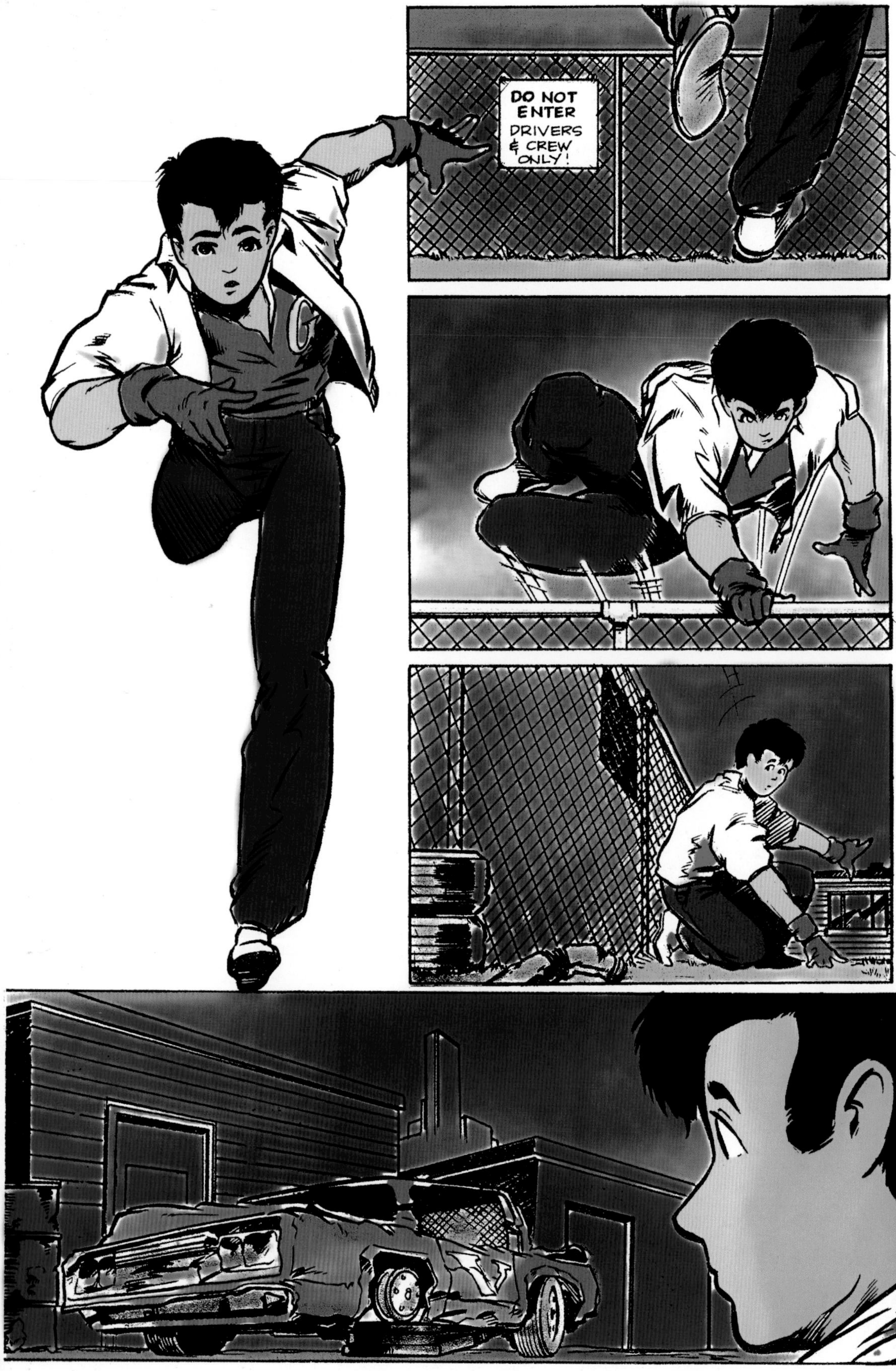
DO NOT ENTER
DRIVERS & CREW ONLY!

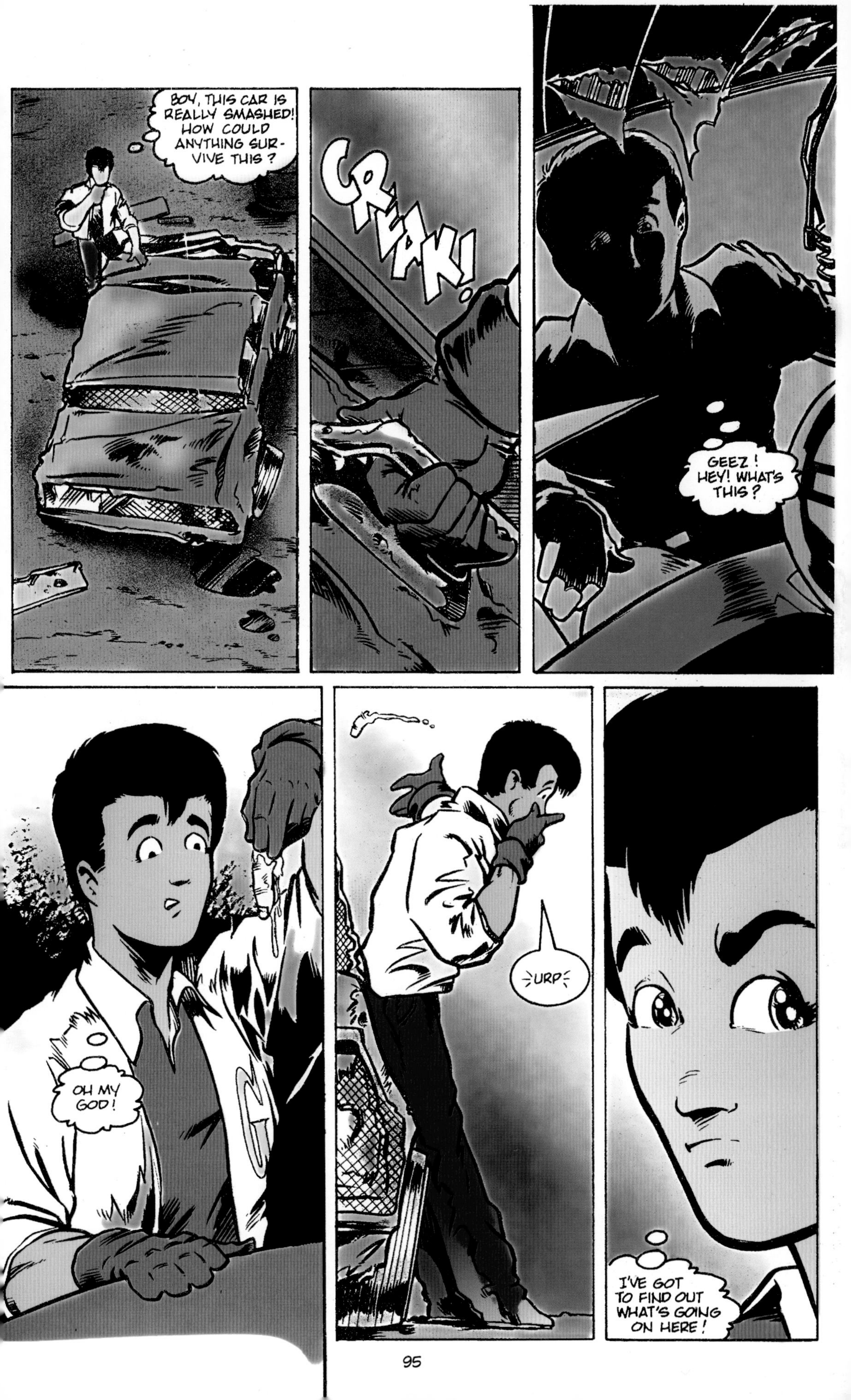
BOY, THIS CAR IS REALLY SMASHED! HOW COULD ANYTHING SUR-VIVE THIS ?
CREAK!
GEEZ ! HEY! WHAT'S THIS ?
OH MY GOD !
URP
I'VE GOT TO FIND OUT WHAT'S GOING ON HERE !

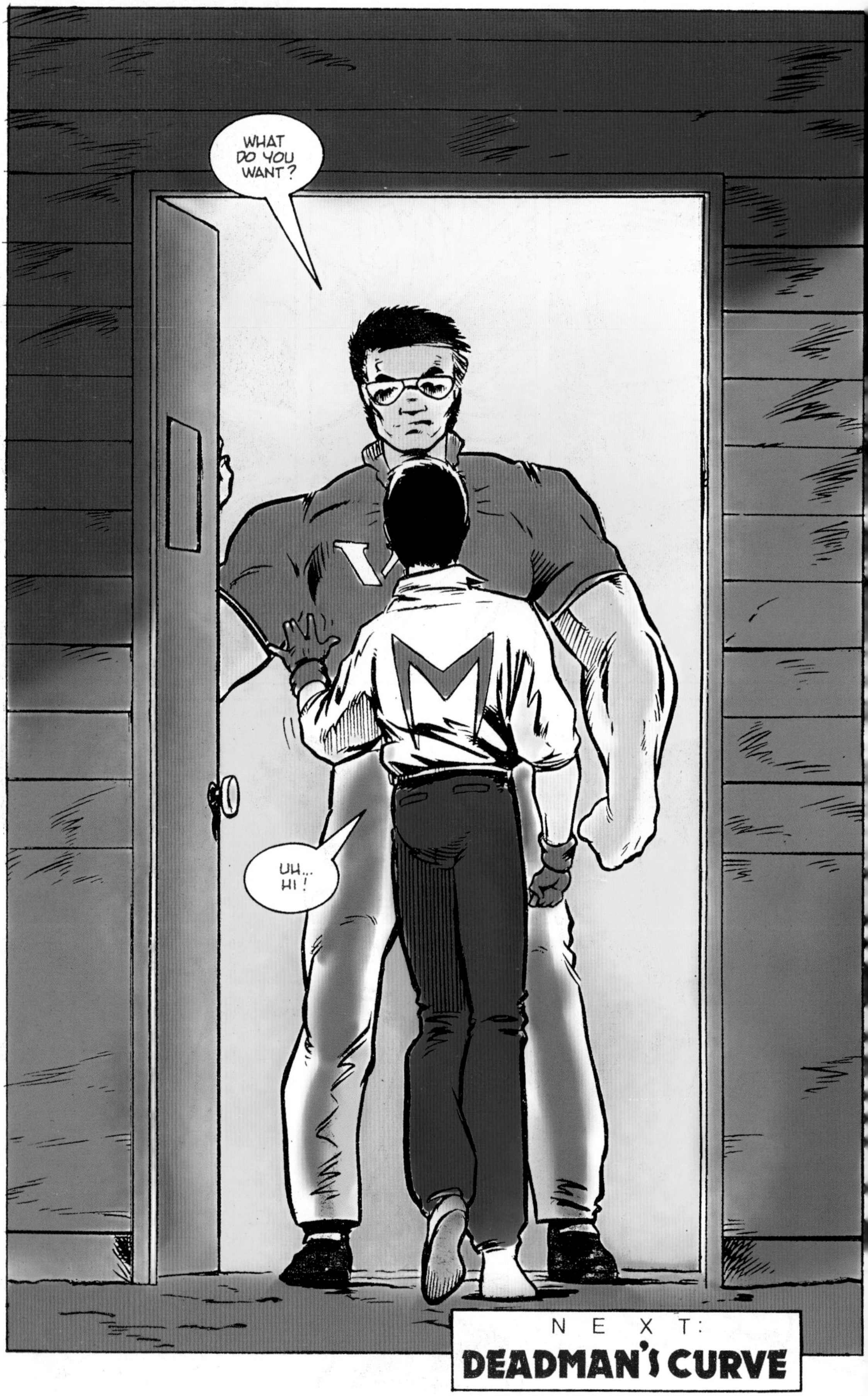

WHAT DO YOU WANT?
UH... HI!
NEXT:
DEADMAN'S CURVE

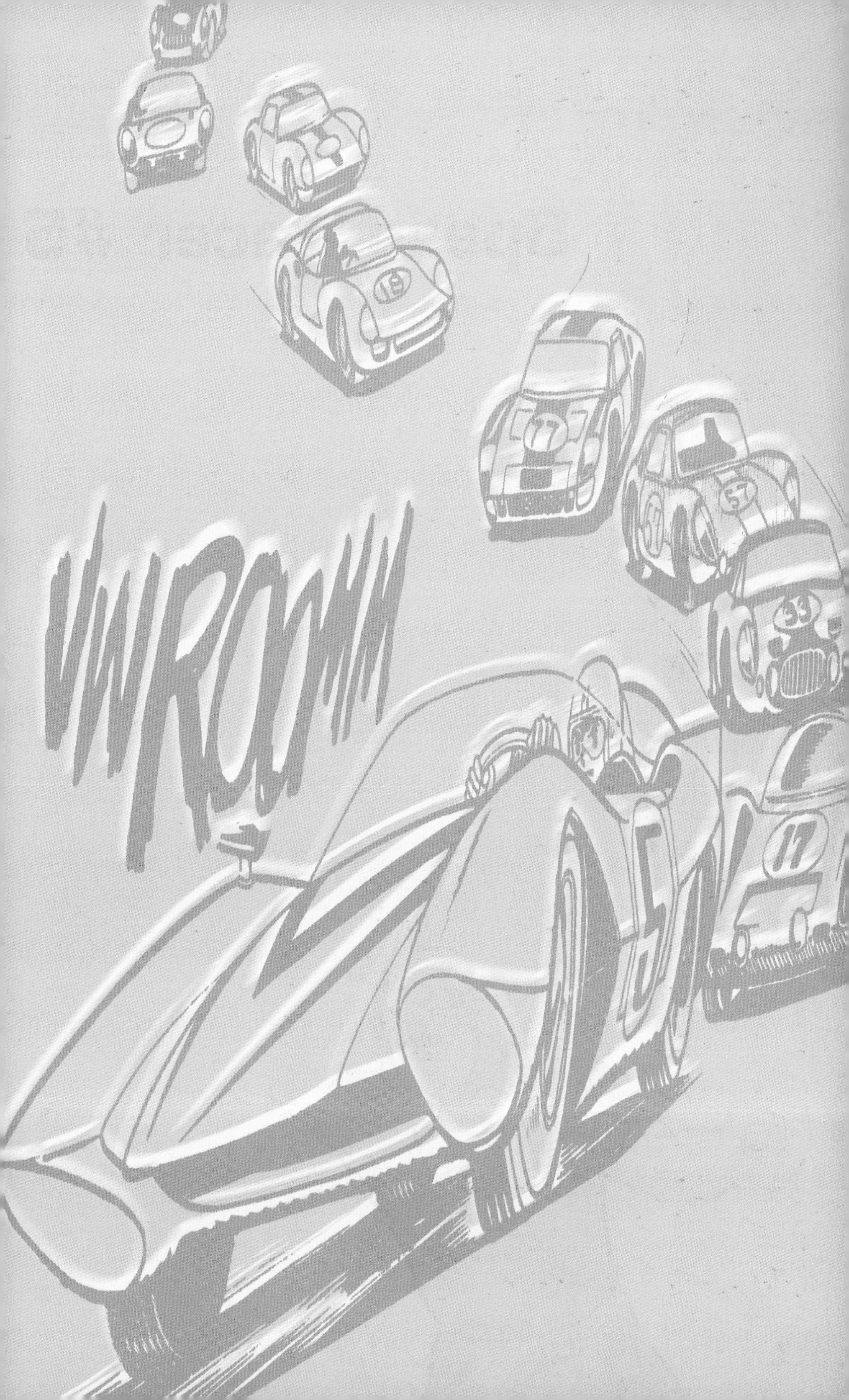

Speed Racer #5

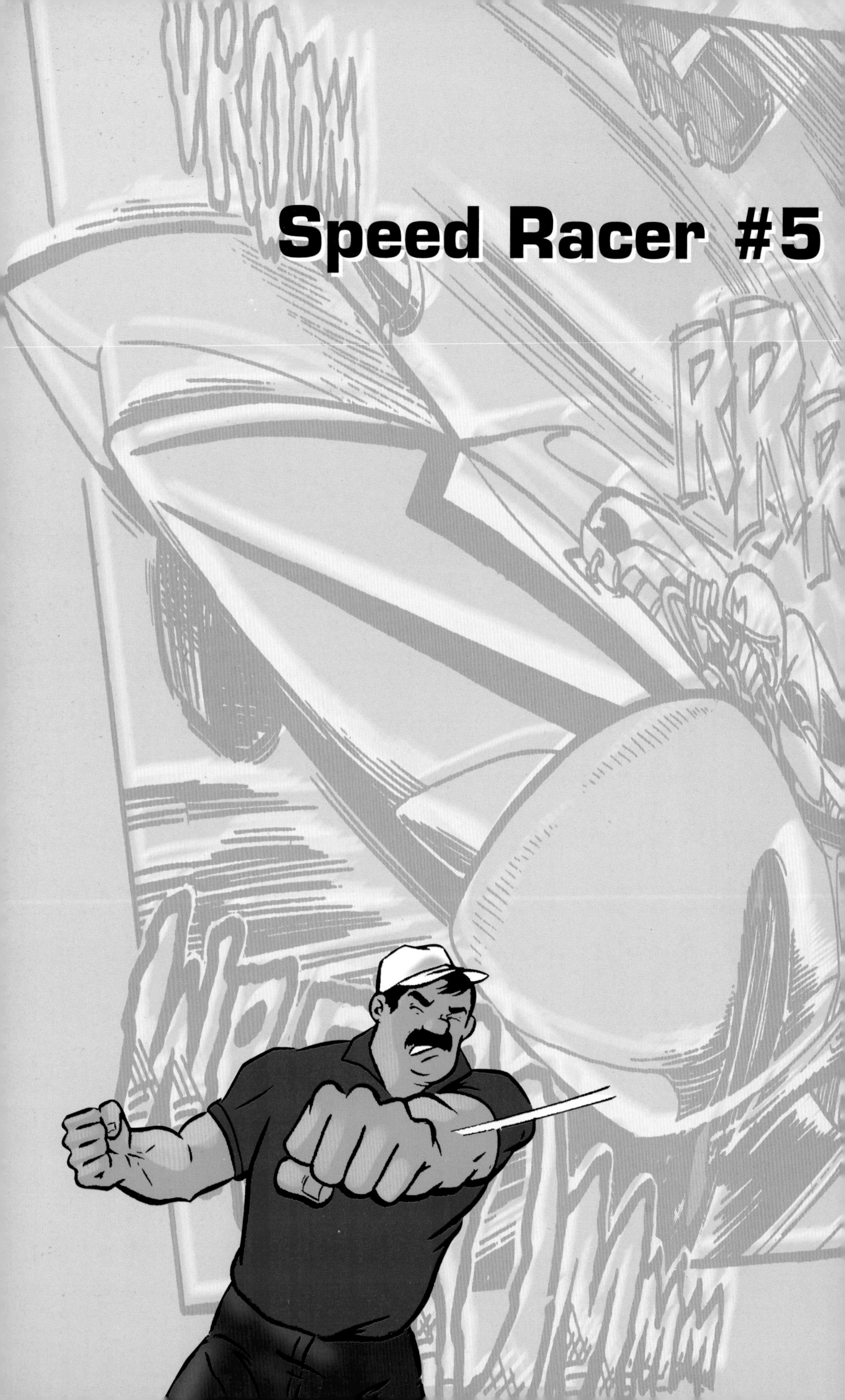

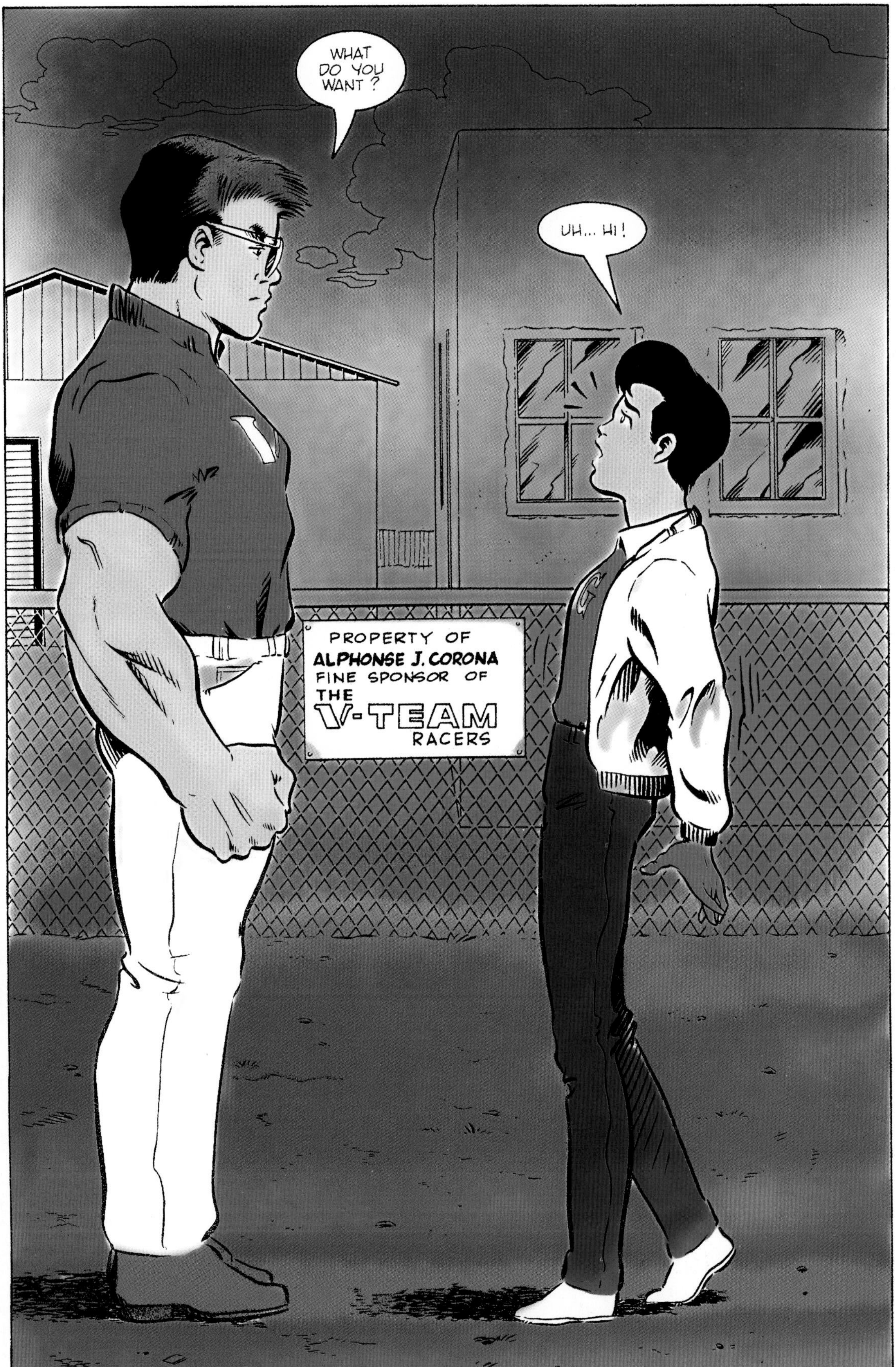
WHAT DO YOU WANT?
UH... HI!
PROPERTY OF
ALPHONSE J. CORONA
FINE SPONSOR OF
THE
V-TEAM
RACERS

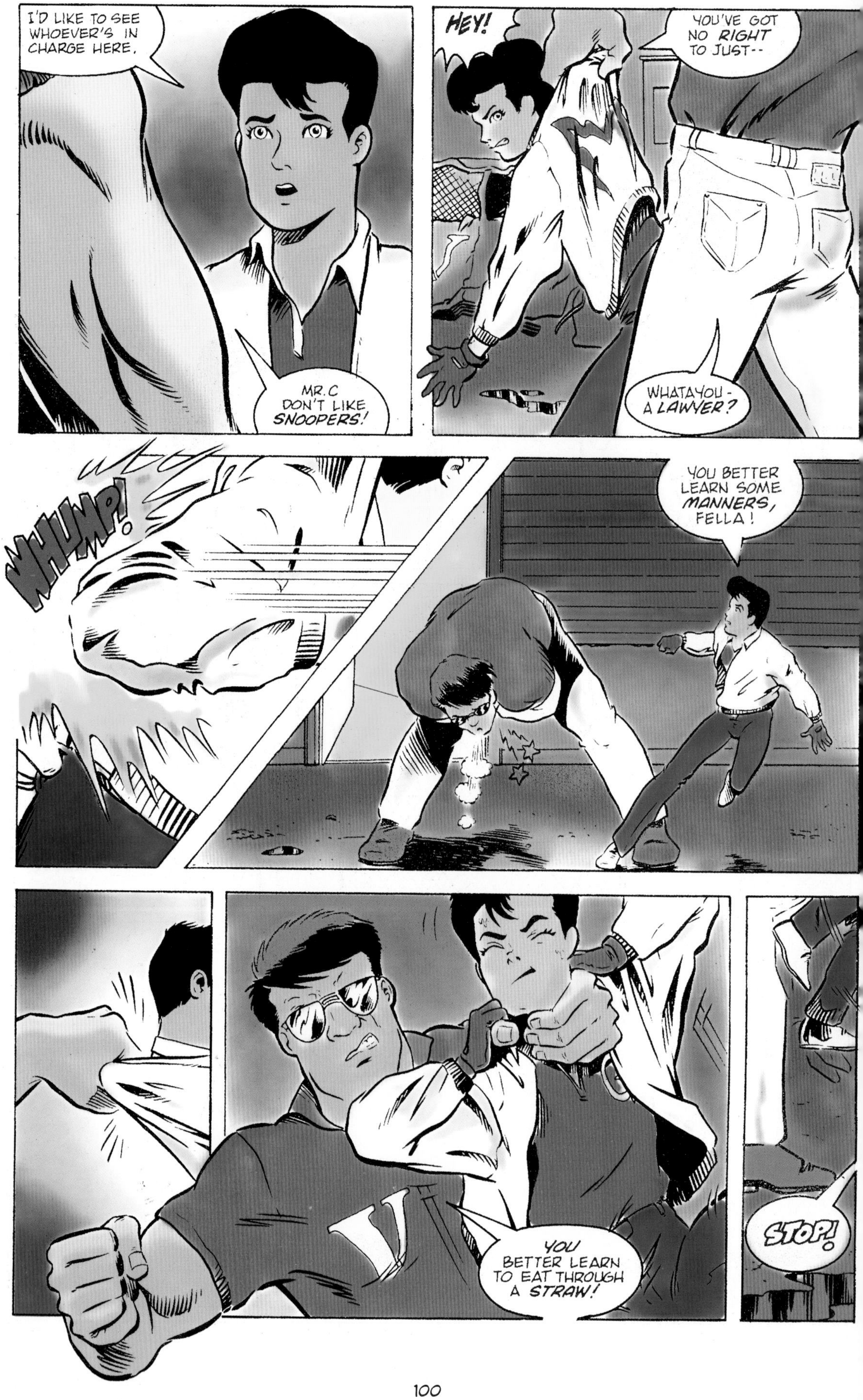
I'D LIKE TO SEE WHOEVER'S IN CHARGE HERE.
MR. C DON'T LIKE SNOOPERS!
HEY!
YOU'VE GOT NO RIGHT TO JUST--
WHATAYOU - A LAWYER?
WHUMP!
YOU BETTER LEARN SOME MANNERS, FELLA!
YOU BETTER LEARN TO EAT THROUGH A STRAW!
STOP!

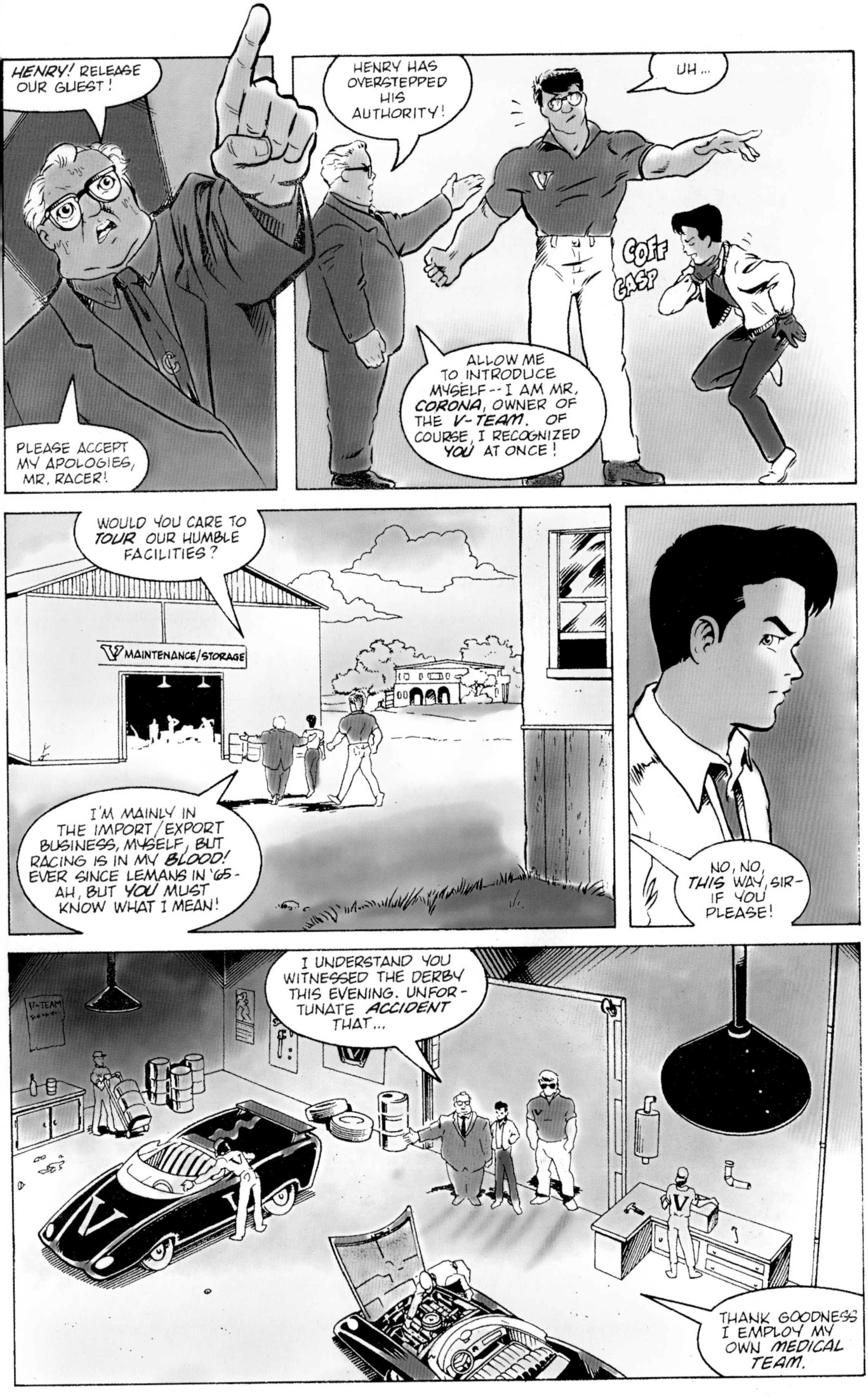
HENRY! RELEASE OUR GUEST!
PLEASE ACCEPT MY APOLOGIES, MR. RACER!
HENRY HAS OVERSTEPPED HIS AUTHORITY!
UH...
COFF
GASP
ALLOW ME TO INTRODUCE MYSELF -- I AM MR. CORONA, OWNER OF THE V-TEAM. OF COURSE, I RECOGNIZED YOU AT ONCE!
WOULD YOU CARE TO TOUR OUR HUMBLE FACILITIES?
V MAINTENANCE/STORAGE
I'M MAINLY IN THE IMPORT/EXPORT BUSINESS, MYSELF, BUT RACING IS IN MY BLOOD! EVER SINCE LEMANS IN '65- AH, BUT YOU MUST KNOW WHAT I MEAN!
NO, NO, THIS WAY, SIR- IF YOU PLEASE!
I UNDERSTAND YOU WITNESSED THE DERBY THIS EVENING. UNFORTUNATE ACCIDENT THAT...
V-TEAM
THANK GOODNESS I EMPLOY MY OWN MEDICAL TEAM.

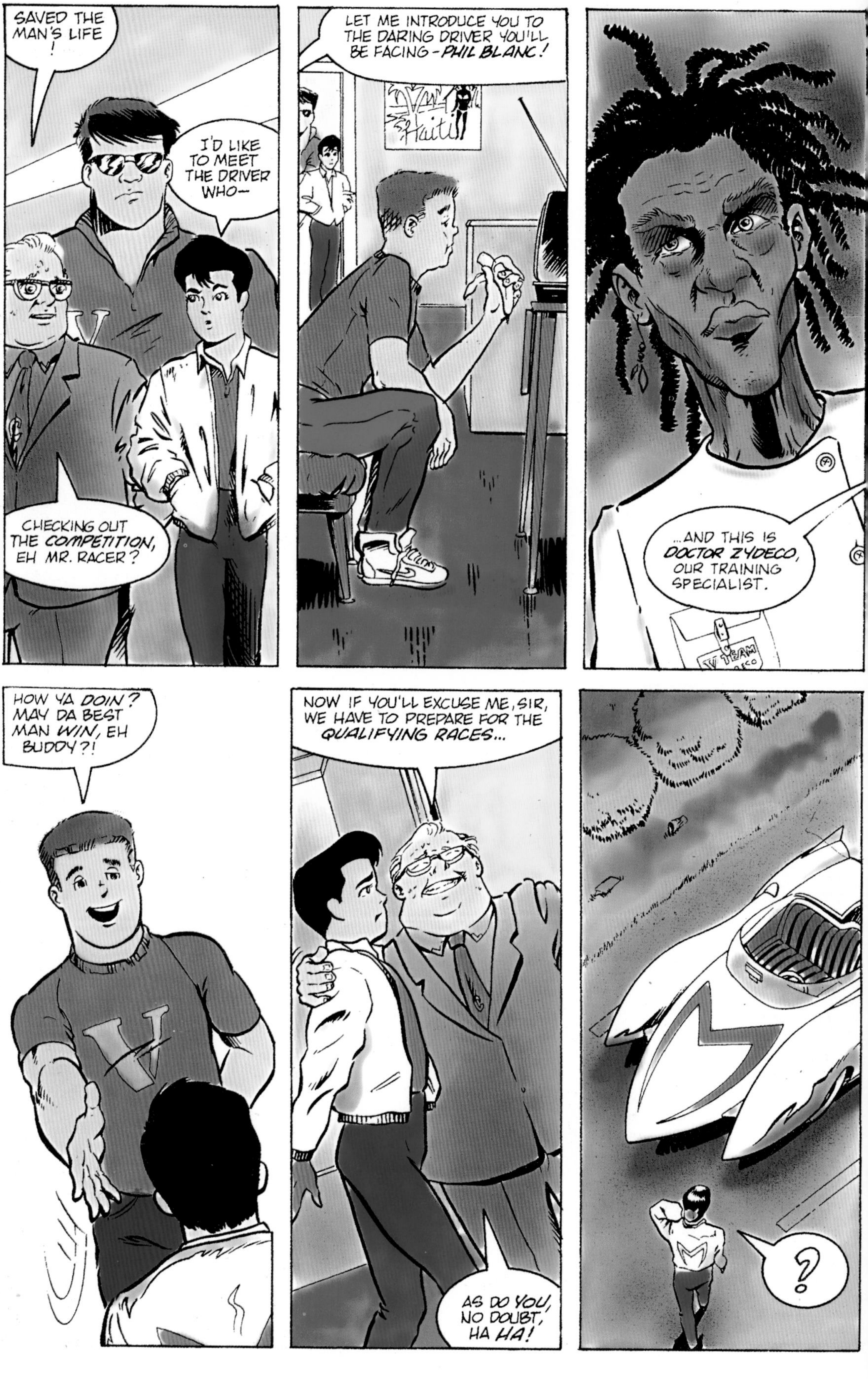
SAVED THE MAN'S LIFE!
I'D LIKE TO MEET THE DRIVER WHO--
CHECKING OUT THE COMPETITION, EH MR. RACER?
LET ME INTRODUCE YOU TO THE DARING DRIVER YOU'LL BE FACING - PHIL BLANC!
...AND THIS IS DOCTOR ZYDECO, OUR TRAINING SPECIALIST.
V TEAM
HOW YA DOIN? MAY DA BEST MAN WIN, EH BUDDY?!
NOW IF YOU'LL EXCUSE ME, SIR, WE HAVE TO PREPARE FOR THE QUALIFYING RACES...
AS DO YOU, NO DOUBT, HA HA!
?

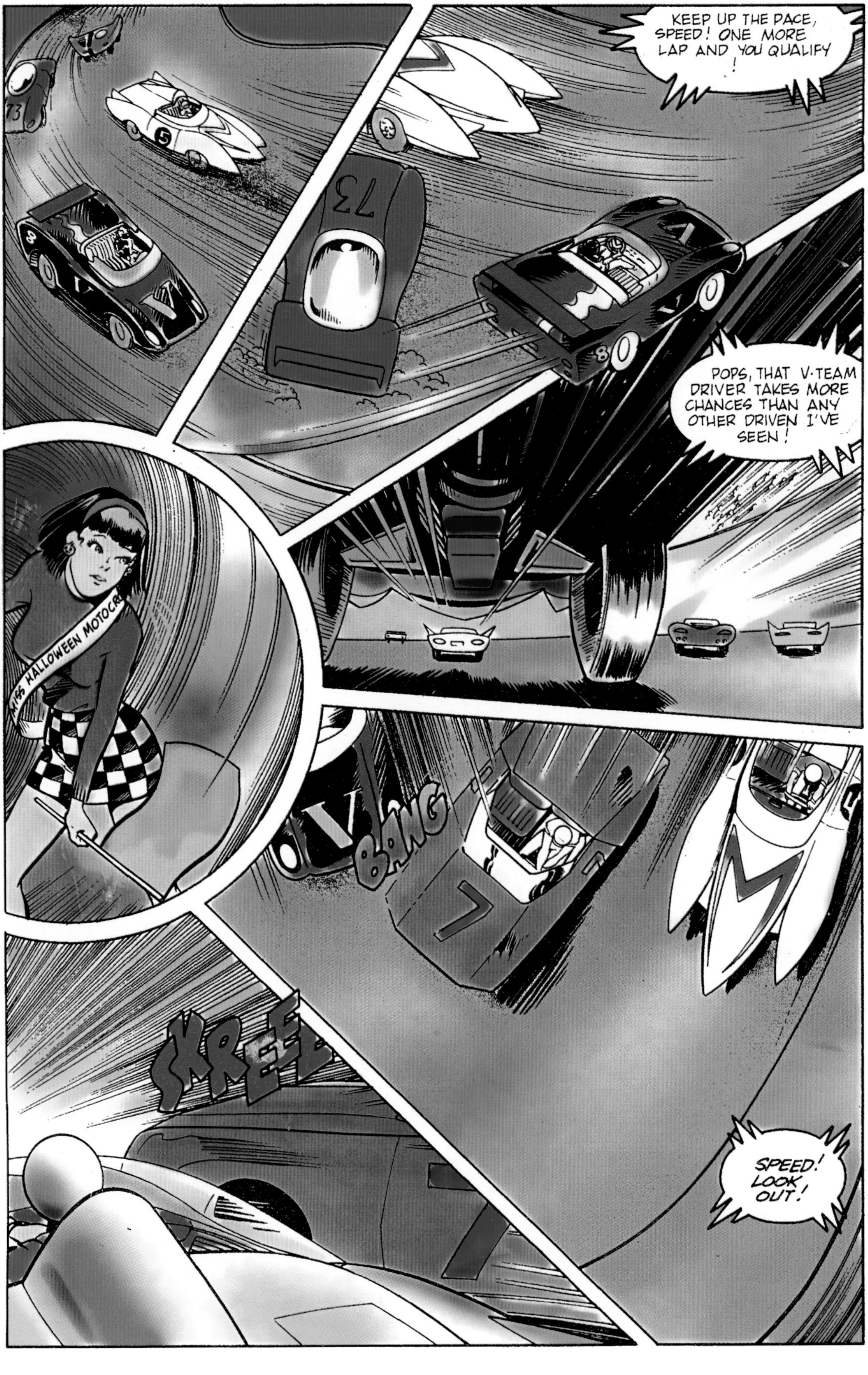

KEEP UP THE PACE, SPEED! ONE MORE LAP AND YOU QUALIFY!
POPS, THAT V-TEAM DRIVER TAKES MORE CHANCES THAN ANY OTHER DRIVEN I'VE SEEN!
MISS HALLOWEEN MOTOCR
BANG
SKREE
SPEED! LOOK OUT!

DEAD HEAT

BOINTH A NAKIT!

BRIAN THOMAS
STORY / INKS

JILL THOMPSON
PENCILS

KEN HOLEWCZYNSKI
LETTERS / COLORS

TONY CAPUTO
EDITOR

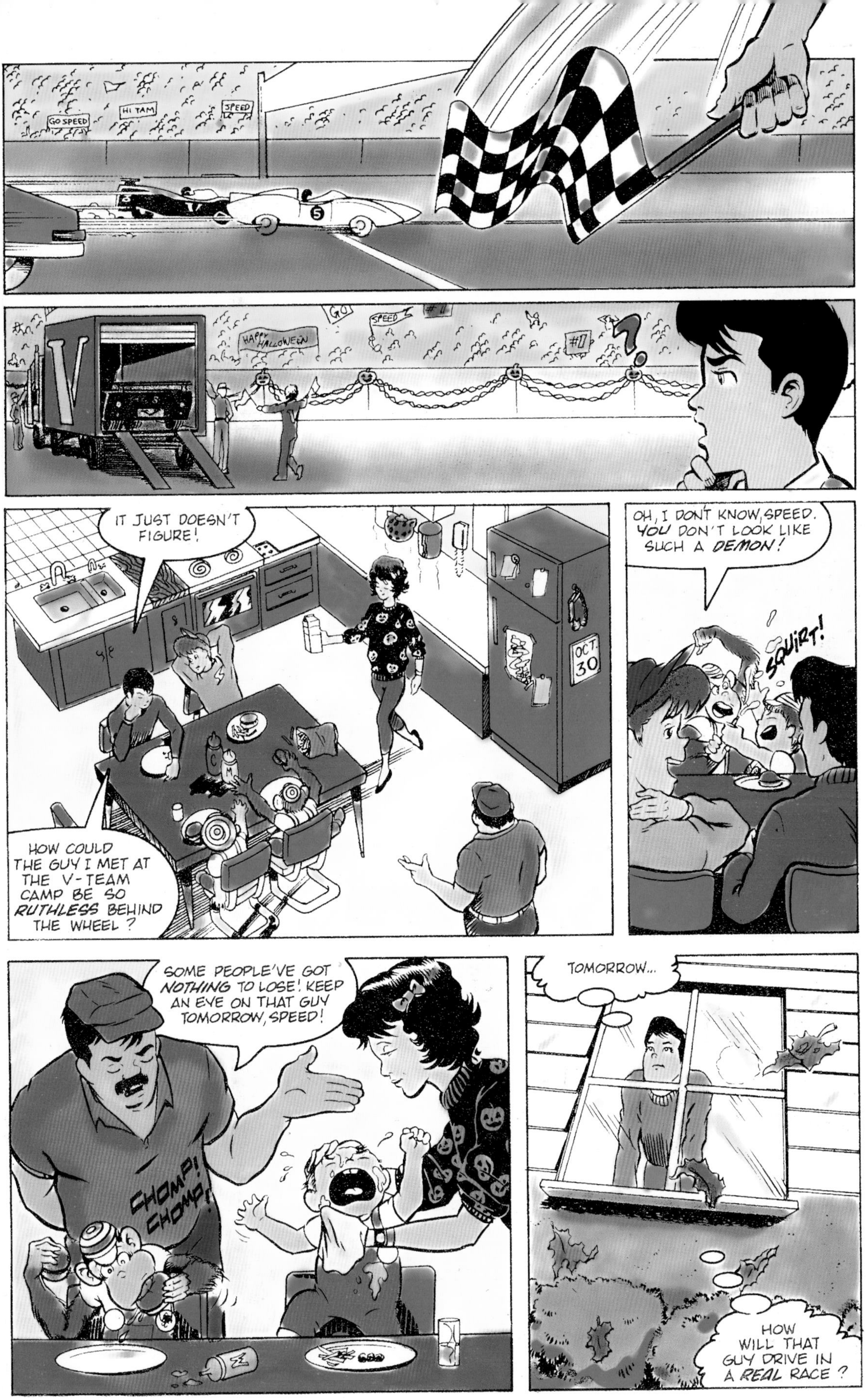
GO SPEED
HI TAM
SPEED
GO
SPEED
#1
HAPPY HALLOWEEN
#1
IT JUST DOESN'T FIGURE!
HOW COULD THE GUY I MET AT THE V-TEAM CAMP BE SO RUTHLESS BEHIND THE WHEEL?
OCT. 30
OH, I DON'T KNOW, SPEED. YOU DON'T LOOK LIKE SUCH A DEMON!
SQUIRT!
SOME PEOPLE'VE GOT NOTHING TO LOSE! KEEP AN EYE ON THAT GUY TOMORROW, SPEED!
CHOMP! CHOMP!
TOMORROW...
HOW WILL THAT GUY DRIVE IN A REAL RACE?

—AND NOW THE CARS ARE LINING UP FOR THE FIRST ANNUAL *HALLOWEEN MOTOCROSS!*

A RECORD CROWD IS ON HAND TO SEE WHO *is...*

HEY! SPARKY, ARE YOU THERE?

WHAT? YOU SPOTTED THE V-TEAM DRIVER IN THE *STANDS?*

WHAT SECTION?

YOU SURE?

THAT'S THE DEVIL DRIVER?

"HEY! SO WHO'S DRIVING THEIR CAR?"

SPEED'S RIGHT...

SOMETHING'S FISHY ABOUT THOSE GUYS. I'D BETTER FOLLOW THEM!

WHEREYAGOIN' SPARKY! CAN I COME TOO? I'M TELLIN' POPS! PLEASETAKEME WITHYOU*PLEASE*!

AWRIGHT! AWRIGHT! JUST KEEP IT DOWN, OKAY?

NO CHIM-CHIM, YOU *STAY* HERE!

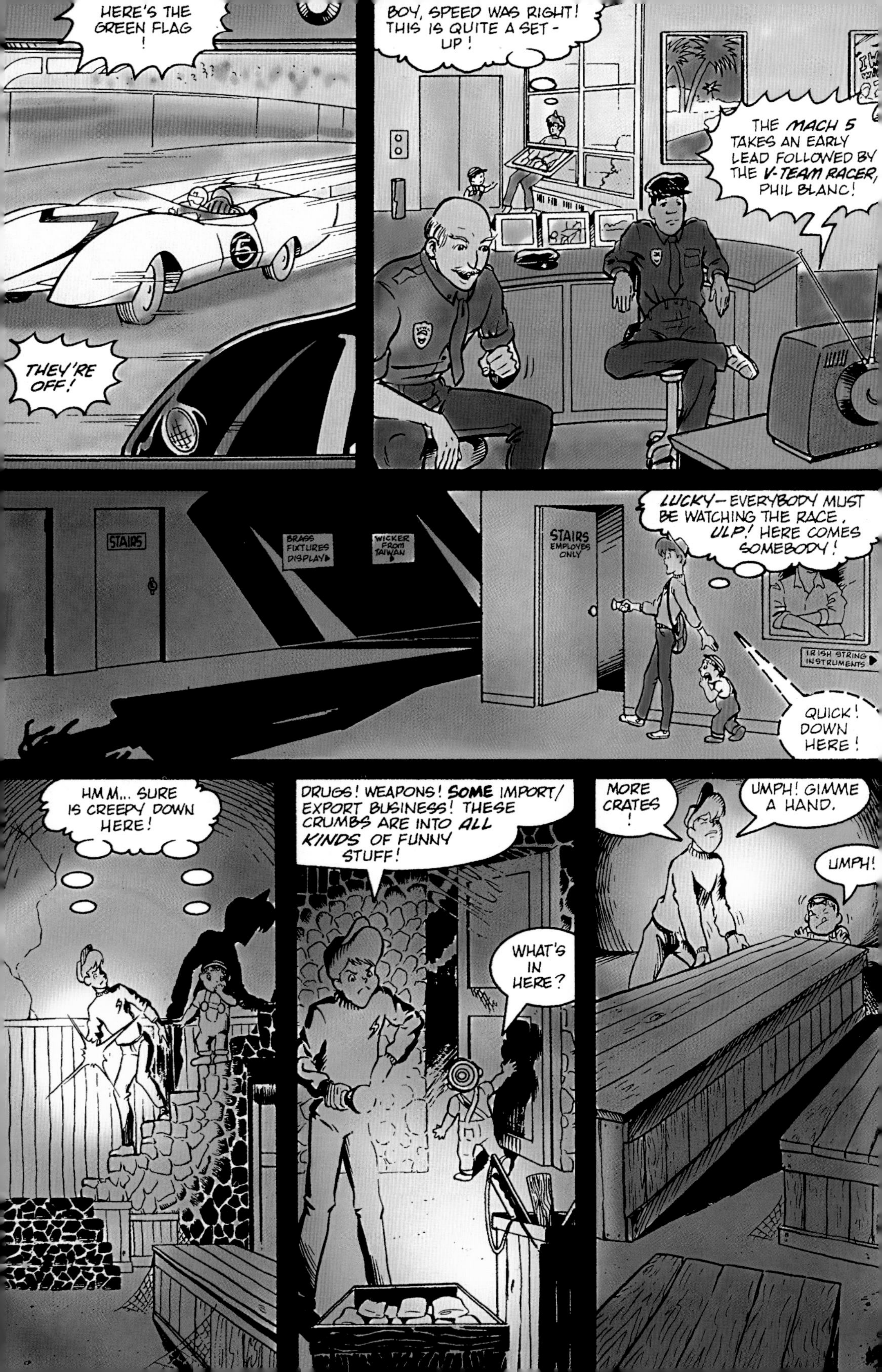
HERE'S THE GREEN FLAG!
THEY'RE OFF!
BOY, SPEED WAS RIGHT! THIS IS QUITE A SET-UP!
THE MACH 5 TAKES AN EARLY LEAD FOLLOWED BY THE V-TEAM RACER, PHIL BLANC!
STAIRS
BRASS FIXTURES DISPLAY
WICKER FROM TAIWAN
STAIRS EMPLOYEES ONLY
LUCKY—EVERYBODY MUST BE WATCHING THE RACE. ULP! HERE COMES SOMEBODY!
IRISH STRING INSTRUMENTS
QUICK! DOWN HERE!
HMM... SURE IS CREEPY DOWN HERE!
DRUGS! WEAPONS! SOME IMPORT/EXPORT BUSINESS! THESE CRUMBS ARE INTO ALL KINDS OF FUNNY STUFF!
WHAT'S IN HERE?
MORE CRATES!
UMPH! GIMME A HAND.
UMPH!

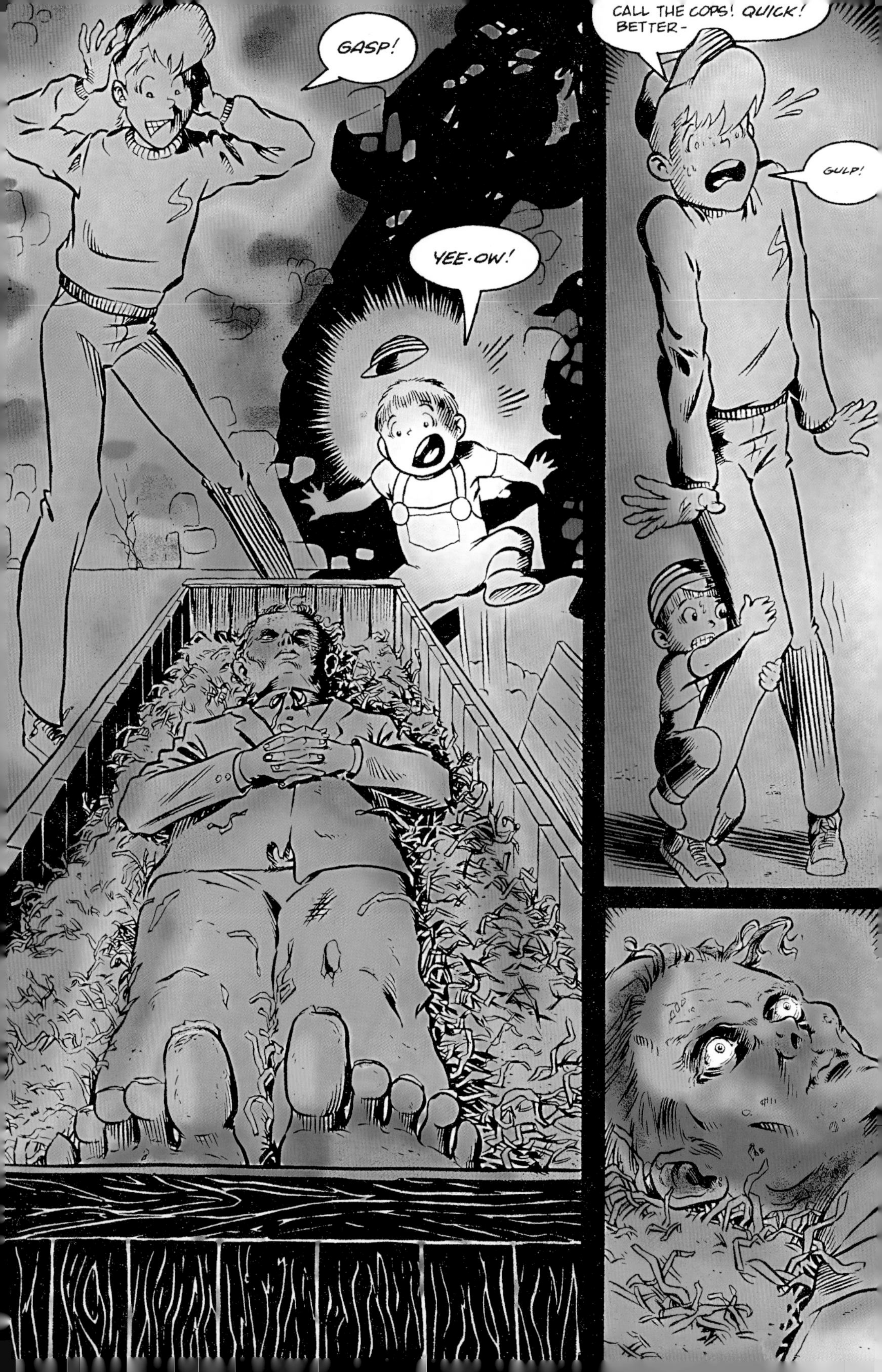
GASP!
YEE-OW!
CALL THE COPS! QUICK! BETTER-
GULP!

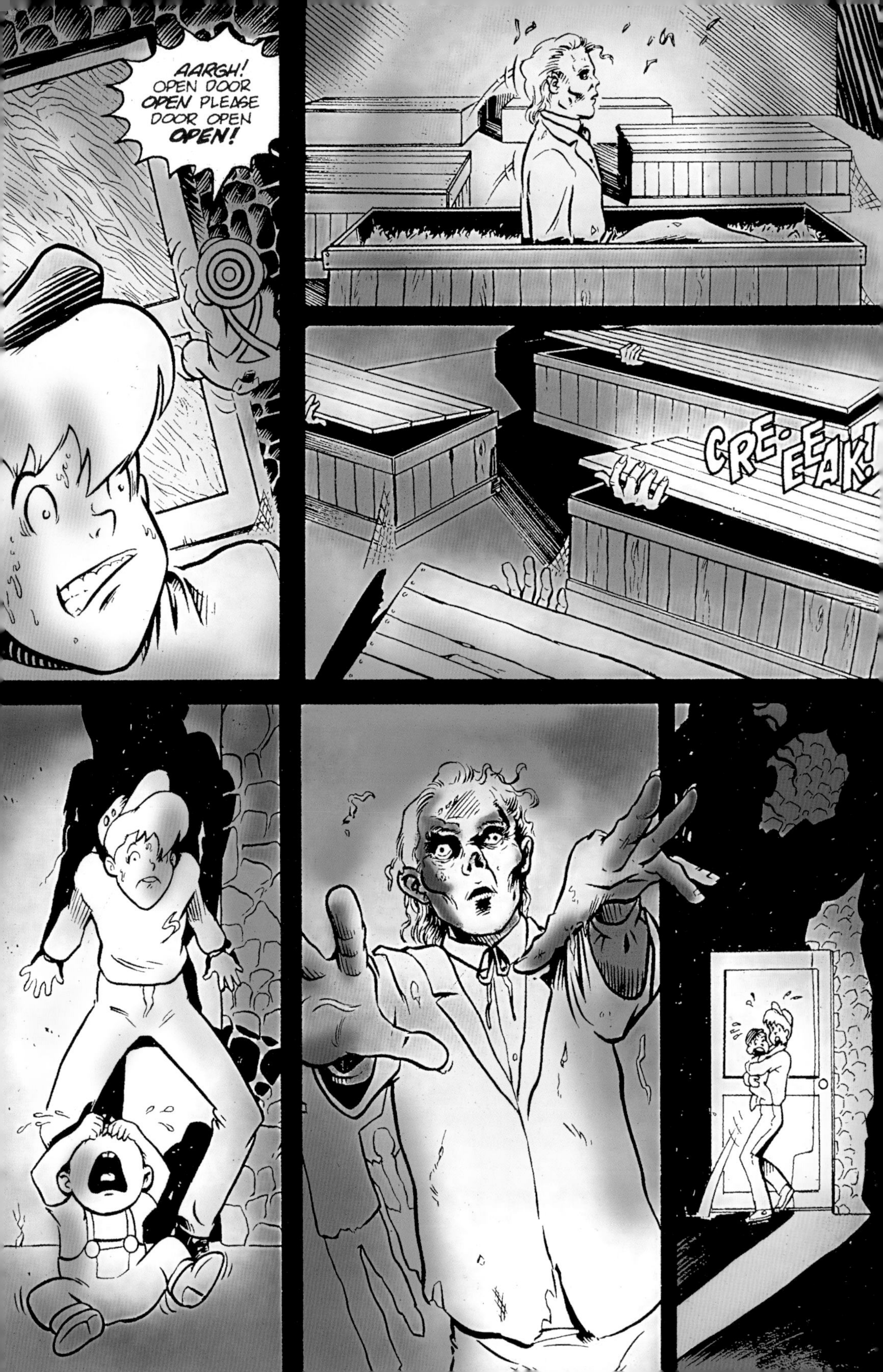
AARGH! OPEN DOOR OPEN PLEASE DOOR OPEN OPEN!
CRE-EEAK!

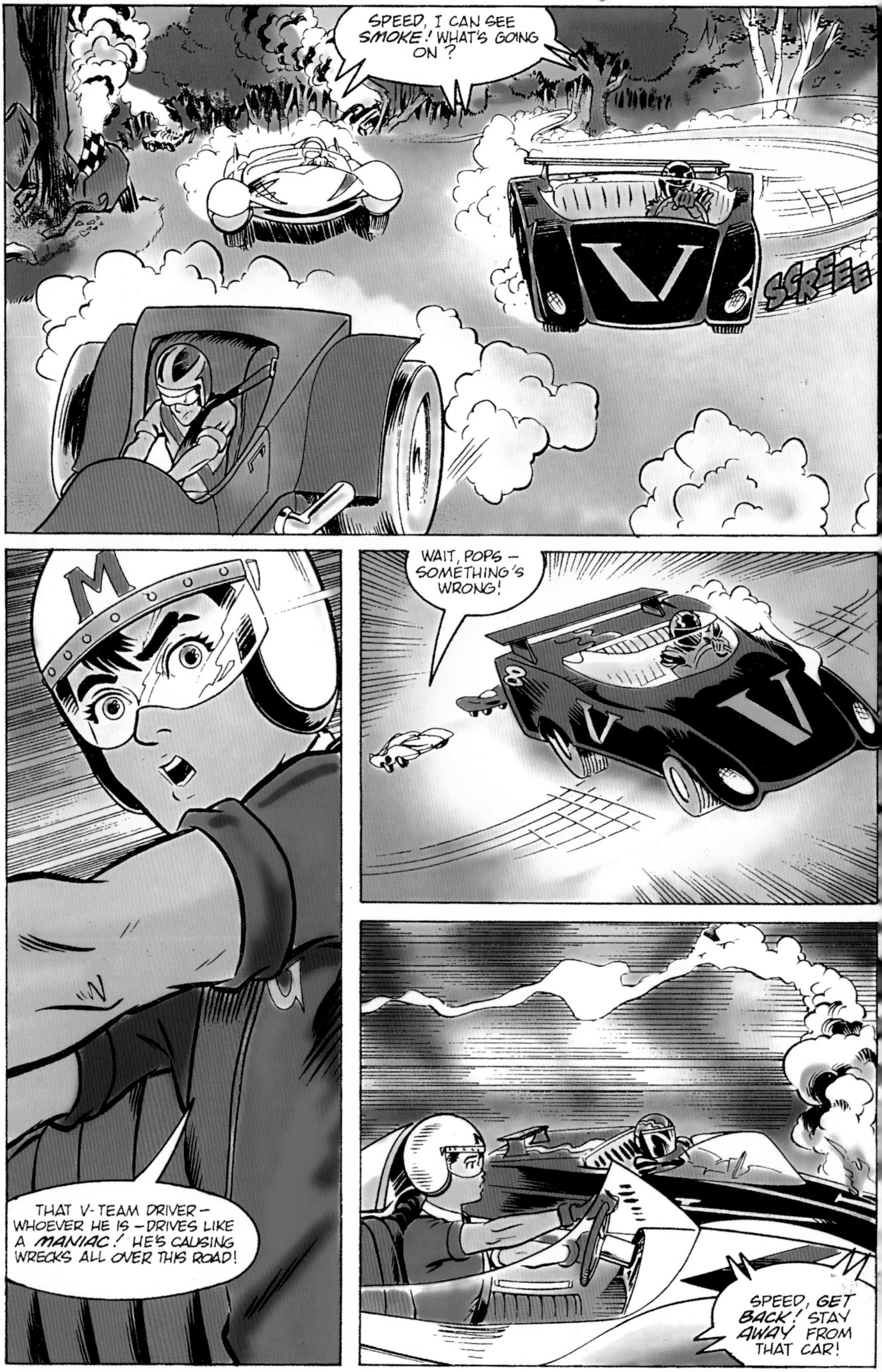
SPEED, I CAN SEE SMOKE! WHAT'S GOING ON?
SCREEE
WAIT, POPS — SOMETHING'S WRONG!
THAT V-TEAM DRIVER — WHOEVER HE IS — DRIVES LIKE A MANIAC! HE'S CAUSING WRECKS ALL OVER THIS ROAD!
SPEED, GET BACK! STAY AWAY FROM THAT CAR!

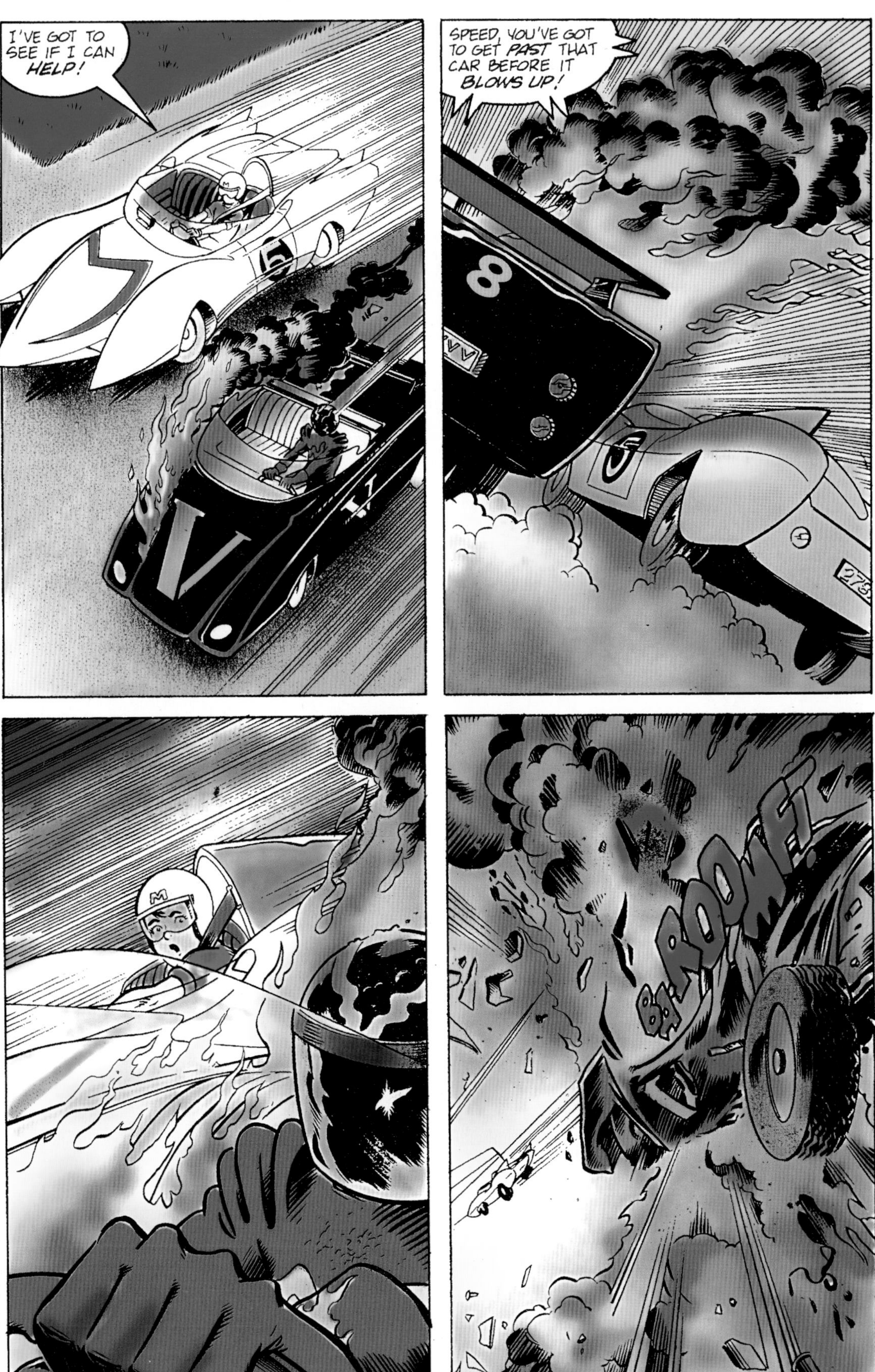
I'VE GOT TO SEE IF I CAN HELP!
SPEED, YOU'VE GOT TO GET PAST THAT CAR BEFORE IT BLOWS UP!
BA-ROOM!

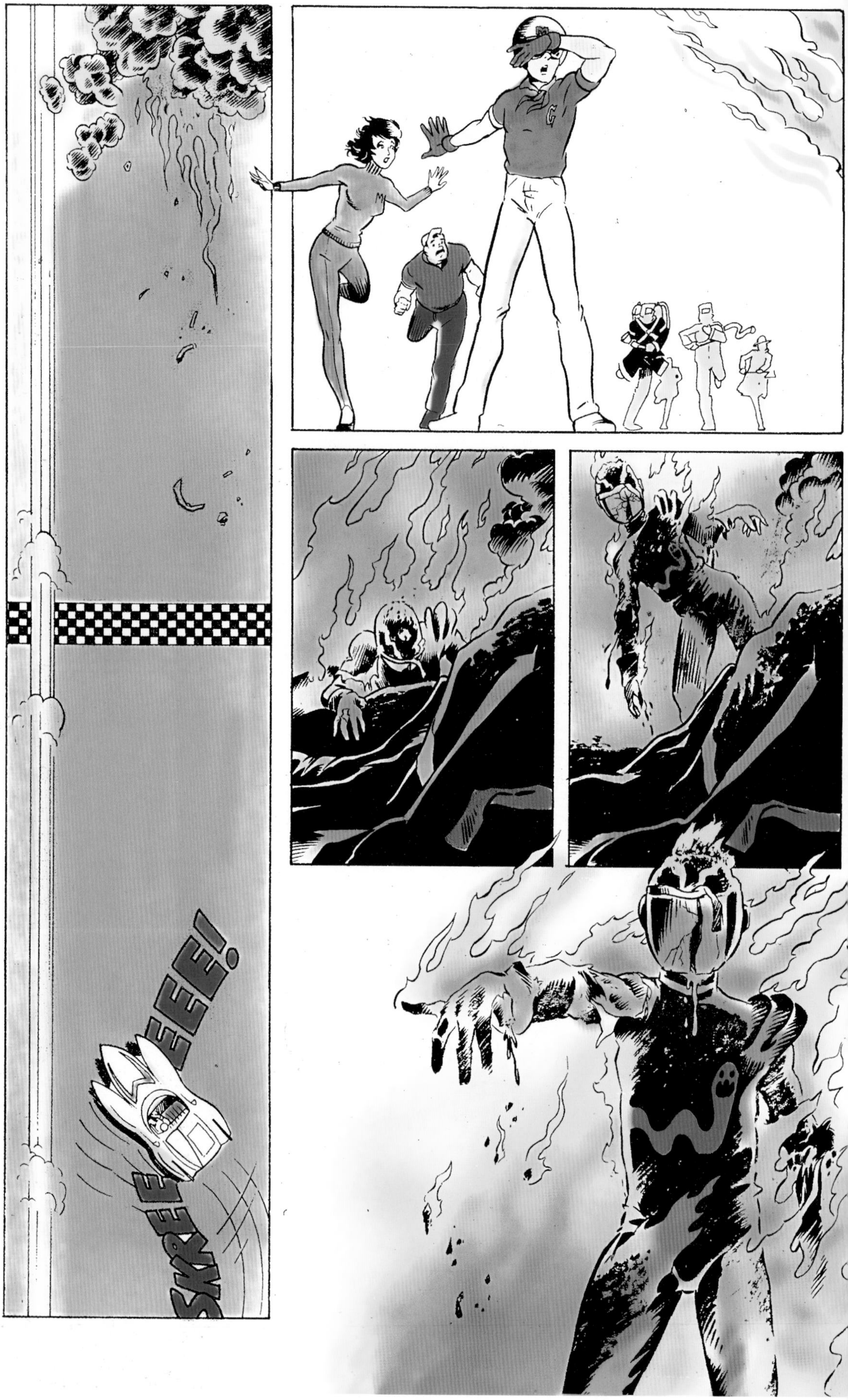
SKREEEEE!

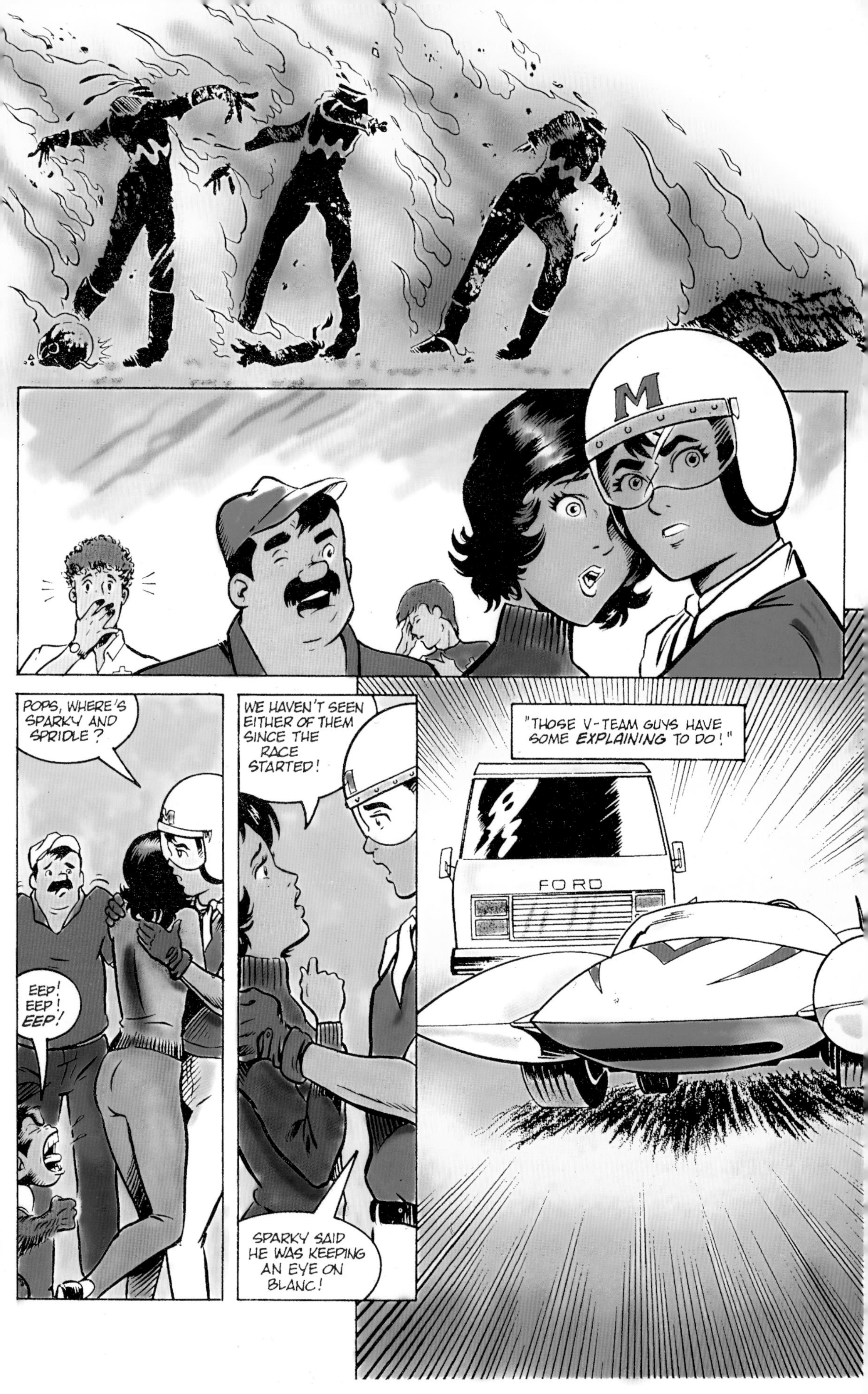
POPS, WHERE'S SPARKY AND SPRIDLE?
EEP! EEP! EEP!
WE HAVEN'T SEEN EITHER OF THEM SINCE THE RACE STARTED!
SPARKY SAID HE WAS KEEPING AN EYE ON BLANC!
"THOSE V-TEAM GUYS HAVE SOME EXPLAINING TO DO!"
FORD

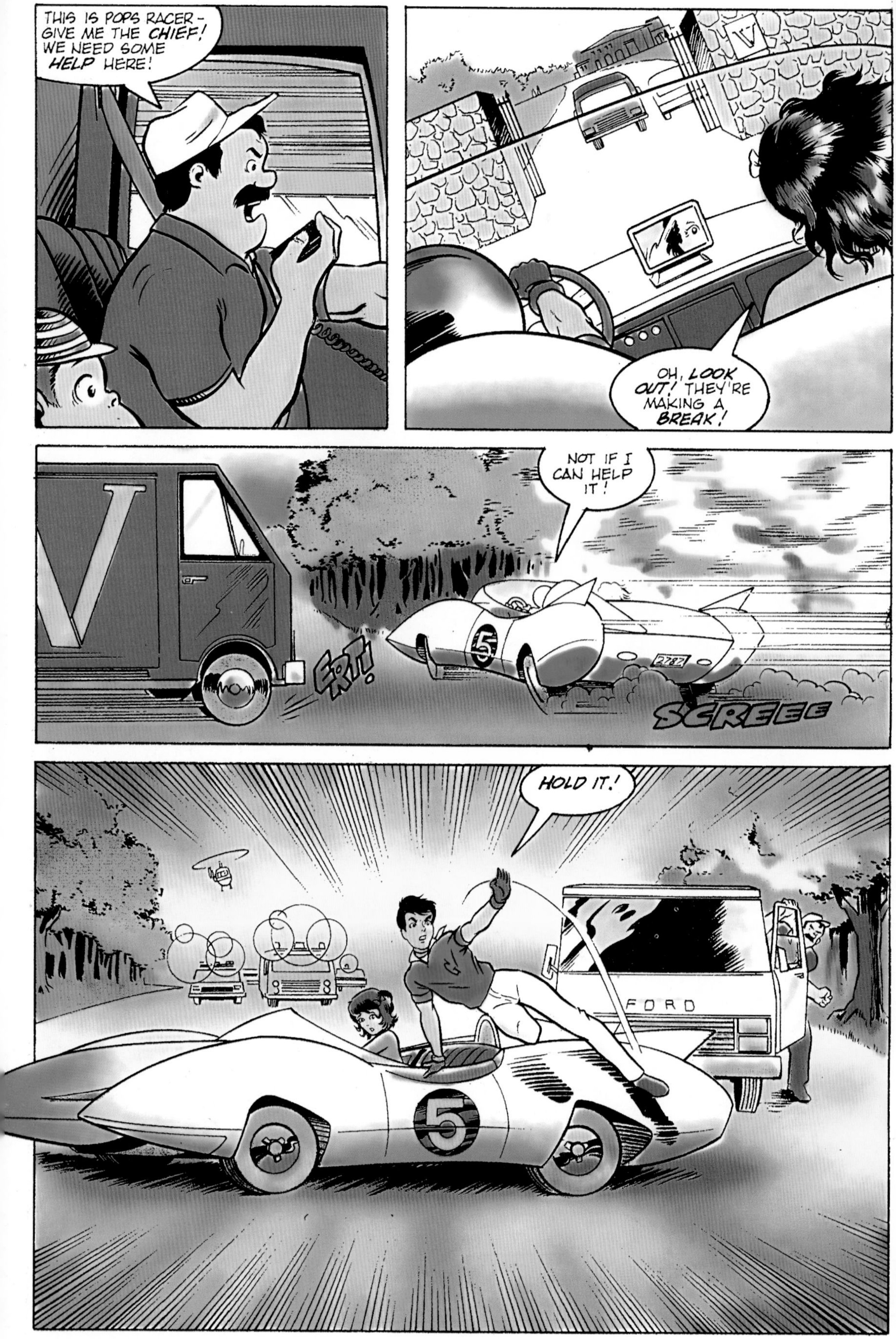
THIS IS POPS RACER - GIVE ME THE CHIEF! WE NEED SOME HELP HERE!
OH, LOOK OUT! THEY'RE MAKING A BREAK!
NOT IF I CAN HELP IT!
ERT!
2782
SCREEE
HOLD IT!
FORD

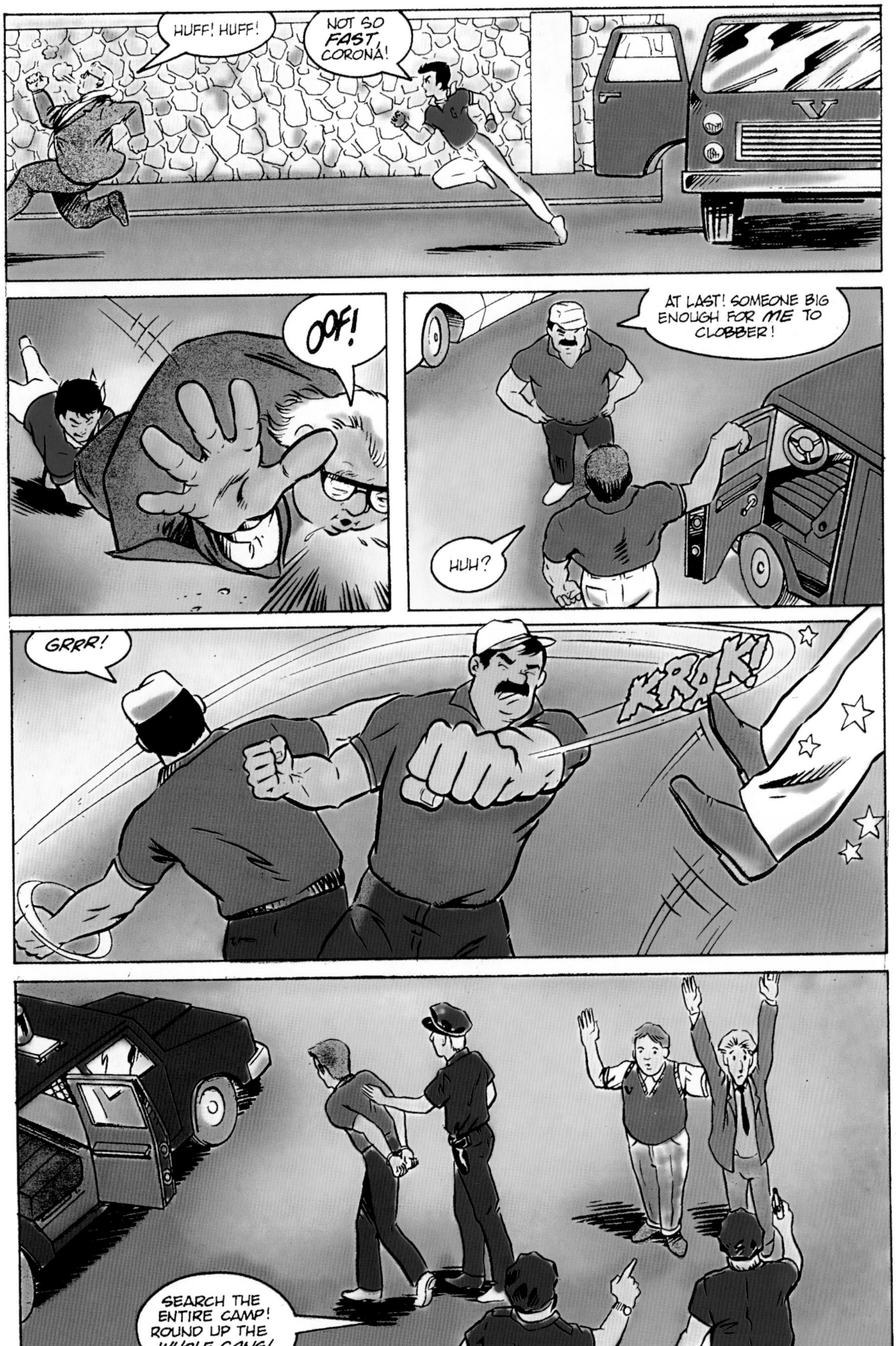
HUFF! HUFF!
NOT SO FAST, CORONA!
OOF!
AT LAST! SOMEONE BIG ENOUGH FOR ME TO CLOBBER!
HUH?
GRRR!
KRAK!
SEARCH THE ENTIRE CAMP! ROUND UP THE WHOLE GANG!

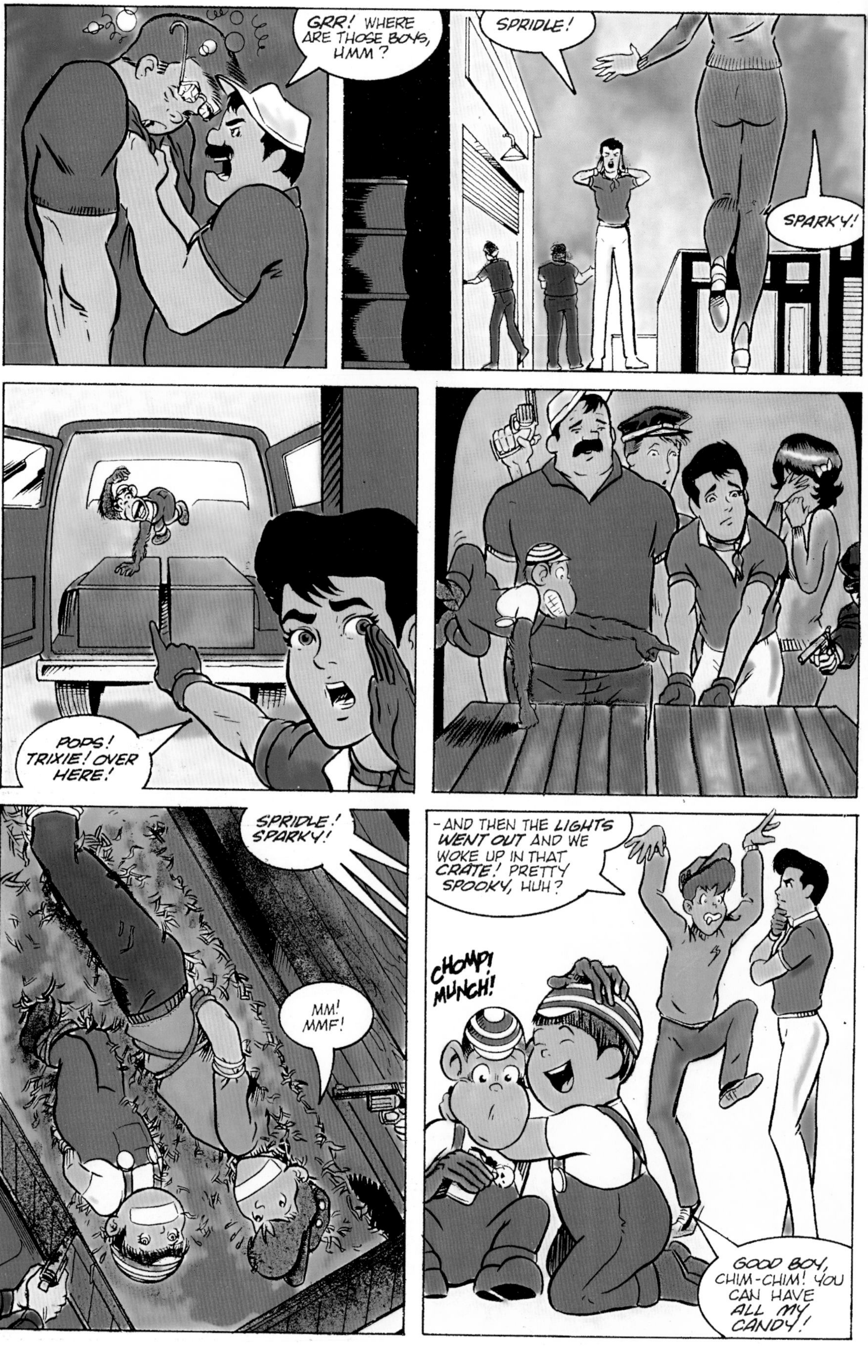
GRR! WHERE ARE THOSE BOYS, HMM?
SPRIDLE!
SPARKY!
POPS! TRIXIE! OVER HERE!
SPRIDLE! SPARKY!
MM! MMF!
-AND THEN THE LIGHTS WENT OUT AND WE WOKE UP IN THAT CRATE! PRETTY SPOOKY, HUH?
CHOMP! MUNCH!
GOOD BOY, CHIM-CHIM! YOU CAN HAVE ALL MY CANDY!

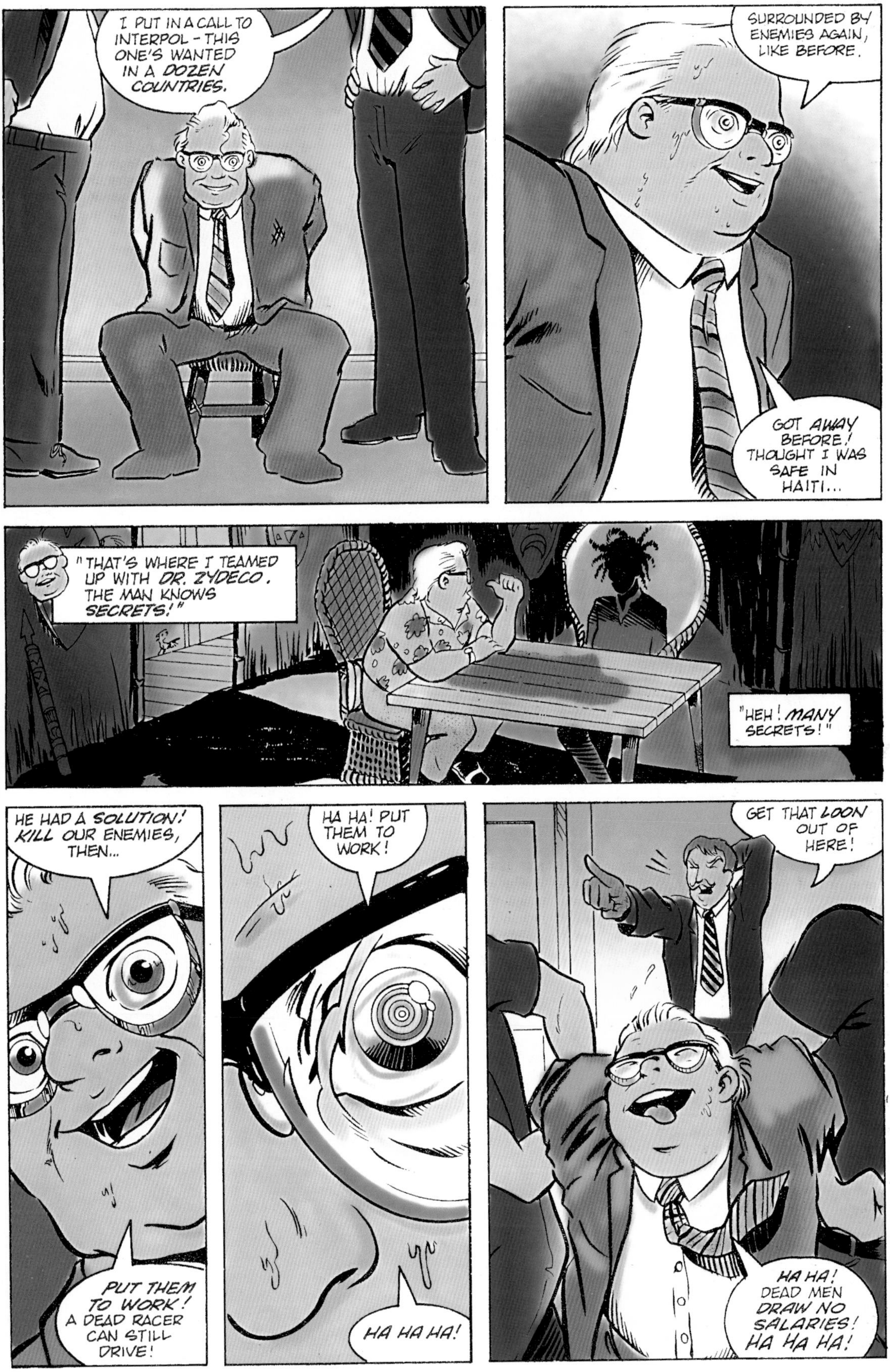
I PUT IN A CALL TO INTERPOL - THIS ONE'S WANTED IN A DOZEN COUNTRIES.
SURROUNDED BY ENEMIES AGAIN, LIKE BEFORE.
GOT AWAY BEFORE! THOUGHT I WAS SAFE IN HAITI...
"THAT'S WHERE I TEAMED UP WITH DR. ZYDECO. THE MAN KNOWS SECRETS!"
"HEH! MANY SECRETS!"
HE HAD A SOLUTION! KILL OUR ENEMIES, THEN...
PUT THEM TO WORK! A DEAD RACER CAN STILL DRIVE!
HA HA! PUT THEM TO WORK!
HA HA HA!
GET THAT LOON OUT OF HERE!
HA HA! DEAD MEN DRAW NO SALARIES! HA HA HA!

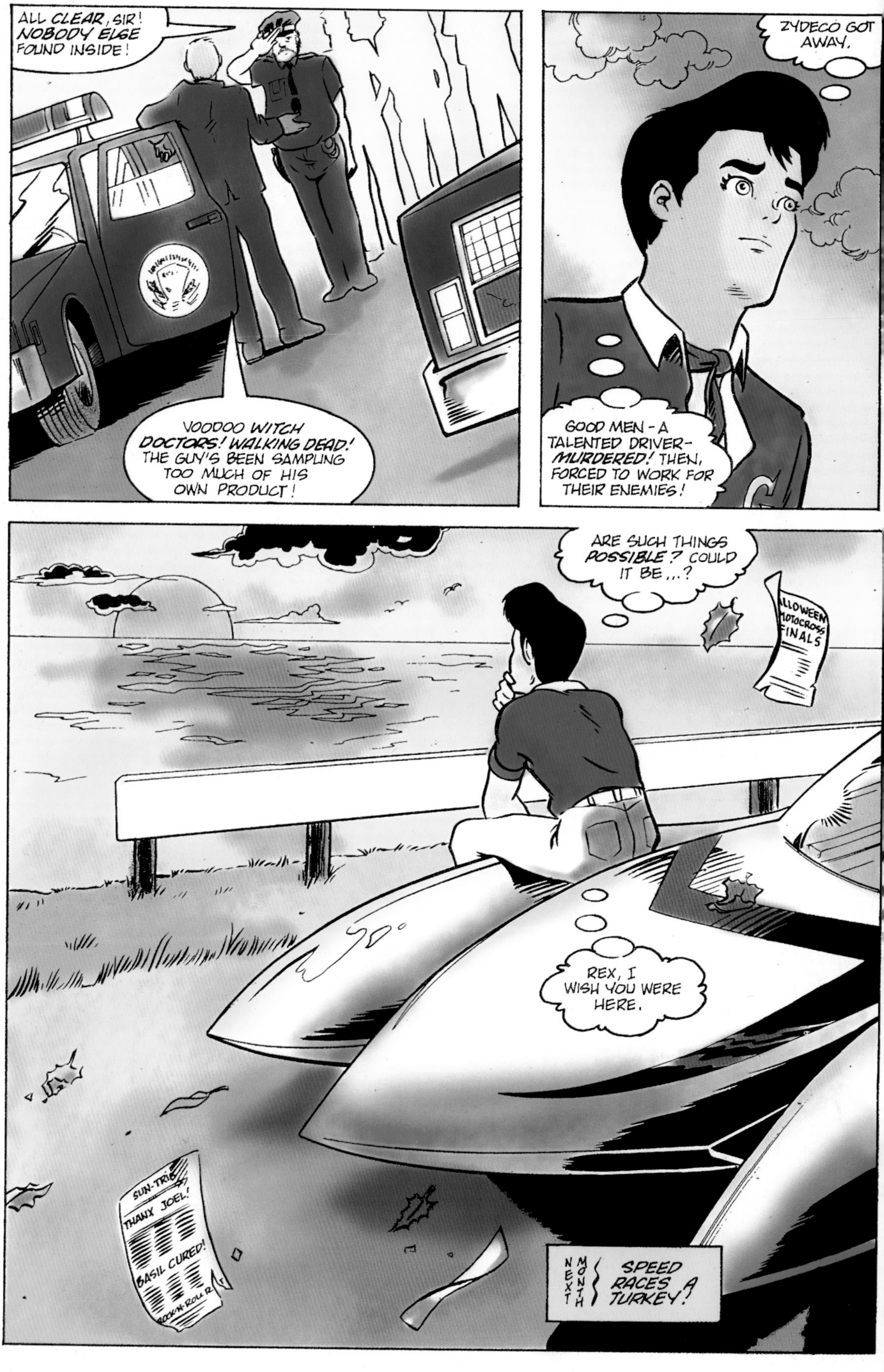
ALL CLEAR, SIR! NOBODY ELSE FOUND INSIDE!
VOODOO WITCH DOCTORS! WALKING DEAD! THE GUY'S BEEN SAMPLING TOO MUCH OF HIS OWN PRODUCT!
ZYDECO GOT AWAY.
GOOD MEN - A TALENTED DRIVER- MURDERED! THEN, FORCED TO WORK FOR THEIR ENEMIES!
ARE SUCH THINGS POSSIBLE? COULD IT BE...?
HALLOWEEN MOTOCROSS FINALS
REX, I WISH YOU WERE HERE.
SUN-TRIB
THANX JOEL!
BASIL CURED!
ROCK-N-ROLL R
NEXT MONTH SPEED RACES A TURKEY!

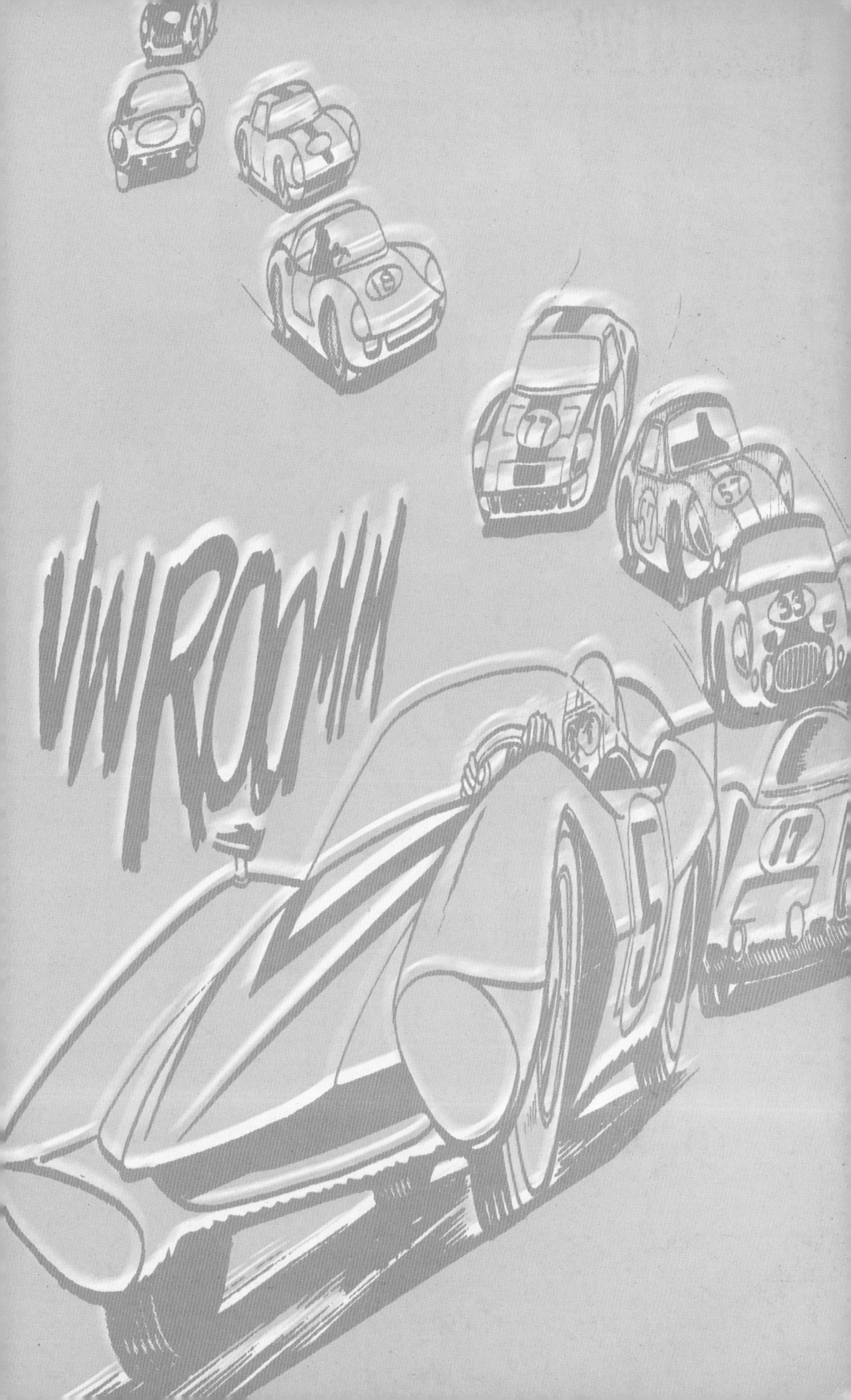

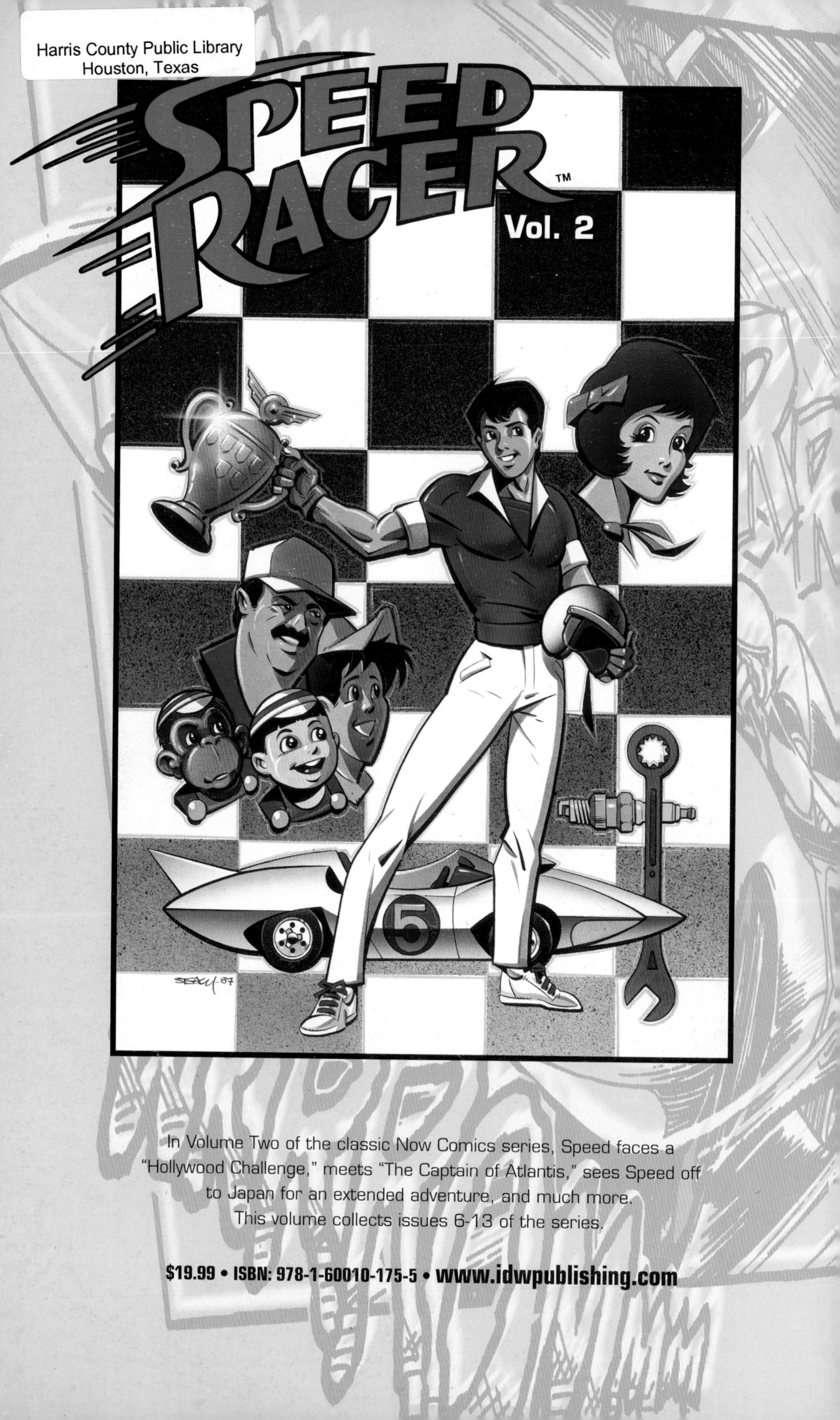
SPEED RACER™
Vol. 2
5

In Volume Two of the classic Now Comics series, Speed faces a "Hollywood Challenge," meets "The Captain of Atlantis," sees Speed off to Japan for an extended adventure, and much more.
This volume collects issues 6-13 of the series.

$19.99 • ISBN: 978-1-60010-175-5 • www.idwpublishing.com